T0330456

Corporate Strategies Under International Terrorism and Adversity

To David, Chantal and Caroline

Corporate Strategies Under International Terrorism and Adversity

Edited by

Gabriele G.S. Suder

Professor in International Business, CERAM Sophia Antipolis European School of Business, France

Edward Elgar
Cheltenham, UK • Northampton, MA, USA

Published by
Edward Elgar Publishing Limited
Glensanda House
Montpellier Parade
Cheltenham
Glos GL50 1UA
UK

Edward Elgar Publishing, Inc.
136 West Street
Suite 202
Northampton
Massachusetts 01060
USA

A catalogue record for this book
is available from the British Library

Library of Congress Cataloging in Publication Data

Corporate strategies under international terrorism and adversity / edited by Gabriele
    G.S. Suder.
      p. cm.
      1. International business enterprises—Security measures. 2. Terrorism—
    Economic aspects. 3. Risk management. 4. Emergency management. I. Suder,
    Gabriele G.S.

    HD61.5.C67 2006
    658.4'77—dc22   2005052764

ISBN-13: 978 1 84542 241 7
ISBN-10: 1 84542 241 4

Typeset by Cambrian Typesetters, Camberley, Surrey
Printed and bound in Great Britain by MPG Books Ltd, Bodmin, Cornwall

Contents

Figures

Tables

Contributors

Nancy J. Adler is a Professor of Organizational Behavior and Cross-cultural Management at McGill University, Montreal, Canada.

Raj Aggarwal is Professor and Chair in Finance, at Kent State University, Kent, OH, USA.

Ilan Alon is Associate Professor of International Business at the Crummer Graduate School of Business, Rollins College, FL, USA.

Max Boisot is Adjunct Professor of Asian and Comparative Management at INSEAD, Fontainebleau, France and Associate Fellow at Templeton College, Oxford, UK.

Mason A. Carpenter is the Keller Associate Professor in Strategic Management at the University of Wisconsin-Madison, Madison, WI, USA.

Claude Chailan is a Professor of Marketing at CERAM Sophia Antipolis, France.

Luis Felipe Calderon-Moncloa is a Professor of Management at ESAN, Lima, Peru.

David Gillingham is Pro-Vice-Chancellor, Dean and Professor of Management Education at Coventry University, Coventry, UK.

John R. McIntyre is Executive Director and Professor of the Georgia Tech DuPree College of Management Tech Center for International Business Education and Research, Atlanta, GA, USA.

David L. McKee is Professor of Economics in the Graduate of School of Management at Kent State University, Kent, OH, USA.

Bill McKelvey is Professor of Strategic Organizing at the University of California Los Angeles Anderson School of Management, Los Angeles, CA, USA.

Alexander D. Stajkovic is an Assistant Professor of Organizational Behavior at the University of Wisconsin-Madison, Madison, WI, USA.

David A.C. Suder is an Environment Expert at CANCA, Nice, France.

Gabriele G.S. Suder is a Professor of International Business and Risk Management at CERAM Sophia Antipolis, France.

Eric Ford Travis is a Research Fellow of the Georgia Tech Center for International Business Education and Research, Atlanta, GA, USA.

David A. Wernick is Research Director of the Knight Ridder Center for Excellence in Management at Florida International University's College of Business Administration, Miami, FL, USA.

Preface

Corporate Strategies Under International Terrorism and Adversity examines the impact of modern global terrorism on the international environment that results in significant adaptations of international firms in terms of risk and disaster management. This collection of chapters significantly contributes to the understanding of the networked economy, of the challenges to corporate and sector level that discerns asymmetries and symmetries in the analysis of networks in internationalization and international operations. While each industrial sector, each business structure, and each geographic region on the globe has to cope with interdependencies and risk management on its own behalf, contributors to this book modellize ways in which corporations may tackle international implications of a global terrorism that business has to deal with in the long term. We hence write about complexity and uncertainty, and conceptualize qualitative and quantitative research that was conducted since 09/11, and around key crisis points and moments such as those of the attacks of New York, Bali, Madrid, London and others.

The underlying theme is that terrorism is a global phenomenon in many different ways. The statistical probability that a firm is subject to direct physical damage is relatively small; that of indirect consequences of threat, act and aftermath of terrorist attacks, however, are high in terms of operations and management.

Analyses and revisions will have been made that encourage more active international cooperation in risk and disaster management, for closer convergence in the face of international terrorism and its impact on the International Business environment.

If we assume that globalization will continue and that corporations will continue to strive for profit and opportunity maximization, then terrorism risk has become part of corporate risk management and scenario planning in its own right, and will remain so.

This book is to be used in the present and in the future. The sequence of themes discussed in this volume guarantees an understanding of the main topics that are vital to international business research and to management training.

Gabriele G.S. Suder

Acknowledgements

The editor would like to express thanks for the patient and never-ending comprehension, love and goodwill of David, Chantal and Caroline during this second book project in regard to terrorism – I hope that they estimate that it was worth it. Also, the particular support of her parents, Ingrid and Rudolf Schmid, have made this volume possible.

The project for this book has crystallized since 11 September 2001, and, though self-standing, complements the works conducted for *Terrorism and the International Business Environment – The Security–Business Nexus* (Suder, 2004). It took shape and was launched at the Academy of International Business Annual Conference in Stockholm, July 2004, whose members I would like to thank for their involvement and support.

This volume contributes significantly to efforts in adapting corporate strategy and international operations to contemporary risk scenarios that are made by academia and professionals. It evolved into a collective undertaking due to a productive match of contributors coming together in a critical effort to undertake a cross-border and cross-disciplinary exercise. As editor, I was helped by a dynamic and very competent groups of contributors. Our gratitude also goes to the many colleagues and institutions whose participation and advice in our research and discussions was very welcome. At Edward Elgar Publishing, I benefited in particular from the professionalism of Francine O'Sullivan, who was once again of great help, and from the confidence of Edward Elgar.

Dr phil Gabriele G.S. Suder
CERAM, Sophia Antipolis

1. Introduction

Gabriele G.S. Suder

Corporate Strategies Under International Terrorism and Adversity is an edited volume representing a collection of important original research papers about the impact of 09/11-type terrorism on the international firm.

The preceding volume *Terrorism and the International Business Environment: The Business-Security Nexus*, had set the basis of this research. We studied and analysed the geopolitical, economic and financial structures on the one hand, and the insight into post-09/11 developments of selected business sectors on the other hand. Since then, events such as the terrorist attacks in Madrid, Bali and London have increased the awareness within both academia and the business sector that international strategies need to anticipate and to assure resilience to two eventualities that arise from risk and uncertainty: direct and indirect damage and disruption through terrorism. The potentiality of those damages and disruptions forces the corporation to adapt to a risk that is broader, wider and more important than it was defined in the classical concept of political risk. It is a risk that has globalized.

Terrorism, in its threat, its acts and its aftermath, has far-reaching implications on international business; these implications are not necessarily local or regional because 09/11-type terrorism originates from and is based on global networks. It utilizes and disrupts networks. The main task for business consists therefore on conceptualizing the possible location of disruptions in a given network and its linkages that may be crucial to the company, and to create just enough flexibility of those points of potential weakness to ensure the proper operation of a given business network, without excessive cost. In our contributions we use different useful approaches that were developed within international business research, such as network and portfolio theory.

International terrorism is a long-term challenge. The prime targets and 'costs' of it are those that bear the innocent parties stricken so as to achieve a maximum of media diffusion and impact on the population's psyche. This translates into a terrible human cost. Post-09/11 terrorism is governed by this search for media impacts through the killing of innocents at symbolic locations, yet it appears that it has entered a new phase with the July 2005 attacks in London: instead of hitting where it would surprise, terrorists now hit where security intelligence expects it – this gives the impression that a development is taking place in a manner that want to express that everything and anything is possible, any time and at any frequency. For the collectivism and community-orientation of any terrorist group this may be an illustration of force and power that aims to enhance the terrorism structures; for the victims and the society as a whole, this is meant to undermine the collective and individual feeling of security. Peripheral groups free-ride on the terrorism networks established with 2001, and utilize the phenomena created herewith. For the firm, and in particular for the international firm, this increases the importance of appropriate risk assessment and management tools.

It is always very sensitive to tackle the issues of terrorism and its impact because any discussion is potentially influenced by strong beliefs and sentiments. The emotional variables that may interfere are those of sentiments in regard to – most importantly – compassion with the victims and their families, in regard to culture and in regard to religion. This book does not represent any particular subscription to a political or ideological belief. Rather, and quite practically, it aims to reflect a variety of approaches to corporate strategies in times of international terrorism and adversity. The central thesis is that the international firm has no choice but to include terrorism risks into management and business concepts. Hence this volume proposes different models that have the potential to contribute to this effort. Terrorism is, as any risk, a challenge that leads to adaptation. The objective here is to help the corporate sector in this effort, and to thereby contribute to academic international business research that has a duty of being at the service of the business community.

For business, the immediate direct loss concerns physical damage and variations in the stock market. But costs are in no case restricted to this. Just like the transnational enterprise, international terrorism is globally connected and transnationally managed. Therefore, international business is first in line to terrorism's indirect consequences, and has to deal with issues such as alterations in consumer behaviors, disruptions of the international value chain (procurement, shipping, etc), and also cross-cultural and HR issues (staff recruitment, security and motivation issues, etc), and strategic management decisions such as concerning locations, investments and disinvestments. There is much to learn from the political science and international relations literature in this field. This literature is complemented by international business research. For instance, we note that the cartography of hot spots (that is, places of high risk to business operations) has altered, and so has the risk–return appreciation (for example, in the US and in England).

A number of international companies still focus on recovery rather than on redundancy and back-up solutions to, for instance, computer data or supplier diversification. Yet, more and more firms – in particular airlines, transport networks, big events management and oil and chemical industries – have increased their safety net, recognizing that insurance needs to be complemented by the flexibility of strategic management decisions in face of terrorism's unpredictability. Insurances, for instance, try to calculate the risk and put figures onto that unpredictability. We do not know when and where a strike will happen again, but we know that the phenomenon is a long-term one, and that terrorism (amid its painful direct impacts) vastly and painfully strikes international business indirectly as well.

PART I

The International Environment and its
Networks

2. Social network theory and methods as tools for helping business confront global terrorism: capturing the case and contingencies presented by dark social networks

Mason A. Carpenter and Alexander D. Stajkovic

INTRODUCTION

Global terrorism is a concern for all. In this chapter, we propose that new research on social network theory can help us fight it. We elaborate on what new research is needed, how such research can be conducted at home and across cultures, and the potential social implications of the results of this research in helping the fight against global terrorism.

Many different means and ways can be used to address global terrorism. The US-led conflict and eventual overthrow of Iraqi leader Saddam Hussein is one example of a military approach to battling terrorism. However, Pulitzer-prize winning author Seymour Hersh recently noted that, while 'one way to fight terrorism is with guns, it is as important to try to do it with brains'. Indeed, United States government agencies like the Center for International Business Education and Research and the National Science Foundation are increasingly calling for conceptual (grant) proposals from social sciences that address terrorism.

We offer one such conceptual approach, social network theory, which is studied in sociology, psychology, and management fields, and coupled with the latest research methodology. Our proposal is based on the following reasoning. Given the nature of their clandestine activity, terrorists live embedded in their social networks. As former Secretary of State, George Schultz, recently stated, 'The movement is not centrally controlled, but is an effectively coordinated loose global network' of social ties. Few terrorist experts disagree with the premise that terrorists can hardly operate without support from such networks.

The social network is the key construct of study in social network theory. This theory has been used to explain and predict criteria ranging from passing the common cold among the members of the social network to forming business alliances. We suggest that new research on social network theory can provide findings that can be potentially useful to numerous new outcomes, but one of which, we feel, may be better understanding and predicting of terrorist behavior. Our idea and this chapter are not about trying to find a 'magic bullet'. Rather, they are about our belief that it is important to try to make small strides and gain early small but important wins in getting the conceptual handle on the terrorist phenomena. In that light, we propose the following research program:

1. Meta-analysis is at the core – we believe a meta-analytic synthesis of all relevant social network studies (about 3,000 studies) is needed. Such a study will quantitatively examine which social network attributes are the most predictive of performance for individuals, as based on data from all relevant studies.
2. Use leading-edge military simulations – based on the results from meta-analysis, experiments need to be conducted under circumstances as relevant as possible to terrorist activities without actually endangering human life. The solution is to employ a military simulation task with terrorist behaviors, measured as saboteur actions aimed at destroying the military resources and obstructing operations.
3. Model the simulated engagements in culturally heterogeneous contexts – the United States has been identified as a highly individualistic society. How social networks operate in such culture context may not be the same as how they function in more collectivistic environment. Thus, experiments, as described above, are also needed under culture circumstances more closely resembling attributes (collectivism) of societies in which terrorists have been shown to originate, that is, in which their social networks may have their roots.

Taken together, we believe that this research approach may help us: (a) identify what social network attributes are the most conducive to effective performance in general; (b) better understand how saboteur actions may unfold in networks with certain attributes; and (c) what are some cultural boundary conditions of social network dynamics. We next outline theoretical background and explain how proposed research can be undertaken.

THEORETICAL BACKGROUND

Social network research in the field of management has proliferated to the point that more studies on the topic have been published in the last five years than in the prior 20 years (Kilduff and Tsai, 2003; Stajkovic et al., 2005). Figure 2.2 summarizes this dramatic increase in social network research. Most organizations researchers will recognize the field of social networks for its emphasis on the benefits individuals gain through network membership, vis-à-vis the resources, contacts, information and reputation that their membership in a network affords them. Indeed, Granovettor's (1973) work on networks, particularly the strength of weak ties, is often pointed to as one of the seminal studies highlighting the personal and interpersonal benefits of social network membership. Burt's later (1992) work on structural holes and other network features elaborated on network mechanics again reiterates the positive role played by networks in individual and organizational outcomes. Recent research on social networks continues in this positive vein. For instance, Stajkovic, Carpenter and Graffin (2005) showed that certain individuals exhibited a greater propensity to develop extensive social networks and in a follow-on study the same authors reported that individuals with extensive social networks were much more likely to set challenging personal career goals. Moreover, both studies showed that these relationships were robust

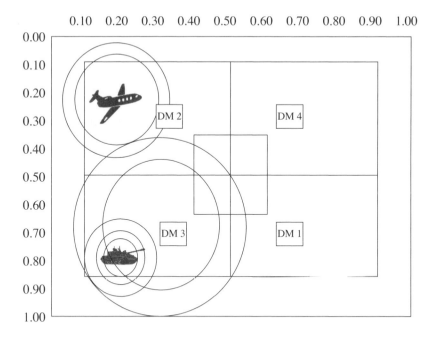

Source: Xu et al. (2003).

Figure 2.1   DDD tactical simulation

across samples of subjects from individualistic (USA) and collectivistic (China) cultures.

In contrast to this apparent flood of important research on the benefits and related methodological issues related to social networks we take a strikingly different tack in this chapter. While we do indeed focus on the outcomes of social networks, the social network outcome of pressing concern to us in this work is global terrorism and terrorist activity. Ironically, a successful terrorist attack is the epitome of social network effectiveness, at least that of a terrorist network. This assertion is true particularly given that many of the recent terrorist attacks have been coordinated through Granovettor's 'loose ties' embedded in a deeply shared and collectivist ingroup culture of animosity toward a well-defined outgroup (Schein, 2004). Even the vernacular describing terrorist groups fits the social network frame – for instance, the social network literature refers to nodes and links, whereas experts in military intelligence circles have long referred to terrorist networks in terms of their component terrorist cells (that is, nodes) and conduits (links).

Throughout this volume, our colleagues will make the case as to why terrorism and terrorist networks are an important business and societal concern, so we do not intend to restate that valid case here. As should be clear by now, terrorism impacts purely domestic firms and transnational organizations alike. Instead, our objective is to present terrorist activity in the context of social networks possessing common and systematically observable social network characteristics. Based on this presentation, we then move on to outline a social network-based methodology for better understanding, and perhaps predicting, terrorist activity. This methodology is novel in that it adapts complex but tractable existing military simulation games to reshape the field of battle to reflect a terrorist and his or her terrorist network's perspective. It is our hope that the interplay of theory and methodology proposed here helps tomorrow's business and political leaders combat the insidious threat of terrorism to global and regional economic recovery and development.

AN EMERGING THEORY OF TERRORISM AS DARK NETWORKS IN ACTION

Social networks exist when people interact, when they form social ties (Salancik, 1995). The preponderance of social network research falls into a category that Raab and Milward (2003) refer to recently as bright networks – that is, networks where the outcomes are considered beneficial for individuals, groups, businesses, and society at large. Dark networks, in contrast, refer to social networks where the network achieves its objectives but at great cost to individuals, groups, businesses and social welfare. It would be unfair and untrue to say that no research relevant to dark networks has been undertaken. In fact, it is probably not surprising that academic interest in management/ organized labor relations during the last century and the potential impact of labor unrest on business effectiveness spawned research which considered the role of social networks.

Among the earliest of such network studies is one documenting the emergence of conflict, changes in interpersonal networks, and an eventual strike by workers in an African garment factory (Kapferer, 1972). Importantly, we are not equating labor unrest or labor action with global terrorism, but instead noting that Kapferer's work clearly shows how changes in social network structures predicted the destabilization of an ongoing business operation. In period 1 of his study circa mid-1964, Kapferer noted how little leadership centralization existed among the African workers at one particular factory, as evidenced by a centralization score of .28. In social network terms, centralization essentially denotes, mathematically, the extent to which a network is centralized around one or a few central actors (Freeman, 1979). The value varies between 0 and 1, and higher values denote greater activity or relationships around one to several central individuals. As such, the measure is both a practically useful and intuitively logical indicator of an important characteristic of social networks.

During period 1, senior workers in the African factory were unable to secure wage and work improvements despite their orchestration of organized walkouts. Consistent with the low centralization score of .28, Kapferer (1972) surmised that this failure was due to a lack of overall support from the many skilled and unskilled workers at the factory. However, seven months later in period 2, the workers' centralization score had jumped to .45, suggesting that some central group of leaders had grown in terms of their influence as demonstrated by a greater number and centralization of social network ties. In Kapferer's terms, the African workers were now 'more linked into a common set of interactional relationships' (1972, p. 180). In reviewing Kapferer's (1972) early study, Kilduff and Tsai (2003) also noted that the social networks documented in period 2 were also more multiplex in that they spanned more clusters in the factory, and hence further enhanced the power and potential influence of the senior labor leaders. The notion of multiplexity of social ties implies that a link between two actors may serve multiple interests (Barnes, 1979), such as the case where two individuals are both friends and co-workers. The outcome of this more robust social network was the senior workers' ability to incite a strike in 1965 where the workers realized a £1 wage increase.

Again, we are not equating organized labor movements with global terrorist networks but instead aim to draw attention to an early, relatively neglected study of what business leaders at the time would likely refer to as a dark network, based on its effect on their business's operations and profitability.

Complementing and at the same time complicating Kapferer's (1972) observation of the effects of centralization is Granovetter's (1973) introduction of the notion of weak ties, and their power in furthering the influence of social networks on important outcomes. The weak ties concept was developed in the vein of bright networks, and suggests that relationships that are infrequent and distant can also allow individuals to benefit from social network membership as viewed by the achievement of their objectives, though the weak-tie notion is most often invoked in contexts where such ties provide access to more diverse information sources and contacts. In contrast, strong ties are those typically characterized by Krackhardt (1992) and others as relationships that are frequent, long-lasting and affect-laden.

DARK NETWORKS COMPARED TO BRIGHT NETWORKS IN SOCIAL NETWORK RESEARCH

Social networks operate to further their members' objectives. In that sense, it is the members objectives and how they differ between bright and dark networks that requires us to adjust how we apply social network concepts in the context of dark networks. For instance, in bright networks the members are typically not fearful that their membership is known and may even be overt in highlighting it. An individual who is seeking a job or new knowledge will thus openly address the members of the network, make their intentions and network affiliations known, and in so doing attempt to broaden the reach and effectiveness of their social network. While it is true that some individuals may try to manage their network positions such that they are in positions of greater relative power (Burt and Ronchi, 1990), ultimate network structure and membership are typically not hidden or covert.

In contrast, members of dark networks typically only want their membership in such networks known after the fact, as seen in factional claims of responsibility of suicide bombings. And yet, given the nature of their clandestine activity, terrorists are embedded deeply in social networks, albeit dark ones. While membership becomes public knowledge, the extant members go to great lengths to hide and protect the structure of the network so that future actions by network members are not thwarted. As a result, even though the social ties among dark members are highly affect-laden, a characteristic typically attributed to strong-tie social networks, the clandestine nature of their work typically leads members to foster a weak-tie structure, where each tie is multiplex in nature. Some key dimensions of social networks and their differing roles from bright and dark network perspectives are summarized in Table 2.1. While this listing is far from exhaustive, the key point is that network constructs may play out very differently in bright versus dark network contexts.

Table 2.1 *Network constructs in bright versus dark network contexts*

Network construct	Definition	Bright network context	Dark network context
Size	Simply the number of individuals that comprise the social network. Importantly, size can be calculated in a narrow sense, where membership only includes active network members. It can also be calculated in a broader sense to include currently inactive but potentially active at any given point in time in terms of their relationship with network outcomes or network members' desired outcomes.	Relatively easy to calculate active network through common network survey intruments (Wasserman and Faust, 1994); inactive network can be identified by asking members who is active and inactive in the network they have reported.	Since members desire to hide their membership in the network, the narrow and broadly-defined network size must be estimated based on socio-economic geographic, cultural, religious, or political characteristics.
Density	This characteristic represents the degree to which each member of the network has ties to other members of the network. Mathematically this characteristic is captured in a matrix where the maximum number of ties are divided by the actual number of ties, with the maximum value being one. A value of one would mean that every member in the network knows every other member of the network.	Work using the density measure typically emphasizes the ideas of diversity of ideas versus behavioral integration. A dense network, values closer to 1, implies the group is fairly cohesive. Low density networks, values closer to zero, signify few common ties and thus diversity of information sources.	Dark networks will favor low density as a survival mechanism since high density would mean that any captured member could reveal a significant number of other dark network members.

Table 2.1 *(continued)*

Network construct	Definition	Bright network context	Dark network context
Centrality	This characteristic can take on one of four potential values. Degree centrality, closeness centrality, betweenness centrality, or eigenvector centrality. Degree centrality means an actor has connections to many other actors in the network. Closeness centrality means the actor is connected to many other actors, but those other actors have few connections among themselves. Betweenness centrality is this latter feature which captures the degree to which an actor's ties are linked to each other. Finally, eigenvector centrality captures the number of connections across centrally connected actors.	Most actors wish to have high degree of closeness centrality and, if they desire power, to also have low closeness centrality among their ties but at the same time have high eigenvector centrality.	Dark networks may strive to have common beliefs serve as substitutes for degree centrality and use indirect communications to achieve the benefits of betweenness and eigenvector centrality to coordinate their actions.

PROPOSED EMPIRICAL RESEARCH

Meta-Analysis

The research on social networks spans across disciplines in social sciences (anthropology, sociology, psychology, management, economics), and has been frequently conducted in recent years as we note above (see also Borgatti, 2005). However, despite the large number of individual studies, little is known in terms of research synthesis, that is: What is the average effect size of different network attributes on performance? Are such network attributes different (in terms of average effect sizes) from each other? What type of network attributes has the strongest impact on performance? Such findings based on empirical synthesis have been lacking to the point that some (for example, Salancik, 1995) have even questioned the very existence of social network theory. Meta-analysis would quantitatively provide such answers for the first time in the social networks research literature. Meta-analysis is the only method to quantitatively examine a set of relationships across multiple studies. Meta-analytic technique has been described in detail elsewhere (Hedges and Olkin, 1985; Hunter and Schmidt, 1995) and we will not repeat such content here. We will just note that our preliminary search identified over 3,000 studies on social networks that may be applicable to be meta-analysed.

Experiments

The next question is: do meta-analytic findings that may be obtained apply to such idiosyncratic behaviors as terrorist activity? Such dangerous behaviors belong to the rare group of activities (punishment may be another) that cannot be purposely manipulated and then tested in the field settings (for example, as one may do with, say, performance in organizations). However, social network attributes and terrorist behaviors can be manipulated experimentally in the laboratory. Findings from such experiments may indicate if meta-analytic results regarding social networks apply to manipulated terrorist behaviors. An important aspect of these experiments would be to find an activity that may be conducive to studying and manipulating terrorist behaviors.

Recent research on teams (see Hollenbeck et al., 1998, 2002; Johnson et al., 2006) has used a complex, dynamic computer simulation of military operations that we believe may also be used to experimentally manipulate terrorist activities. The complexity of this simulation is high. The simulation we suggest is a modified version of the distributed dynamic decision-making (DDD) operation developed for the United States Department of Defense for research and training purposes (for a more complete description of this simulation see Miller et al., 1998; and Xu et al., 2003). The version of the simulation we suggest here (MSU-DDD) is customized for participants with little or no military experience. A graphical rendering of the simulation is provided in Figure 2.1. Because this simulation has been described in detail previously (Hollenbeck et al., 2002), we provide only a summary overview here.

The job is that of military operation in which study participants must defend a certain area from incoming enemy targets. The task presents participants with a simulated representation of a radar screen encompassing the area they must defend. The participant has a 'base' in the center of the area they must monitor and defend. In monitoring their area on-screen, participants can only 'see' enemy vehicles in the area near their base. A portion of the area that must be defended does not have radar coverage, and approaching enemy vehicles cannot be detected in that area. In addition to base radar, subjects have access to four assets/vehicles of varying capabilities (tank, AWACS plane, jet plane, helicopter) which can extend radar capabilities beyond the base radar area and be used to destroy incoming enemy targets. Participants in the simulation must dispatch a vehicle with the right set of predetermined capabilities. For example, simulation sets as a rule that tanks have slow travel speed and a high level of firepower, while jet planes travel quickly but have the least firepower. Thus, study participants would achieve the best results by dispatching

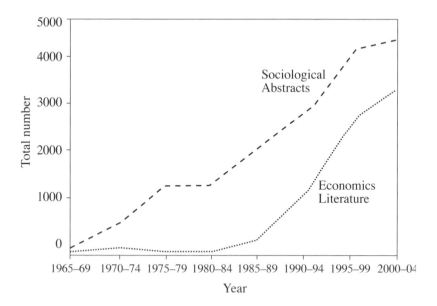

Source: Sociological Abstracts, Econ Lit.

Figure 2.2   Articles with network keyword

vehicles that can reach and then can actually destroy a target with the minimum required firepower in the shortest amount of time.

Two distinct capabilities are needed to successfully complete the task of keeping a protected area clear. First, participants need to use response speed to attack quickly and destroy incoming targets. The longer an enemy vehicle is allowed to stay near a participant's base area, the lower a participant's overall performance, as scored in this simulation. Second, participants must accurately identify, shoot and destroy the enemy targets – breaking rules of engagement or hitting own targets ('friendly kills') results in lower performance, that is, inaccuracy is penalized.

The roles in this simulation can be programmed (reversed) to have a terrorist/saboteur who tries to do harm (do opposite of desired activities described above) and who needs to be identified. One × 6 ANOVA in each sample can be used to identify under which of the six network attributes the terrorist/saboteur performance is the most effective. The same design can be used to identify under which of the six network attributes the defense against terrorist/saboteur is most effective.

CROSS-CULTURAL MODERATION

The United States is characterized as an individualistic culture, characterized, in short, by focus on self, individual actions, one's own benefits (House et al., 2004; Hofstede, 1980). The first set of experiments would address the following question: if terrorists were to act (manipulated) in an individualistic culture (for example, US study participants), would such culture characteristic moderate the meta-analytic results, and if so, how? The flip side of individualistic culture characteristic is collectivistic culture, characterized by focus on group actions, social interconnectedness, and communal good (Triandis, 2004). Thus, we propose a second set of experiments to address the following questions: (a) if terrorists were to act (experimentally manipulated in the proposed simulation) in a collectivistic culture (for example, with study participants from such cultures), would such culture characteristic moderate the meta-analytic results, and if so, how, and (b) how will these results be different from results we obtained in an individualistic culture? We propose examining individualism/collectivism culture characteristics as a moderator because terrorism is a global phenomena and these two culture characteristics have been shown to be moderators of many relationships (for example, what works here may not work everywhere) (Trompenaars, 1998).

Taken together, these findings may help us: (a) as a starting point, identify what social network attributes are the most conducive to effective performance in general (meta-analysis), (b) better understand how saboteur actions may unfold in networks of certain attributes (experimental manipulations and theory testing based on a highly complex and realistic military simulation), and (c) discover some cultural boundary conditions (same simulation with different participants).

CONCLUSION

We feel that the program of research we propose here has a potential to make a contribution to social network theory, and perhaps offer practical suggestions for a topic of social relevance – better understanding and predicting terrorist behaviors. We believe that the proposed program of research based on social network theory offers a feasible set of academic and practitioner tools to study something so idiosyncratic, clandestine, and hazardous to the public under-taking – terrorist activity.

Our objective was to emphasize the importance of social network theories and social network research methodologies to the study of global terrorism and its relationship with both purely domestic and transnational business orga-nizations. To achieve this objective we used the contrasting lenses of bright versus dark social networks to show how social network structure and theo-retical constructs might be viewed differently from a dark social networks perspective. Building on this conceptual framework, we proposed specific methodologies by which social network may be empirically studied. Our hope is that this framework and analytical tool may foster future research and substantive progress in combating the global terrorist threat.

REFERENCES

Barnes, J.A. (1979), 'Network analysis: orientation notion, rigorous technique or substantive field of study?', in P.W. Holland and S. Leinhardt (eds), *Perspectives on Social Network Research*, New York: Academic Press, pp. 403–23.

Borgatti, S.P. (2005), 'Centrality and network flow', *Social Networks*, **27**(1), 55–71.

Burt, Ron S. (1992), *Structural Holes: The Social Structure of Competition*, Cambridge, MA: Harvard University Press.

Burt, Ron S. and D. Ronchi (1990), 'Contested control in a large manufacturing plant', in J. Wessie and H. Flap (eds), *Social Networks Through Time*, Utrecht, Netherlands: ISOR, pp. 121–57.

Freeman, L.C. (1979), 'Centrality in social networks: I. Conceptual clarification', *Social Networks*, **1**, 215–39.

Granovetter, M. (1973), 'The strength of weak ties', *American Journal of Sociology*, **78**, 1360–80.

Hedges, L.V. and I. Olkin (1985), *Statistical Methods for Meta-analysis*, San Diego, CA: Academic Press.

Hofstede, G. (1980), *Culture's Consequences*, London: Sage.

Hollenbeck, J.R., J.A. Colquitt, D.R. Ilgen, J.A. LePine and J. Hedlund (1998), 'Accuracy decomposition and team decision making: testing theoretical boundary conditions', *Journal of Applied Psychology*, **83**(3), 494–500.

Hollenbeck, J.R., H. Moon, A. Ellis, B.J. West, D.R. Ilgen and L. Sheppard (2002), 'Structural contingency theory and individual differences: examination of external and internal person-team fit', *Journal of Applied Psychology*, **87**(3), 599–606.

House, R.J., P.J. Hanges, M. Javidan, P.W. Dorfman and V. Gupta (eds) (2004), *Culture, Leadership, and Organizations: The GLOBE Study of 62 Societies*, Thousand Oaks, CA: Sage.

Hunter, J.E. and F.L. Schmidt (1995), *Methods of Meta-analysis: Correcting Error and Bias in Research Findings*, Beverly Hills, CA: Sage.

Johnson, M.D., J.R. Hollenbeck, S.E. Humphrey, D.R. Ilgen, D. Jundt and C.J. Meyer (2006), 'Cutthroat cooperation: asymmetrical adaptation to changes in team reward structures', *Academy of Management Journal*, in press.

Kapferer, B. (1972), *Strategy and Transaction in an African Factory*, Manchester: University of Manchester Press.

Kilduff, M. and W. Tsai (2003), *Social Networks and Organizations*, London: Sage.

Krackhardt, D. (1992), 'The strength of strong ties: the importance of Philos in organizations', in N. Nohria and R.G. Eccles (eds), *Computational Organizational Theory*, Hillsdale, NJ: Erlbaum, pp. 89–111.

Miller, D.L., P. Young, D. Kleinman and D. Serfaty (1998), *Distributed Dynamic Decision-making Simulation: Phase I. Release Notes and User's Manual*, Woburn, MA: Aptima.

Raab, J. and H.B. Milward (2003), 'Dark networks as problems', *Journal of Public Administration Research and Theory*, **13**(4), 413–39.

Salancik, G. (1995), 'Wanted: a good network theory of organization', *Administration Science Quarterly*, **40**: 345–9.

Schein, E. (2004), *Organization Culture and Leadership*, 3rd edn, London: Wiley.

Stajkovic, A., M.A. Carpenter and S. Graffin (2005), 'Individual differences as predictors of social network extensiveness', working paper, University of Wisconsin-Madison.

Stajkovic, A., M.A. Carpenter and S. Graffin (2005), 'Social network extensiveness as a determinant of self-set career goal difficulty', working paper, University of Wisconsin-Madison.

Stajkovic, A., M.A. Carpenter, M. Maltarich and A.J. Nyberg (2005), 'Meta-analysis of 20 years of network research', working paper, University of Wisconsin-Madison.

Triandis, H.C. (2004), 'The many dimensions of culture', *Academy of Management Executive*, **18**, 88–93.

Trompenaars, A. (1998), *Riding the Waves of Culture*, 2nd edn, New York: McGraw-Hill.

Wasserman, S. and K. Faust (1994), *Social Network Analysis: Methods and Applications*, New York: Cambridge University Press.

Xu, D., M. Miller, R.A. Volz and T.R. Ioerger (2003), 'Collaborative agents for C2 teamwork simulation', International Conference on Artificial Intelligence (ICAI), Las Vegas, pp. 723–9.

3. Speeding up strategic foresight in a dangerous and complex world: a complexity approach

Max Boisot and Bill McKelvey

Recently some emergent nonlinear events of historical proportions occurred, three of which were al-Qaeda's September 11 attack on the World Trade Center, the collapse of Enron, and the disintegration of NASA's space shuttle, Columbia. At the FBI there was a failure to 'fill in the dots', that is, failure to discover the early predictive patterns in a timely fashion. The failure was the result of spatial dispersion, hierarchy and jurisdictional disputes. At Enron the problem stemmed from illegal activities, 'don't ask; don't tell' managerial attitudes, and self-serving 'reinterpretations' of accounting rules, coupled with conflict of interest between the CPA firm's and Enron's accountants. At NASA, budget cuts, flight schedules and a lackadaisical organizational culture meant that top-management's responses were even slower than the steady accumulation of evidence pointing to the Columbia shuttle's vulnerability. In each case the rate at which the pattern pointing to an emergent problem progressed was higher than the rate at which top managers (of the FBI and NASA) or government regulators (of Enron) could appreciate the emerging patterns and take action. Similar historical failures come to mind: Pearl Harbor, the Cuban Missile Crisis and the Challenger shuttle explosion – all showing the same failure of foresight to detect emerging patterns – in a timely fashion.

All of the foregoing triggered national crises. Failure to find patterns because of space, hierarchy, and speed effects is also endemic to most firms. Decades ago, Ashby (1956) put it in terms of building internal requisite variety to match environmental variety in a timely fashion. For March and Simon (1958) the issue is framed in terms of bounded rationality. Williamson (1975) blames asymmetric information and opportunism. McKelvey (1997) talks about the problem in terms of rate dynamics. Boisot (1998) talks about it in terms of abstraction and codification in the Information-Space (the I-space). Fine (1998) discusses competitive advantage in terms of 'clock speed'.

Emergent complexity events progress at different speeds. Firms don't need to reach for the moon, they just need to find instructive patterns faster than their competitors. More generally, firms need to uncover patterns at a rate faster than that at which the emergence process is unfolding. But, there are potentially hundreds or thousands of 'dots'. Not all can be targets of attention and not all possible patterns are important. Yet the vast number of dots, the geometric increase in patterns, and the need for speedy pattern finding combine to create the foregoing failures.

Getting ahead of kinds of danger comparable to the build-up of terrorist cells – in a timely fashion – is demonstrably difficult, as is evident in the FBI's response to pre-09/11 events. It may very well be beyond the capability of a human organizational hierarchy, absent some kind of distributed intelligence processing capability coupled with high-speed computational help. In this chapter we first describe the threat of dangerous emergent events progressing at speeds beyond the pattern processing capabilities of most human hierarchies. We then turn to Ashby's (1956) Law of Requisite Variety and complexity science to outline an approach for:

1. Reducing the problem imposed by quadrillions of possible patterns; and
2. Changing organizational bureaucracies from hierarchical command-and-control structures dating back to the Fordist Industrial Era to Knowledge Era structures style featuring distributed intelligence.

We argue that these two redesign approaches are recursive; the functioning of each is speeded up through improved performance by the other. Before concluding the chapter we return to the problem posed by hierarchies and silo effects. We turn to high-speed computational help in Chapter 4.

THE FORESIGHT PROBLEMATIQUE

> [Foresight is] the ability to see through the apparent confusion, to spot developments before they become trends, to see patterns before they fully emerge, and to grasp the relevant features of social currents that are likely to shape the direction of future events [and being able to] . . . look for generality where there is variety, and to look for idiosyncrasy where there is generality. (Alfred North Whitehead, 1967, p. 89)

In this quote, Whitehead gives us a fairly elaborate definition of foresight. We see four component problems facing firms trying to cope with the new and complicated dynamics characterizing the dawn of the 21st century, many of which are discussed in Halal and Taylor (1999). They are (1) danger, (2) speed and (3) complexity both internal and external. We discuss each in turn.

Danger

The following could be from Charles de Gaulle to Paris, or Dulles to Washington DC, or anywhere:

> The year is 2010. You are an MI-6 special agent traveling by Tube from Heathrow to Piccadilly. The time is 9.20am; the subway train is moderately crowded. London has gone Condition Red. 'Chatter' from here and there around the world has accumulated recently suggesting that a possible terrorist action may be aimed somewhere in London, involving either the explosion of a dirty nuclear bomb, anthrax, bird-flu or a sarin-gas attack. A number of years back, however, special security organizations were created throughout Europe and the US – composed of 'official' special agents as well as all sorts of other employee-agents who routinely take public transportation, with each member carrying a bio-chemical/radiation detection device, a beeper and a mobile phone with photo capabilities. London is a large city and has several thousand members, any one of whom can be contacted via the network.
>
> You are hanging onto the overhead handgrip when your mobile phone emits a faint beeping sound. It does so because a chemical sensor in your computer bag has detected the possible presence of a PETN-based material in the subway car (a chemical used in the manufacture of a sophisticated form of C4, the kind of explosive Richard Reid hid in his shoes when he boarded American Airlines flight 63 out of Paris in December 2001). Looking around, you spot a beat-up looking rucksack under a seat at the far end of the car. You wonder whether you should act. It is a difficult decision. Your beeper has occasionally sounded in the past, as you have traveled here and there around London. By questioning passengers, you could end up making a fool of yourself. You might also be revealing that you are a special agent.
>
> For the time being you decide to do nothing, knowing that your beeper has already fired off a signal to MI-6's computer. At the next stop, two women board at the far end of the car. One of them is a railroad employee who is, on the side, also a member of a special rail-security organization. Now her beeper also goes off – with a more intense beeper code, which also goes to the MI-6 computer. The computer 'sees' that the two signals come from the same cell district. It signals back to the beeper units with a code asking you each to independently 'text-message' back your location and what you see, or you each immediately receive a phone call from an agent at MI-6. You each describe the situation – independently of each other.[1]

As a special government, intelligence, military, or corporate-employee 'agent' (hereinafter just 'Operative'), you are an intelligent communication node embedded in a distributed network of sophisticated sensors. Your first responsibility when your beeper goes off is to register the possibility of a threat. Once this has been established, the next step is to assess its plausibility. For this one needs further corroborative evidence. In our Tube example, this was provided by the second Operative's beeper also firing – at a greater intensity. In effect, she provided MI-6 with a Bayesian update on what was initially a fairly low a priori probability estimate. If your beeper had gone off when you were alone in the middle of a field, for example, the degree of corroboration required for establishing plausibility would have been higher than for the Tube.

Its faintly futuristic quality apart, how realistic is the above scenario? In an invited article in *The Economist* commenting on the findings of the US and UK commissions of inquiry, the former head of Mossad, Israel's intelligence service wrote the following:

> There is an inherent understanding. . .that the shortage of information on the threats – from Islamic terrorism and from Iraq's weapons of mass destruction – was at the root of the intelligence breakdown on these two fronts. It seems only logical that the more you know, the safer you are and the greater the chance that you will get things right.
>
> Yet Israel's most costly and fateful failure was its mistaken estimate of Egyptian and Syrian intentions, on the eve of the Yom Kippur war in 1973, when the two armies unexpectedly attacked Israel in a bid to regain the territories lost in the 1967 war. At the time, Israel had it all: superior intelligence coverage, excellent human resources with good access, high-level and discreet dialogue with more than one Arab or Muslim leader, and an intelligence-evaluation arm that had provided an early warming several months before the war, thus preventing it from breaking out at that time. But despite all of the above, we got it all wrong. The abundance of information led us to intelligence 'hubris': we trusted our superior analytical prowess rather than ominous indicators on the ground. (Efraim Halevy, 2004, p. 21)

Clearly, sufficiency of information is not the only issue. The ability to rapidly link different items of information together is also recognized as important. To this end, the Final Report of America's September 11th Commission (2004) proposed the creation of the National Counter-Terrorism Center (NCTC) that would concentrate all the analysts and spies working on counter-terrorism in one place. The 09/11 attacks were made all the easier, argues the Commission, because not enough information was shared among the agencies. The proposed new centre ". . . will help to connect the dots" (*The Economist*, 2004, p. 30). Yet the CIA emphasized that it had warned senior policy-makers of the terrorist threat well before it happened: "Our fundamental flaw was not withholding information. The flaw was in not recognizing the significance of the information that we did have and acting on it promptly", one senior official said (Kean, 2004). In both the US and the UK, intelligence assessment is acknowledged to have been as much of a problem as intelligence gathering (*Financial Times*, 2004).

Speed of response

> The only thing that gives an organization a competitive edge – the only thing that is sustainable – is what it knows, how it uses what it knows, and how fast it can know something new! (Prusak, 1996, p. 6)

A concern with speed has become a priority for all organizations – not just those facing emergent terrorist cells. In business, for example, good strategy is no longer just about picking the right industry; it is about being at the cutting edge of industry evolution, of new technology, of new markets, of new moves to counter competitors. For firms in high-velocity environments this shifts competitive dynamics from industry selection and interfirm competition to intrafirm rates of change: *It's not the BIG that eat the SMALL . . . it's the FAST that eat the SLOW.*[2]

Recent writing about competitive strategy and sustained rent generation parallels Prusak's emphasis on the speed at which a firm must develop new knowledge. As high-velocity product life-cycles (Eisenhardt, 1989) and hyper-competition (D'Aveni, 1994) have increased in recent decades, speed of knowledge appreciation has become a central attribute of competitive advantage (Leonard-Barton, 1995) with learning fundamental to change in knowledge (Fiol, 1994; Argote, 1999). Rents are seen to stem from industry trends (Hamel and Prahalad, 1994), staying ahead of the efficiency curve (Porter, 1996), and value migration (Slywotzky, 1996). Eisenhardt and colleagues have focused on 'high-velocity' high-tech firms for some time (Bourgeois and Eisenhardt, 1988; Eisenhardt and Tabrizi, 1995). In these firms the classic 'organic' organizing style (Burns and Stalker, 1961) is just too slow to keep pace with changes in high-velocity firms, as Eisenhardt (1989) and Brown and Eisenhardt (1997) observe.

Learning is seen as a key element of core competence (Barney, 1991). Much of the concern about human capital appreciation bears on high-technology based industries (Leonard-Barton, 1995; McMaster, 1996; Dosi, Teece and Chytry, 1998). Further, advocates of the resource- and competence-based view emphasize unique resources, distinctive/dominant/core competencies, dynamic capabilities, learning, and knowledge creation (Teece, Pisano and Shuen, 1994; Heene and Sanchez, 1997). They advocate moving firms toward more sophisticated skills and technologies. Becker (1975) defines knowledge/skills held by employees and their intellectual capabilities as human capital (H), and having given knowledge and capability economic value, adds it to the production function.

Human capital is a property of individual employees. Taken to the extreme, even geniuses offer a firm only minimal adaptive capability if they are isolated from everyone else. A firm's knowledge requisite for competitive advantage increasingly appears as networks of human capital holders (Carley and Hill, 2001). These knowledge networks also increasingly appear throughout firms rather than being narrowly confined to upper management. Employees have become responsible for adaptive capability rather than just being bodies available to carry out orders. Here is where networks become critical. Especially in the last two decades, much of the effectiveness and economic value of human capital held by individuals has been shown to be subject to the nature of the social networks in which the human agents are embedded (Granovetter, 1985, 1992; Burt, 1997), as a reading of the various chapters in Nohria and Eccles (1992) also suggests. Burt (1992) goes so far as to move networks into the realm of economic value by terming them social capital (S), saying that competitive advantage is a function of network relations, not individual knowledge attributes (1992, p. 3). Combining the need for both H and S, the Cobb Douglas production function, thus, becomes Y = f(K, L, H, S), where Y = income, K = capital and L = labor. But, since Porter (1996) now argues that K and L portions of the equation no longer guarantee sustainable rents, this leaves all the emphasis on H and S.

In this new world, fast-acting distributed learning and intelligence capabilities are crucial.

Complexity

Internal complexity

Ross Ashby's Law of Requisite Variety states that 'only variety can destroy variety' (Ashby, 1956, p. 207). More specifically, his Law holds that for a biological or social entity to be efficaciously adaptive, the variety of its internal order must match the variety of the environmental constraints that it confronts. In defining variety, Ashby pointed to the following series: c, b, c, a, c, c, a, b, c, b, b, a. He observed that a, b, and c repeat, meaning that there are only three 'distinct elements' – three kinds of variety or three degrees of freedom. In the language of patterns, however, this is variety at the level of 'dots'. Suppose, instead, we define variety in terms of the number of patterns instead of the number of dots. Then, using the formulae from Table 3.1, we see that four dots lead to six possible links; they also generate 64 possible patterns. With ten dots one gets 45 possible links and approximately 3.5 trillion possible patterns. Twelve dots produce 66 possible links and approximately 4,700 quadrillion possible patterns! Even supposing 99 percent of these are not worth paying attention to, trillions are left, and one still doesn't know, up front, which ones are trivial and which are not.

Table 3.1   Relation of dots to patterns

Number of dots: N	Number of possible links: $L = (N)N - 1)/2$	Number of possible patterns: $P = 2^L$
N = 4	L = 6	P = 64
N = 10	L = 45	P = 3.5 trillion
N = 12	L = 66	P = 4,700 quadrillion

Despite this computational reality, six of America's most experienced intelligence practitioners, writing in *The Economist* (2003, p. 30), argue that although there had been "... an inability to connect the dots", what is really needed are more useful dots to connect, more fine-grained and better quality data, and more monitoring based on the data. We believe, however, that simply pleading for more and better dots is to mistake the nature of the problem. An arithmetic increase in the number of 'dots' – high quality or otherwise – leads to a geometric increase in the possible connections that one can establish between them. It also leads to an exponential increase in the number of patterns to decipher.

The implication of the quadrillions of possible patterns is that despite whatever we feel about the need for more high quality dots to connect – and we don't deny the need is real – if we are not to drown in a sea of unprocessable data, we need to zero in on meaningful patterns whilst simultaneously filtering out the much larger number of those that are meaningless. We illustrate this in Figure 3.1. Pattern processing divides into two kinds of processing capability: the ability to (1) reduce the vast external complexity above the 'Ashby Line' (represented by the inverted pyramid); and (2) increase internal

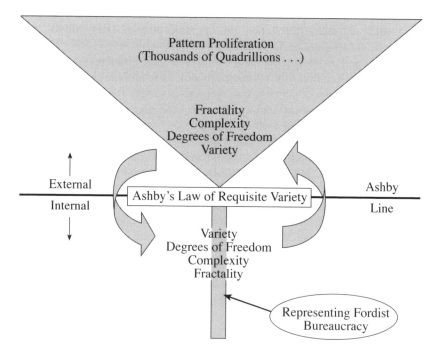

Figure 3.1　Pattern proliferation above; Fordism below the Ashby Line

complexity below it (Fordist bureaucracy is represented by the thin column below the line). As the Figure depicts, there is usually far too much complexity above the line and not enough below. We discuss each processing approach in turn.

External complexity

Since variety is but the phenomenological manifestation of complexity at work, we extend Ashby's treatment of variety to complexity and argue that only complexity can destroy complexity (McKelvey and Boisot, 2003). How might we apply our reformulation of Ashby's Law?

Any living creature survives by first scanning its environment for data on the threats and opportunities that confront it. It must then extract the relevant information from such data and interpret it according to its prior experience before acting on it. Where it scans from depends on what data it is sensitive to. In the case of humans, the range of data that we are sensitive to has been considerably expanded by technologies that allow us to capture the very small via microscopes or the very large via telescopes. These technologies often create problems of data overload that require us – now aided by computer imaging – to separate out what is informative data from what is noise. Effective scanning, thus, calls for selectivity with respect to what will count as data, what information will be extracted from it, and what information will be acted upon.

Any agent operates a set of tuneable filters, both perceptual and conceptual, that allow past knowledge, values and preferences to shape both what will register as data as well as what information will be extracted from such data. Information then modifies an agent's knowledge, viewed as a set of probability distributions or conditional expectations (Arrow, 1984). We can think of these filters as expressing a set of hypotheses as to what to look for in environmental signals. Unfortunately, the tuneable filters that shape our hypotheses can sometimes function too well. When confronted with a radically novel situation, relying solely on past experiences to tune the filters can end up unduly narrowing the compass of one's scanning efforts.

The cognitive approach (Boisot, 1998; Boisot and Child, 1999) to variety reduction brings us back to the distinction between data, information and knowledge (Boisot and McKelvey, 2004). Simplifying here, dots are environmental signals that register with an agent as data. Links between dots constitute information that an agent extracts from the data, and the patterns that can be derived from such information when properly filtered can become knowledge that the agent can act upon. Patterns, however, only acquire the status of knowledge for an agent when they have graduated from being merely possible to being sufficiently probable to justify action.

Data, however, are not patterns and, indeed, nor are dots. The problem is well known in science. The Duhem-Quine thesis holds that we never test hypotheses in isolation but in patterned clusters or chunks (Duhem, 1914; Quine, 1969). But as we have just seen, from a few dots and links a huge number of patterns become candidates for testing. The patterns that survive the testing – that is, that are now judged to be either 'plausible' or 'probable' – will subsequently orient us in an iterative fashion towards attending to particular dots and particular links now deemed to be relevant (Hanson, 1958). Yet, given the unimaginably large number of patterns that we have to start with, how does the process ever get going? How do we winnow out unviable patterns and process the rest in a time frame that allows for efficacious action and adaptation?

The challenge is to improve one's pattern recognition skills rather than one's data collection skills. If one's existing repertoire of patterns or paradigms is inadequate for interpreting incoming data, then it has the effect of converting information-bearing data into noise. Collecting more data under such circumstances ends up exacerbating the problem since it merely increases the level of noise.

But what does pattern recognition involve? It requires matching the patterns suggested by incoming data to stored templates. Do we, therefore, need to hold in memory quadrillions of pattern templates to cope with the whole range of possible patterns generated by the data we collect? No! We adopt the strategy of our immune system (Kauffman, 1993) and exploit the combinatorial power of a limited number of pattern elements already in our repertoire. Providing we can mix and match these flexibly and rapidly to incoming data, we greatly reduce the number of patterns that we need to store.

Even so, such pattern reducing strategies may still not be enough. Our own memory, its combinatorial powers notwithstanding, may still end up filtering out as meaningless, patterns that are potentially significant. In effect, we run the danger of reducing complexity too quickly.

One way of improving our pattern recognition skills is to harness those of other agents so as to create a distributed processing capacity. This is what the institutions of science are designed to do. In spite of its competitiveness, science is essentially a collaborative enterprise in which all players share a concern to extract meaningful information from data in order to come up with novel patterns – a form of socially distributed information processing.

Increasing internal complexity below the Ashby Line

My work is in a building that houses three thousand people who are essentially the individual 'particles' of the 'brain' of an organization that consists of sixty thousand people worldwide. (Zohar, 1997, p. xv)

Zohar starts her book by quoting Andrew Stone, a director of the retailing giant, Marks and Spencer. Each particle has some intellectual capability –

Becker's (1975) human capital, H, and some of them talk to each other – Burt's (1992) social capital, S. Together, H and S comprise distributed intelligence, what McKelvey (2000, 2005) terms 'Corporate IQ'. Intelligence in brains rests entirely on the production of emergent networks among neurons – intelligence is in the synaptic network structure, not in the neurons; they behave as simple 'threshold gates' that have one behavioral option – fire or not fire (Fuster, 1995). As intelligence increases, it is represented in the brain as emergent connections (synaptic links) among neurons.

The lesson from brains is that organizational intelligence is best seen as 'distributed' and that increasing it depends on fostering network development along with increasing the human capital of agents. In contrast, command and control systems, and even leadership theory, date back to the mentality of Henry Ford (quoted in Hamel, 2000, p. 102), who said, 'Why is it that whenever I ask for a pair of hands, a brain comes attached?'

We represent the silo-generated, command and control, bureaucratic hierarchy, one-brain-at-the-top mentality of Industrial Era organizations with the narrow vertical column below the line in Figure 3.1. The FBI is the perfect example or such an organization. Even though its command and control 'hierarchy' had been given all of the right cues, it was incapable of filling in the dots by shrinking down to the correct patterns, and certainly not fast enough to stay ahead of the 09/11 disaster. Ironically, even visionary, charismatic leadership theory motivates top managers to pursue activities that recreate Fordist organizations at the expense of distributed intelligence (Uhl-Bien, Marion and McKelvey, 2004).

How, then, to organize? Specifically, we believe that bottom-up self-organizing networks with a capacity to engage in distributed information processing are called for. Such networks are described in Boisot and McKelvey (2004).

With the advent of the internet, there has been a growth of interest in so-called 'network' forms of organization. These are said to differ from more traditional forms of organization by the looseness of their coupling (Weick, 1976). Yet all organizational forms, markets, bureaucracies, clans, adhocracies, fiefs, etc, can be described as networks (Boisot, 1998). What distinguishes them one from another is the structure of the network. Whereas bureaucracies, for example, will have an extended hierarchical reach and will be tightly coupled, a clan network will typically exhibit dense and restricted non-hierarchical connections (Simon, 1962), and will be loosely coupled. A market network, by contrast, will reach out, will be sparse, non hierarchical, and will be loosely coupled.

Different network structures favour different processes. Miles et al. (1999) outline the importance of 'cellular network' forms of organization. Their definition of 'cells' and self-organizing entrepreneurial subunits (really firms) closely fit Simon's (1962) theory on the evolutionary advantage of complex hierarchical designs based on 'nearly decomposable', that is, modular, designs (Sanchez and Mahoney, 1996; Schilling, 2000). Computational organizational theory allows us to focus on the computational properties of these distributed intelligence processes and to think of organizations as computational devices (Prietula, Carley and Gasser, 1998). Parallel processing strategies can allow these to substantially speed up and simultaneously corroborate pattern processing, an idea we further develop in Chapter 4 and in Boisot and McKelvey (2004).

Strong command and control systems associated with top-down serial computing strategies are necessary for organizational focus and efficiency. We note, however, that they frequently and inadvertently destroy heterogeneity and hence adaptive variety, thereby leading to fossilization (McKelvey, 2001, 2005). Yet heterogeneity, valuable as it may be for the generation of variety and hence for adaptation, if excessive, could, in fact, undermine corporate control and efficiency. Recent research shows that both top-down and bottom-up ideas and influences are in fact, necessary (Romme, 1999); Thomas, Kaminska-Labbé and McKelvey, 2005).

What is so great about heterogeneity? The value of heterogeneity in any system depends on how much it needs to cope with change and novelty. Heterogeneity underpins the generation of variety and variety, in turn, facilitates novel combinations and hence the emergence of new patterns (Holland, 1988; Johnson, 2000; Allen, 2001). Agents and organizations that can rapidly generate new interpretative patterns to match those in a changing environment enjoy a survival advantage in that they can more easily adapt to such an environment. Heterogeneity is essential to improved distributed intelligence and corporate functioning (McKelvey, 2001, 2005).

ORGANIZATIONAL IMPLICATIONS

What are the organizational implications of the above analysis for intelligence services and firms? As we now know, the quality of intelligence assessment was identified as a major problem in post-09/11 analyses. Who does it? How is it managed? Returning to our earlier scenario, should the assessment of what is going on – that is, pattern recognition – be centralized in some distant office, or should it be decentralized to locally 'situated' Operatives? What if one was dealing with a train station in Peshawar (Pakistan) rather than Washington? And how fault-tolerant should such pattern recognition be?

The new NCTC aims to bring all analysts and agents working on counterterrorism under a single authority. The hope is that this will help to 'fill in

the dots' more rapidly and accurately next time by promoting a better sharing of information among the experts – and thus to find more dots more
quickly. Unfortunately, this proposal leaves intelligence assessment –
pattern recognition again – essentially undisturbed at the top of the hierarchy, and thus subject to the same problems of data overload and of filtering
biases that we discussed earlier.

Furthermore, putting the intelligence services under a single authority
does nothing to remove the silo mentality that operates both within and
between these services. While the 09/11 Commission's Final Report
describes the CIA, the FBI, and more than 13 other intelligence units as
'cast-iron stovepipes' at the agency level (p. 403), silos also exist within
these agencies. The FBI, for example, already had one boss, and yet people
from different parts of the organization – its internal silos – didn't talk to
each other (Posner, 2003). In effect, the 'stronger management' that the
Commission calls for to unify all the intelligence-gathering agencies (p. 411)
will simply replicate at a higher level the silo-generating management
processes, structures and cultures already existing at the CIA, NSA, FBI, and
DOD. The UK experience with MI-6 has been little different (Butler, 2004).

By connecting Operatives directly to a new pattern-processing technology, and by taking advantage of thousands of 'open source' information
opportunities, our 'distributed' socio/computational approach gets around
silo thinking (see Chapter 4). How? A hierarchical organization deploys
information filters in such a way that information is extracted from data
collected at the base and is then passed up to the next hierarchical level. That
is, dots (data) collected at the base get 'joined' or linked (creating information) by intelligence analysts in the middle of the hierarchy before being
'assessed' – that is, wrought into patterns (actionable knowledge) – at the
top. The finer the lower level filters the slimmer and steeper the hierarchy,
as depicted in stylized form in Figure 3.2a. By contrast, the filtering of dots
in a distributed approach would produce an organizational structure looking
more like Figure 3.2b. Whereas in Figure 3.2a, Operatives at the bottom
eliminate dots at a rapid rate in order to limit the data processing load of
those higher up the hierarchy, in Figure 3.2b, lower-level Operatives deploy
a limited – that is, filtered – number of dots to generate a larger number of
links and a vastly larger number of pattern elements requiring higher-level
processing.

The difference between the two figures reflects fundamentally different
data processing strategies. In Figure 3.2a, relevant information is presumed
to reside primarily in the mean of a data distribution. Under assumptions of
a normal distribution and independent events, the variance is mostly treated
as an error term, that is, noise that has to be got rid of as quickly as possible.
In Figure 3.2b, by contrast, relevant information is presumed to reside

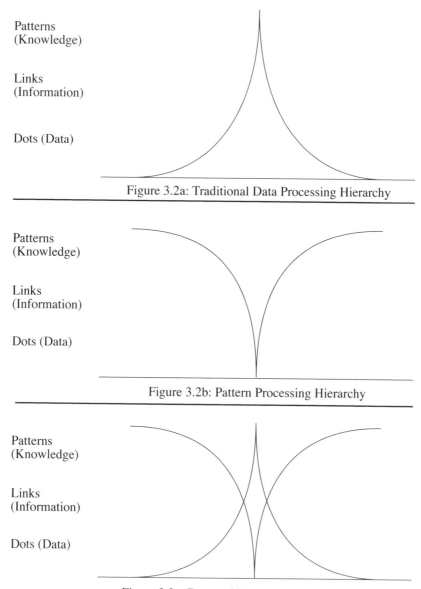

Patterns
(Knowledge)

Links
(Information)

Dots (Data)

Figure 3.2a: Traditional Data Processing Hierarchy

Patterns
(Knowledge)

Links
(Information)

Dots (Data)

Figure 3.2b: Pattern Processing Hierarchy

Patterns
(Knowledge)

Links
(Information)

Dots (Data)

Figure 3.2c: Data and Pattern Processing Combined

Figure 3.2   Pattern processing

primarily in the variance – independence of events and a normal distribution is no longer assumed. This is the source of the combinatorial explosion that generates so many patterns for processing further up the hierarchy. In case b a large amount of information-bearing data either has to be processed at lower levels or moved up the hierarchy before anything useful can be extracted from it. Focusing on means is what intelligence services were acculturated to do during the Cold War, when the enemy and its possible range of behaviors were relatively well known and it was relatively easy to tell what was data and what was noise. But as Thomas Kean (2004), the Chairman of the 09/11 Commission, observes, the national security bureaucracy still remains stuck in a Cold War time warp. In a post-Cold War world of asymmetric threats in which small causes can have disproportionately large effects, intelligence services must learn to focus on information-bearing variances as much as on means (Gleick, 1987; Andriani and McKelvey, 2005).

Clearly the volume of data processing implied by Figure 3.2b is many times larger than that implied by Figure 3.2a, too large, we believe, to be effectively processed by any traditional organization or even a limited number of expressly intelligence-oriented ones such as MI-6, the CIA, the FBI, Homeland Security, etc.

Furthermore, we now need to distinguish between traditional hierarchical data processing and socially distributed pattern processing. Whereas the former type of processing still leaves intelligence assessment – that is, pattern processing – exclusively in the hands of a few overloaded, higher-level 'experts', the latter type distributes pattern-processing activities across a much wider community. It replaces the hierarchically located – and thus silo-confined – 'experts' with a diverse set of well equipped public and corporate Operatives scattered across thousands of places outside the official intelligence agencies such as MI-6, FBI, or CIA. Assessment does not thereby disappear, but it now operates across different levels: (1) at the lower levels – even outside the hierarchy – meaningful patterns are intentionally generated and corroborated for subsequent selection and processing; and (2) at higher levels – possibly within MI-6 or the NCTC – the most promising of these are actually put into play and fed back to the lower levels in an interactive fashion. The implication of our scheme – and what our scenario builds upon – is that the NCTC and MI-6 need to involve many more stakeholders than just the existing intelligence services. Yet to avoid information overload, they will also need a way of organizing that takes advantage of emerging socio/computational technologies.

The implication of Figure 3.2c – a superimposition of Figures 3.2a and 3.2b – is that the intelligence process needs to spread outside Fordist hierarchies and take advantage of socially distributed computational methods (Prietula, Carley and Gasser, 1998); we explore the challenge in Chapter 4.

CONCLUSION

As far back as 1945, in a classic paper entitled 'The use of knowledge in society', Friedrich Hayek showed how socially distributed processing could help citizens and organizations cope with a complex and fast-moving, nonlinear world. Such parallel processing strategies, he argued, were to be found in markets. In matters of intelligence, however, government agencies continue to operate exclusively through archaic Fordist organizations – MI-6, CIA, FBI, etc. The proposed solution of the 09/11 Commission – to create a new intelligence Tsar – simply builds on this traditional organizing strategy. This is wrong-headed: by making the silo taller the Commission will actually exacerbate the pattern-processing problem. The complexity of the security challenge suggests that these traditional approaches now need to be complemented by modern socio/computational data processing methods that integrate silicon- and carbon-based agents in novel ways.

We have argued that 'joining the dots', whilst a problem, is not the problem. Finding the computational capability to process and corroborate trillions of possible patterns is the problem. New open-source pattern processing technology will be needed to address it. Yet, since computational strategies are only effective if the underlying organizational capabilities required to implement them are in place, a change in computational strategy implies new organizational capabilities.

In Chapter 4 we propose an approach that integrates new high-speed computational processes with new organizational ones. Our approach suggests that significant organizational and cultural challenges loom if intelligence agencies are ever to efficaciously anticipate and counteract terrorism.

NOTES

1. Alternatively or in addition, detectors could be permanently installed in key locations – like subway cars, train depots, airports, nuclear facilities, container unloading areas, government buildings, etc.; the portable detectors would then corroborate and contextually enrich signals from the stationary detectors.
2. Title of Jennings and Haughton's book (2000).

REFERENCES

09/11 Commission (2004), *Final Report of the National Commission on Terrorist Attacks upon the United States*, New York: Norton.
Allen, P.M. (2001), 'A complex systems approach to learning, adaptive networks', *International Journal of Innovation Management*, **5**, 149–80.
Andriani, P. and B. McKelvey (2005), 'Beyond averages: extending organization

science to extreme events and power laws', presented at the Academy of Management Annual Meeting, Honolulu, HA, 8–10 August.

Argote, L. (1999), *Organizational Learning: Creating, Retaining and Transferring Knowledge*, Norwell, MA: Kluwer.

Arrow, K. (1984), 'Information and economic behavior', in *The Economics of Information: Collected Papers of Kenneth J. Arrow*, Cambridge, MA: Belknap/Harvard University Press, pp. 136–52.

Ashby, W.R. (1956), *An Introduction to Cybernetics*, London: Chapman & Hall.

Barney, J.B. (1991), 'Firm resources and sustained competitive advantage', *Journal of Management*, **17**, 99–120.

Becker, G.S. (1975), *Human Capital*, 2nd edn, Chicago, IL: University of Chicago Press.

Boisot, M. (1998), *Knowledge Assets*, New York: Oxford University Press.

Boisot, M. and J. Child (1999), 'Organizations as adaptive systems in complex environments: the case of China', *Organization Science*, **10**, 237–52.

Boisot, M. and B. McKelvey (2004), 'Counter-terrorism as neighborhood watch: a socio/computational approach for getting patterns from dots', working paper, The Sol Snider Center, The Wharton School, University of Pennsylvania.

Bourgeois, L.J. III and K.M. Eisenhardt (1988), 'Strategic decision processes in high velocity environments: four cases in the microcomputer industry', *Management Science*, **34**, 816–35.

Brown, S.L. and K.M. Eisenhardt (1997), 'The art of continuous change: linking complexity theory and time-paced evolution in relentlessly shifting organizations', *Administrative Science Quarterly*, **42**, 1–34.

Burns, T. and G.M. Stalker (1961), *The Management of Innovation*, London: Tavistock.

Burt, R.S. (1992), *Structural Holes: The Social Structure of Competition*, Cambridge, MA: Harvard University Press.

Burt, R.S. (1997), 'The contingent value of social capital', *Administrative Science Quarterly*, **42**, 339–65.

Butler, Rt. Honorable Lord (2004), *Review of Intelligence on Weapons of Mass Destruction*, London: The Stationery Office, House of Commons.

Carley, K.M. and V. Hill (2001), 'Structural change and learning within organizations', in A. Lomi and E.R. Larsen (eds), *Dynamics of Organizational Societies: Computational Modeling and Organization Theories*, Cambridge, MA: AAAI/MIT Press, pp. 63–92.

D'Aveni, R.A. (1994), *Hypercompetition: Managing the Dynamics of Strategic Maneuvering*, New York: Free Press.

Dosi, G., D.J. Teece and J. Chytry (eds) (1998), *Technology, Organization and Competitiveness: Perspectives on Industrial and Corporate Change*, New York: Oxford University Press.

Duhem, P. (1914), *The Aim and Structure of Physical Theory*, Paris: Marcel Riviere et Cie.

The Economist (2003), 'America needs more spies', 12 July, pp. 30–31.

The Economist (2004), 'No blame, no pain', 31 July, p. 30.

Eisenhardt, K.M. (1989), 'Making fast strategic decisions in high-velocity environments', *Academy of Management Journal*, **32**, 543–76.

Eisenhardt, K.M. and B.N. Tabrizi (1995), 'Accelerating adaptive processes: product innovation in the global computer industry', *Administrative Science Quarterly*, **40**, 84–110.

Financial Times (2004), 'The human factor: all is not well in clandestine intelligence collection', 7 July, p. 15.

Fine, C.H. (1998), *Clock Speed: Winning Industry Control in the Age of Temporary Advantage*, Reading, MA: Perseus.

Fiol, M.C. (1994), 'Consensus, diversity, and learning in organizations', *Organization Science*, **5**, 403–20.

Fuster, J.M. (1995), *Memory in the Cerebral Cortex: An Empirical Approach to Neural Networks in the Human and Nonhuman Primate*, Boston, MA: MIT Press.

Gleick, J. (1987), *Chaos: Making a New Science*, New York: Penguin.

Granovetter, M. (1985), 'Economic action and social structure: a theory of embeddedness', *American Journal of Sociology*, **82**, 929–64.

Granovetter, M. (1992), 'Problems of explanation in economic sociology', in N. Nohria and R.G. Eccles (eds), *Networks and Organizations: Structure, Form, and Action*, Boston, MA: Harvard Business School Press, pp. 25–56.

Halal, W.E. and K.B. Taylor (1999), *Twenty-First Century Economics: Perspectives of Socioeconomics for a Changing World*, New York: Macmillan.

Halevy, E. (2004), 'In defence of the intelligence services', *The Economist*, 31 July, pp. 21–3.

Hamel, G. (2000), 'Reinvent your company', *Fortune*, June, 99–118.

Hamel, G. and C.K. Prahalad (1994), *Competing for the Future*, Boston, MA: Harvard Business School Press.

Hanson, N.R. (1958), *Patterns of Discovery: An Inquiry into the Conceptual Foundations of Science*, Cambridge, UK: Cambridge University Press.

Hayek, F. (1945), 'The use of knowledge in society', *American Economic Review*, **35**, 519–30.

Heene, A. and R. Sanchez (eds) (1997), *Competence-Based Strategic Management*, Chichester, UK: Wiley.

Holland, J.H. (1988), 'The global economy as an adaptive system', in P.W. Anderson, K.J. Arrow and D. Pines (eds), *The Economy as an Evolving Complex System*, Proceedings of the Santa Fe Institute, vol. V, Reading, MA: Addison-Wesley, pp. 117–24.

Jennings, J. and L. Haughton (2000), *It's not the BIG that eat the SMALL . . . It's the FAST that eat the SLOW*, New York: HarperBusiness.

Johnson, N.L. (2000), 'The development of collective structure and its response to environmental change', report #LA-UR-02-3125, Los Alamos, NM: Los Alamos National Laboratory.

Kauffman, S.A. (1993), *The Origins of Order: Self-organization and Selection in Evolution*, New York: Oxford University Press.

Kean, T. (2004), 'A "failure" to protect the US', *International Herald Tribune*, 23 July, pp. 3–4.

Leonard-Barton, D. (1995), *Wellsprings of Knowledge*, Boston, MA: Harvard Business School Press.

March, J.G. and H.A. Simon (1958), *Organizations*, New York: Wiley.

McKelvey, B. (1997), 'Quasi-natural organization science', *Organization Science*, **8**, 351–80.

McKelvey, B. (2000), 'Improving corporate IQ', keynote address, Conference on Complex Systems in Industry, International Manufacturing Centre, University of Warwick, UK, 19–20 September, pp. 77–84.

McKelvey, B. (2001), 'Energizing order-creating networks of distributed intelligence', *International Journal of Innovation Management*, **5**, 181–212.

McKelvey, B. (2005), 'Microstrategy from macroleadership: distributed intelligence via new science', in A.Y. Lewin and H.W. Volberda (eds), *Mobilizing the Self-Renewing Organization*, New York: Palgrave/Macmillan.

McKelvey, B. and M. Boisot (2003), 'Redefining strategic foresight: *"fast"* and *"far"* sight via complexity science', presented at the INSEAD Conference on *Expanding Perspectives on Strategy Processes*, Fontainebleau, France, 24–26 August.

McMaster, M.D. (1996), *The Intelligence Advantage*, Boston, MA: Butterworth-Heinemann.

Miles, R., C. Snow, J.A. Matthews and G. Miles (1999), 'Cellular-network organizations', in W.E. Halal and K.B. Taylor (eds), *21st Century Economics: Perspectives of Socioeconomics for a Changing World*, New York: Macmillan, pp. 155–73.

Nohria, N. and R.G. Eccles (eds) (1992), *Networks and Organizations: Structure, Form, and Action*, Boston, MA: Harvard Business School Press.

Porter, M.E. (1996), 'What is strategy?', *Harvard Business Review*, **74**, 61–78.

Posner, G. (2003), *Why America Slept: The Failure to Prevent 09/11*, New York: Random House.

Prietula, M.J., K.M. Carley and L. Gasser (1998), *Simulating Organizations: Computational Models of Institutions and Groups*, Cambridge, MA: MIT Press.

Prusak, L. (1996), 'The knowledge advantage', *Strategy and Leadership*, **24**, 6–8.

Quine, W.V. (1969), 'Naturalized epistemology', *Ontological Relativity and Other Essays*, New York: Columbia University Press, pp. 69–90.

Romme, G.L. (1999), 'Domination, self-determination and circular organizing', *Organization Studies*, **20**, 801–32.

Sanchez, R. and J.T. Mahoney (1996), 'Modularity, flexibility, and knowledge management in product and organization design', *Strategic Management Journal*, **17**, 63–76.

Schilling, M.A. (2000), 'Towards a general modular systems theory and its application to inter-firm product modularity', *Academy of Management Review*, **25**, 312–34.

Simon, H.A. (1962), 'The architecture of complexity', *Proceedings of the American Philosophical Society*, **106**, 467–82.

Slywotzky, A. (1996), *Value Migration*, Boston, MA: Harvard Business School Press.

Teece, D.J., G. Pisano and A. Shuen (1994), 'Dynamic capabilities and strategic management', CCC working paper 94-9, Center for Research in Management, UC Berkeley.

Thomas, C., R. Kaminska-Labbé and B. McKelvey (2005), 'Managing the MNC and exploitation/exploration dilemma: from static balance to dynamic oscillation', in G. Szulanski, Y. Doz and J. Porac (eds), *Advances in Strategic Management: Expanding Perspectives on the Strategy Process*, vol. 22: Elsevier.

Uhl-Bien, M., R. Marion and B. McKelvey (2004), 'Complex leadership: shifting leadership from the industrial age to the knowledge era', presented at the Academy of Management Annual Meeting, New Orleans, LA, 9–11 August.

Weick, K.E. (1976), 'Educational organizations as loosely coupled systems', *Administrative Science Quarterly*, **21**, pp. 1–19.

Whitehead, A.N. (1967), *Adventures of Ideas*, New York: Free Press.

Williamson, O.E. (1975), *Markets and Hierarchies*, New York: Free Press.

Zohar, D. (1997), *Rewiring the Corporate Brain*, San Francisco, CA: Berrett-Koehler.

4. National security as a socio/ computational process

Max Boisot and Bill McKelvey

In Chapter 3 and elsewhere we drew upon Ashby's 'Law' (1956), which we update to the law of requisite complexity, to analyse the nature of the 09/11 or Madrid bombing-type of security challenges that nation states face in the 21st century (Boisot and McKelvey, 2004). The problem of how organizations can stay ahead of unfolding emergent events also lies behind other disasters like NASA's two space shuttle accidents and the Pearl Harbor, Cuban Bay of Pigs or Enron affairs. Under competitive conditions, rapid pattern recognition becomes a weapon in a cognitive arms race between adversaries – requisite complexity calling for the generation of adaptive responses in a timely fashion. We have shown that effective counter-terrorism requires more than just 'filling in the dots'. Given the trillions of possible patterns that a few dots can generate, the cognitive challenge of quickly reducing the vast complexity of externally emergent patterns far exceeds the organizational capacities of a few government agencies, no matter how well equipped these might be. In Chapter 3 we also argued that in the real world the trade-off between generating data and generating meaningful patterns is time-constrained. The need for rapid pattern recognition may thus set a limit to the amount of data that can usefully be collected and processed by a purely human hierarchy. This is a new problem that traditional technologies and ways of organizing were never designed to cope with.

To deal with both pattern finding and rate problems, we develop two related approaches. First, we reduce a potentially infinite proliferation of patterns that generate external variety. We need to find patterns that are indicative of unfolding emergent events before these ever become obvious, that is, before a 09/11 or an Enron. Our proposed socio/computational approach uses state-of-the-art computational methods – coupled with the use of contextual tensions, different vantage perspectives and corroboration over time – to simplify and constrain external pattern proliferation in a timely fashion and thus to reduce Ashby's external complexity.

Secondly, we create, activate and speed up the formation of internal complexity. To do this we develop a socio/computational semi-autonomous human connectionist network consisting of two elements: (1) a distributed intelligence spread across a large number of heterogeneous human agents using state-of-the-art detectors and mobile phones; and (2) the combination of a neural network computational model (Anthony and Bartlett, 1999) and a structural equation model (Kaplan, 2000) located in some central intelligence organization.

In the following section, we outline the relevant computational processing methods – serial and parallel – briefly describing the steps in our socio/computational approach. Our method is designed to take advantage of distributed intelligence – multiple agents, detectors, and mobile phones – so as to improve the corroboration of pattern processing whilst at the same time vastly shrinking the number of patterns calling for action and doing so in a timely fashion. We start with external pattern proliferation, moving in a controlled fashion from possible, to plausible, to probable patterns.

A SOCIO/COMPUTATIONAL SOLUTION OF PATTERN REDUCTION

Given hundreds and possibly thousands of agents in a distributed information processing – corporate intelligence – network, the only way to get ahead of a 09/11 – or Enron-type of disaster is to rely on a semi-automated, parallel, computational technology. New parallel processing computational approaches can accommodate a greater measure of agent heterogeneity and many more agents (even up to a million) in the analysis of organizations than can the more traditional, analytically oriented, top-down decision-science approaches (Carley, 1996). These approaches also appear to be the only ones that can substantially speed up pattern processing and simultaneously corroborate the results. They need to be adaptive and allow for innovation. AI researchers have identified two bottom-up parallel processing strategies that, within a certain range, can meet these requirements, connectionism and evolutionary programming (Mitchell, 1996).

In principle, connectionist computational theory dates back to von Neumann's (1951) seminal work on cellular automata and neural networks. Gilbert and Troitzsch (1999) divide connectionist modelling into three groups:

- *CA models*: These typically consist of cells in a grid; each cell typically has one or two binary inputs and depending on the input combination has a binary output. Classics are Schelling's (1971) study of ethnic segregation, and Conway's *Game of Life* (Berlekamp et al., 1982).
- *Multi-agent models*: In their simplest forms, these may look and behave like CAs, but usually they allow more input options and cells have more

capabilities. Agents[1] may have autonomy, social ability, reactivity, proactivity and intentionality in the form of beliefs, desires, motives, emotions and memory (Gilbert and Troitzsch, 1999).

- *Adaptive learning models*: The best known examples of these are neural networks (NNs) and genetic algorithms (GAs). In these models, agents may change their rules; these may change spontaneously, or the structure of the model may change. Two sophisticated examples of such models are LeBaron's (2000) model of stock market purchasing and Carley's ORGAHEAD model of agent, group and strategic behavior in organizations (Carley and Svoboda, 1996). These models use CA search spaces, GA rules for agent evolution and NN models for learning.

In order to generate the 'pattern' that can 'train' a connectionist model, we also draw on a fourth structural equation model (SEM) (Kaplan, 2000). Our socio/computational approach thus integrates the use of neural net and structural equation models.

THEORY: USING CONTEXT TO COARSE-GRAIN FINE-SCALE STRUCTURE

The concept of distributed intelligence builds on the insight that as individuals in a social network interact over time, they influence each other's behavior, if only in some limited way – they exchange things and ideas; they have agreements and disagreements; they discover common interests, likes, dislikes, shared attitudes, values and prejudices, share past experiences, etc. Like elementary particles in quantum theory, therefore, individuals may be characterized by the history of their interactions with all other individuals they have come into contact with over time – that is, pairs or larger groupings of individuals exhibit correlated social histories (McKelvey, 2003, 2004). We will use the term 'transaction', as opposed to 'interaction', to reflect our interest in meaningful rather than neutral encounters between individuals. As transactions multiply, a person's behavior can be inferred with some probability from the behavior of those s/he has transacted with – that is, through their correlated social histories.

In quantum theory, entanglement occurs when the correlated histories of pairs of electrons are greater than zero. If individual histories are thus correlated, they are said to interfere with each other. Correlated histories across a random collection of heterogeneous individuals will have their predictive effects canceled out due to the randomness of the forces at play. Gell-Mann (1994) refers to a world densely populated with interference-prone histories as having 'fine-grained' structures. The quantum world is just such a fine-grained structure. By contrast, Gell-Mann labels the kinds of patterns that we see in the material world as 'coarse-grained' structures. The question then arises: How do coarse-grained patterns emerge from fine-grained – entangled – structures? More broadly: How does pattern emerge from a background of everything-more-or-less-correlated-with-everything-else that cancels out?

This is equivalent to asking: How can we obtain meaningful patterns from connected dots? According to Gell-Mann, 'A coarse-grained history may be regarded as a class of alternative fine-grained histories, all of which agree on a particular account of what is followed, but vary over all possible behaviors of what is not followed, what is summed over' (p. 144). Researchers exploit this phenomenon every time they assume that the various interrelated effects not specifically hypothesized, or controlled for, are randomized.

Gell-Mann's view is that contextual effects lead some correlated histories in the fine-grained structure to get selected as the basis of probabilistic patterns whilst the remaining histories are washed out – their effects remaining randomized. For example, faced with some urgent, external work-related problem, a project team's decision process focuses on the contextually imposed problem and not on the many incidental concerns of its individual members. Such context-driven coarse-graining emerges from the fine-scale structure of all possible concerns and correlated social histories of team members. Omnès (1999) further emphasizes the role of external context. In the most basic and rudimentary pattern-forming processes, quantum theory illustrates how probable patterns emerge from possible ones. From our 'dot' analysis (in Chapter 3), we know that an almost infinite number of possible patterns can be derived from a modest number of dots. Quantum physics guides our thinking on how patterns first emerge and on how a move from possible to probable patterns via plausible ones can reduce pattern proliferation.

THREE PATTERN FILTERS

To recapitulate the scenario presented in Chapter 3:

> Suppose that a number of years after 09/11, special security organizations were created throughout Europe and the US – composed of 'official' special and other employee-agents who routinely take public transportation, with each member carrying a bio-chemical/radiation detection device, a beeper and a mobile phone with photo capabilities. London is a large city and the organization has several thousand members there, anyone of whom can be contacted via the network.
>
> You are an MI-6 special agent traveling by Tube from Heathrow to Piccadilly. Riding with you on the subway (and on other trains and buses) are other special 'Operatives' on routine patrol, on their way to work, going shopping, etc. Triggered by a chemical sensor your beeper, and several others, have just gone off here and there, sending signals to the MI-6 'Computer' that stores them temporarily. The

Computer text-messages all other Operatives, who then find excuses to leave their
posts and take the nearest public mode of transportation. Based on where beepers
are going off, the Computer begins producing maps showing possible convergence
areas, which suggest possible terrorist target areas.

The first step is to reduce the trillions of possible patterns 'out there' at as low
a cost as possible. As shown in Chapter 3, while 12 dots produce 66 links,
these pale beside the 2^{66} possible patterns that could emerge from these links.
As noted above, it is not 'filling in the (missing) dots' that is the problem.
Instead, given even a relatively few dots, it is the unmanageably large number
of patterns emerging from the 'fine-grained structure' of connected dots that
initially do nothing more than obscure the 'coarse-grained' possibility of some
pending catastrophe.

In our scenario above, a dot is just a data point – a spatio-temporally situated state of nature existing at some given level of complexity. It could range
from, 'a person just entering my subway car may have set off my beeper', to
'a white middle-class woman wearing green sunglasses and wearing a black
leather coat bulging at mid-torso has entered my car carrying a strange
-looking orange bag; my beeper was triggered right after she entered'. The
second 'dot' is clearly more information-bearing than the first – it has more
attributes. The basic pattern-generating matrix thus, consists of d dots × h
attributes. So, the number of possible patterns possibilities may actually turn
out to be far higher than the 2^{66} derivable from 12 dots. Each 'dot' is an h
attribute vector that can connect at one or more points with the vectors associated with other dots in a connectivity matrix. Clearly, the more points at
which two vectors connect on, the stronger the correlated histories of their
respective dots, and, by implication, the stronger the connection between
them. For example, was the 'white middle-class woman wearing a black
leather coat' at school with the Malay-looking young man who entered car
number seven two stops before? He was also carrying a strange-looking
orange bag and also triggered the firing of a beeper. None of this, however,
necessarily constitutes a threat. No one knows. Thus, most of the dot-vectors
interfere with each other to produce entanglements, whilst concealing from
outsiders the connections of possible interest.

Any person may link with another person with respect to each attribute –
sunglasses to sunglasses, common schools, orange bags, etc. At the maximum,
we could see 2^{66} pattern-element connections *multiplied by* the h attributes
comprising each vector = $2h^{66}$. For some large number of agents, there would
be many dissimilar or non-complementary attributes, so in reality a given dot-
vector, x, is a long bit-string containing some 1s and mostly 0s with occasional
1s at the same level as, say, vector y – where some association could be established. Possibly no linking occurs at all, however, so that the number of
patterns remains zero. The basic array of $2h^{N(N-1)/2}$ possible patterns could be

vast indeed but most pattern-elements (or frequencies) will cancel out and disappear into the fine-scale structure.

We now propose a three-step filtering approach to pattern processing, one for each of the possible, plausible and probable worlds. The operation needs to be computationally tractable and performed at a faster rate than, say, the rate at which a given threat or opportunity builds up. Our proposed hi-tech 'socio/computational' approach follows.

Step 1: Identify Contextual Tensions and Possible Worlds

We start with the need for what McKelvey (2001, 2005) calls adaptive tension in the system. New order emerges in a system when the energy differentials within it – adaptive tensions – are of sufficient strength to trigger phase transitions. Emergent events result when this tension, that is, the energy differentials, exceeds some critical value, R. A process of new order creation is then initiated and newly emerging patterns begin to appear. For a simple example, consider a pot of water being heated. When the heat produces a temperature above R, a phase transition occurs and the water molecules begin moving in a rolling boil – a new structure – instead of remaining stationary and increasing their vibration rate. This basic law in complexity science, dating back to Bénard (1901), tells us that only tensions above R cause emergent events to unfold. We hypothesize that limiting our search to contexts in which the tension exceeds R – let's call these k-contexts – offers an effective method for filtering out most of the irrelevant dots, links and possible patterns, leaving only those worth more attention.

Adaptive tension (for example, political Islam, falling profits at Enron, etc) is the motivating force that activates transactions (interactions or links) between 'dots'. The tension has to be high enough to exceed the threshold-activation levels of the relevant dots. If no dot gets activated there cannot be an emergent transaction. Tension, then, separates out relevant transactions from the rest, turning them into candidates for further processing – that is, they belong to some possible world, one that provides some k-context in which they have relevance. It follows that, in a k-context, if the adaptive tension remains below R, the transactions will not form part of the emerging coarse-grained structure of relevant patterns. Adaptive tension can sometimes be increased or diminished through pragmatic action. In the case of the beeper, for example, just going and asking the white middle-class female, 'Is this your (orange) bag?' may be effective in generating the required level of adaptive tension – how might she react? It is unlikely to do so, however, if one simply puts the question at random to other passengers that happen to be in the subway car.

Step 2: Identify Corroborating Vantage Points and Plausible Worlds

Having established a pattern's relevance in one of the k-contexts, that is, a possible world, additional corroboration from unbiased perspectives is essential to turn possible patterns into plausible ones. We need multiple vantage points, v, for this added corroboration. A possible pattern gains in plausibility if it makes sense from the 'situated' perspectives of different agents – that is, it gets triangulated.

By summing over non-corroborated tension-driven transactions and relegating them to the fine-scale structure, corroboration through v-vantage points further narrows the field of possibly relevant coarse-grained pattern-elements. As a second filter that moves us towards coarse-graining, it offers two advantages: (1) v-vantage points, say four, offer corroboration that a particular emergent transaction, activated by some tension, is relevant and not a random transaction driven by some tension below R; (2) v-vantage points offer the chance of retrieving a relevant transaction that might have been missed by one agent's k-context filter but picked up by another's.

In our beeper example, if a third Operative's beeper had fired at the station where the woman boarded the train – besides yours and the other Operative's – and if she had been observed to behave suspiciously by a station employee (four corroborating beepers), then, from four distinctive v-vantage points, one would have reason to process her data further. It may be that the third passenger ignored his sensor's signal, no pattern suggesting itself given his k-context. But now we have triangulation and the first sensor's signal needs to be retrieved and attended to.

Step 3: Identify Time-based Robustness and Probable Worlds

Ashby (1962) observed that chaotic environments do not impose the kind of variety (the degrees of freedom defining levels of complexity) that an organism or an organization can easily respond to. Just as a teapot on a stove requires a continuous source of heat to come to the rolling boil, so our dots, for the most part, only get configured into patterns exhibiting some stability if the adaptive tension remains consistent over a number of time periods. A transient and shifting tension is chaotic and, thus, cannot consistently instigate the progressive emergence of intelligible patterns over time. Consequently, tracking phenomena across somewhat differentiated (mildly chaotic) time-periods accomplishes two things: (1) Patterns that are robust enough to persist for some time under adaptive tension and in mildly chaotic conditions, that is, they remain correlated across sequential time periods, are indeed worth worrying about; and (2) even after testing d × h dot-vectors for k-contexts and v-vantage points, a large number of transactions could remain that do not lead to an identifiable emergence sequence. Further filtering may be achieved by looking for correlated elements that yield patterns across a number of t-time periods.

But what value for t should we choose? Patterns specifically presaging 09/11 were discernible months before the event (Strathern, 2003). How far back should one go? To the Gulf War of 1990? To the creation of the Israel in 1947? Alternatively, across how many future time periods should one wait for events to unfold? Waiting too long could allow the emergent pattern to crystallize, with the result that some emergent event such as 09/11 actually occurs. Arguably, the FBI waited for the nth time period, which, as it turned out, was (obviously) at least one time period past the date of the 09/11 attack. No magic formula will tell us what the appropriate number of t-time periods should be. Nevertheless, t-time-period filters will reduce the set of plausible patterns to one of probable patterns by only focusing on those that recur over time.

To summarize, we can represent our matrix of interlinked dots as a densely connected network that is gradually thinned out by successive filtering, that is, by a sequence of matrix multiplications that reflect the selective influence of k, v, and t. Such a network can then be imported into a connectionist computational model.

COMPUTATIONAL STRATEGIES

In moving from possible to probable worlds via plausible worlds, one confronts the problem of computational overload. Two overload-reducing computational strategies have been established over the past 30 years: Serial and parallel computing:

Serial Computing

A serial computer program (SC) uses a 'top-down' process that takes symbolic material as its input, that is, data that have already been processed into information in the form of symbolic patterns. It emits symbolic material as its output after having submitted it to a set of well-defined operations. A sophisticated example of such a process is structural equation modelling (SEM) (Kaplan, 2000), illustrated in Figure 4.1.

1. For those familiar with questionnaire design, our text-messages correspond to scale items that act as inputs; our pattern elements – part of a pattern-structure – correspond to those variables that make up the theoretical explanatory structure. The dependent variables get 'chunked' into prospective 'training models' that, when finalized, will constitute inputs for the neural net model. In Figure 4.1a, the k-contexts show text messages getting processed

and filtered into a number of candidate-dependent variables. In Figure 4.1b, the v-vantage points further filter these 'plausible' patterns, with some now becoming more dominant; Figure 4.1c shows the filtering effects of the t-time periods, generating one or two pattern elements that now become plausible training models for parallel processing by the neural net.

2. In the SEM, text messages are first filtered by the context in which different Operatives find themselves, then by vantage point provided by individual Operatives' perspectives, and finally over successive time periods. The program starts with specified contexts, such as: terrorists, cults, rebels, pandemic disease indicators, new technological elements, etc. Or, it may find contexts as it analyses messages. As texts are passed through k-, v-, and t-filters, the emerging candidate patterns become fewer and more focused. Through successive iterations, the SEM provides ever better training patterns to the neural net parallel processor. The objective of the SEM computation is to reduce candidate patterns generated by countless possible input data/patterns.

Parallel Computing

A parallel processor (PP) or connectionist computer program uses a 'bottom-up' process designed to deal with sub-symbolic material as its inputs. The neural network processor (Hassoun, 1995) depicted in Figure 4.2 is a typical example. By processing this material through a set of 'hidden layers', the PP generates plausible patterns as its outputs. Through successive iterations, these eventually coagulate into probable, and therefore actionable, hypotheses. In order to find plausible patterns more rapidly, PPs need a 'training pattern' against which to test those that they generate for goodness-of-fit. The training patterns act as 'Bayesian priors' that, through a series of iterations, get gradually updated. Where do such patterns come from? In our case, the SC provides them.

1. Our PP is a neural net that takes a 'chunked' output from the SEM as a temporary training pattern. It keeps adjusting its 'hidden variables' in an attempt to achieve a goodness-of-fit between the patterns that it generates and those it has received as inputs. Initially it achieves a number of plausible fits and then later very few. Its 'Bayesian updates' generate the best matches with the training patterns (the 'chunks') produced by the SEM. Eventually they become identifiable actionable patterns for reaching back into the real world to uncover the links among terrorist 'dots', that is, 'dot-links'. The objective of the neural net computation is to find the few relevant terrorist *dot-links* from among all those that match the training pattern.

As already suggested, if it is to act as an efficient pattern processor, a PP requires the guidance of training patterns. The difficulty is that training

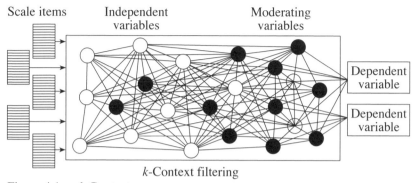

Figure 4.1a   *k*-Contexts

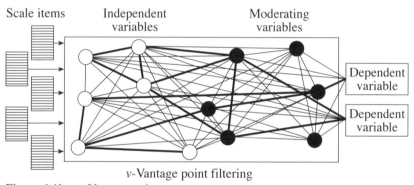

Figure 4.1b   *v*-Vantage points

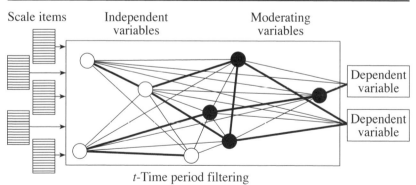

Figure 4.1c   *t*-Time periods

Figure 4.1   Pattern filtering via serial computing

Input units
Text terms

Hidden units

Output units
Actionable pattern

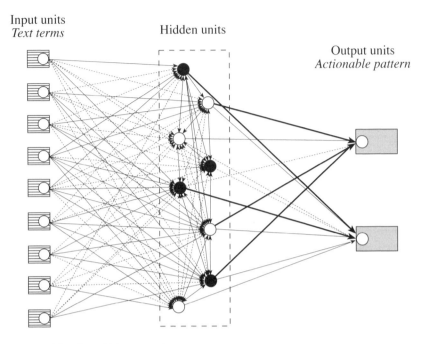

Figure 4.2   Parallel computing

patterns themselves need to get updated dynamically as time progresses in response to new text message inputs – the world does not come to a halt whilst we try to figure it out! The PP and SC therefore have to work in tandem, as depicted in Figure 4.3, in order to achieve convergence on some increasingly probable pattern.

So far, we have described the computational process in the abstract. How is it going to be made to work in practice? What we need to do is to combine the remarkable pattern-processing skills of human agents with the high-speed data-processing capacities of computers, a hybrid socio/computational approach involving Operatives equipped with detectors, beepers, mobile phones, phone photos, etc, providing inputs – both dots and patterns of dots – to the two computational processing components described above. We detail the computational steps next.

OUR SOCIO/COMPUTATIONAL PROCESS USING A TEST SCENARIO

By passing them through k, v, and t filters, the SEM cycles the continuously

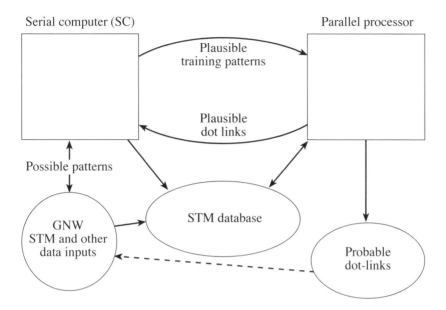

Figure 4.3   Serial and parallel processing combined

upgraded inputs being received (beeper signals, text messages, photos, conversations, etc) in order to help the PP to select out the key links (and dots) from among the trillions of possible patterns – that is, patterns that have coherence, are recognizable, and result in actionable dot connections. The acronyms that we use to save space are defined in the table below.

Stage One: k-contexts and Possible Worlds

When two or more beepers, that is, dots, go off at the same time, a correlation is established. Does it suggest a possible pattern?

- Most of the time, the beepers go off here and there in a random fashion. Typically, no inter-dot connections are implied by such false positives.
- If the triggering of two beepers more or less coincides – say caused by the action of a chemical sensor – then the signals automatically get registered in the Computer. An agent located at MI-6 can then either communicate directly via short-text-messaging (STM) with the relevant Operatives through their mobile phones, or it can alert a higher-level Operative who then 'conference' calls both of them.
- At this point an exploration of possible patterns is initiated. Operatives in the subway train look around the cars they are in. One sees a man and

woman with a baby carriage. The man has a 'Mediterranean' look. The MI-6 agent asks the Operatives to get nearer; the beeper signals from their detectors get stronger.

Only possible patterns (some subset of correlated input signals) are generated at this stage. In this case, two beepers (dots) firing in a subway car initiate a pattern generation process between them. This instance of correlation between firing beepers need not be a purely local affair. It could conceivably extend to international locations such as a garden in Perak (Malaysia), Singapore's Changi Airport, a school playground in Karachi or a casino in Macau. No coherent story, or pattern, can yet account for these correlated beeper firings. That is, the pattern cannot yet be recognized. A huge number of possible candidate input patterns, therefore, are in need of processing. The vast majority of them will get eliminated when passed through k-context filters.

When it can correlate incoming beeper signals over space and time – even if only weakly – the SC initiates a top-down process. The next step is to automatically call back the relevant Operatives and get them to briefly describe the different contexts in which the beeper signals were emitted. Pattern recognition now becomes both a local and a human affair.

Stage Two: v-vantage Points and Plausible Worlds

Beepers going off at random here and there can, for the most part, be ignored. But if several go off in some correlated fashion, then keywords can be derived from the different vantage points of Operatives to guide further data processing and interpretation. In this way patterns become more plausible:

- The MI-6 agent calls the Operatives whose beepers initiated the process and asks them to describe in some detail what they see. In this specific case, the MI-6 Operative then alerts other Operatives who happen to be either on the subway train or in the vicinity of its destinations – Piccadilly station and the other stations the train is due to stop at – to become more alert and to converge toward these stations, etc. Given some corroborating overlap in the description of Operatives located at v-vantage points, candidate input pattern elements are identified and processed. These are evolved in an iterative fashion through the continuing interaction of the MI-6 agent and the SC on the one hand, with the socially distributed network (SDN) of Operatives, and PP on the other.
- Upon receiving beeper signals, the SEM is programmed to request text messages from Operatives using as many standard code words as possible – that is, central Asian, young male, bearded, strange expression, box, suitcase, laptop, shopping bag, stroller, etc. The SEM is

programmed to rank these words against Zipf's (1949) power law ranking – looking for frequently used words that are inconsistent with the power law ranking of frequency of use.

- Guided by the MI-6 agent, the SEM keeps cycling through all incoming messages trying to tease out plausible connections – pattern elements – between them (a process depicted in Figure 4.3). The SEM then suggests suitable terms or labels, to 'help' Operatives communicate the pattern(s) they see. Of course, the SEM should not be so 'helpful' as to lead members to 'see' non-existent patterns. As the SEM's 'experience' accumulates it gets better at suggesting appropriate terms – those learnt in earlier training exercises and that Operatives themselves would want to use.

As pattern elements emerge and get corroborated across sensors, Operatives' beepers and v-vantage points – that is, as dots get 'filled in' and links are found – candidate patterns begin to take shape. As pattern elements accumulate and get further defined, the nascent patterns gain in plausibility.

Stage Three: t-time Periods and Probable Worlds

When two (or more) Operative inputs generate correlated keyword-and-context messages across t-time periods, the recurrence justifies the formulation of probabilistically derived expectations. As more Operatives approach the vicinity of the subway train, the number of possible incoming inputs could well increase far beyond the MI-6 agent's capacity to respond. Here is where SEM becomes especially useful. Increasingly plausible patterns recurring across t-time periods now produce temporary training patterns as inputs to the PP:

- At some point the SC runs 'block model' software[2] to more efficiently abstract out training patterns from the myriad inputs. Needless to say, the SEM needs some minimum number of inputs to get going. Via the abstracting process, redundant pattern elements begin to coagulate into candidate pattern elements that get integrated into meaningful 'wholes'. These the SEM consolidates into trial sets of pattern elements, chunks, that are entered into the PP to serve as temporary training patterns (TTPs) for it.
- Each TTP – and there could be many of these instead of just one as with conventional neural net models – now acts as a template against which further inputs can be compared. An emergent pattern would grow in strength to the extent that its constituent elements matched the SDN-generated patterns that now define a TTP. The larger the number of

  spatio-temporal events that match a given TTP, the more probable it
  becomes.
- For each initial set of two (or more) inputs that end in a TTP, the recursive cycling ends when the most successively refined, and thus most
  probable, TTPs are fed back to the SDN for final checking. At this stage
  we have a TTP built up from the various inputs emanating from interactions with situated Operatives. TTPs thus consist of probable patterns
  – alternative configurations of dots and links enjoying a high degree of
  corroboration.

Stage three ends with the emergence of a limited number of sequentially
corroborated TTPs.

Stage Four: Pattern Matching in Actual Worlds

TTPs are testable hypotheses. Sooner or later, nature will show its hand and
test them. By this time, in our scenario we have potentially hundreds of
Operatives converging on Tube stations along the train's route. They have
generated a number of TTPs for the SEM to process as probable scenarios.
Many of these diverge, but some converge to produce chunks.

While cycling through and refining TTPs, the SDN compares them and
looks for chunking opportunities. Chunks are defined by standard bio-taxo-
nomic method: No single term is essential; most – but not all – are included.
TTPs generate chunks in two ways: (1) From overlap with or corroboration by
other TTPs. They gain credibility from redundancy and are now reduced in
number. The block model abstracts and synthesizes multiple patterns into
chunks and the SEM now sends these out to Operatives for further corrobora-
tion/confirmation. (2) From the integration of new incoming recycled STMs
providing further corroboration that individual links between dots constitute
valid pattern elements. TTPs now either: (1) merge into a single chunk; (2) are
cast away as errors; or (3) are maintained as alternative hypotheses.

Here is where SEM 'logic' appears. SEMs 'compute' – that is, they pick
selected pattern elements as inputs and modify their interrelationship thus
producing structural variables – so as to ultimately find the selection of data
inputs and patterns that most accurately define the dependent variable (chunk)
to be predicted. Beeper signals, STMs, photos and taped conversations are the
pattern elements to be input. The actual patterns play the role of the 'structure'
in the SEM. The inter-relationship of their components is constantly changing,
just as independent and moderating variables change position in SEM modelling as correlations strengthen or weaken. The chunks play the role of the
dependent variable(s) – as pattern elements are added or deleted and as structural elements (the TTPs) are rearranged into trial patterns, the chunks become

better defined. The SEM program cycles through the various pattern elements, TTPs, and chunk constructions until one or more coherent chunks emerge. First, following block model theory, the challenge is to represent the commonalities among the TTPs with the fewest chunks. This results from abstracting out the more frequently reoccurring links across the population of patterns – the pattern(s) built from the dominant abstractions (those occurring in the most patterns) become chunks (Wasserman and Faust, 1994). Second, in structural equation modelling (Kaplan, 2000), the challenge is to maximize the correlation of independent variables (the TTPs arising from the STM terms) with emerging chunks. Collapsing similar TTPs into a single chunk accomplishes both.

Chunks, the output of stage four, constitute inferences to the best explanation (Sklar, 1995) – hypothetical patterns systematically evolved to train the PP in what to look for as it sifts through the vast number of dot-vectors supplied by all of the input signals.

CONCLUSION

In Chapter 3 we argue that uncovering terrorist plots before the event is far more difficult than simply 'filling in the dots' – it is a problem of finding meaningful patterns among trillions of possible patterns. We also demonstrate the need for rapid pattern generating and recognition capabilities in the context of security and terrorist prevention. Further, pattern processing has to be accomplished in timely fashion by organizational hierarchies that are siloized and cut off from key detection sources. In this chapter we argue that this calls for building up internal complexity so as to 'destroy external complexity'. We then present a socio/computational method that allows hierarchical organizations to process complexity, that is, carry out decision and pattern processing, at high speed. When dealing with dangerous emergence events – possibly global in scope – speed is what counts. It can only be achieved when the following are in place:

1.   Widely dispersed and highly mobile human Operatives in and outside official intelligence agencies engaged in 'distributed' pattern processing and corroboration activities – that is, 'intelligence' distributed across thousands of Operatives (neurons) acting within a connectionist (synaptic) brain-like network.
2.   Operatives all equipped with portable detectors, beepers, mobile camera phones and STM capability. Only with these resources can agencies move methodically and quickly from possible to probable knowledge via plausible knowledge.

3. A centralized socio/computational technology that:
   a. Can quickly reduce trillions of candidate patterns down to an action-able few to serve as inputs for parallel processors in the form of successively updated training patterns. We suggest structural equation (with block) modelling as a preferred method.
   b. Uses neural net parallel processing, driven by increasingly accurate training patterns, to focus searches through corroborated open-source information for relevant dot-links existing in the world as input data – especially those that foreshadow some imminent security threat.

We frame our argument mostly in terms of security threats. But any firm needing rapid information processing – about new technology, consumer tastes or competitor moves – could take advantage of our proposed method.

NOTES

1. In computational models, 'agent' is a general term used to designate the semi-autonomous entities which comprise a complex system, which may be such things as atoms, molecules, bio-molecules, organelles, organs, organisms, species, processes, individuals, groups, firms, industries, and so on.
2. Block model programs come out of network sociology. They abstract commonalities across multiple networks (Wasserman and Faust, 1994).

REFERENCES

Anthony, M. and P.L. Bartlett (1999), *Neural Network Learning: Theoretical Foundations*, New York: Cambridge University Press.
Ashby, W.R. (1956), *An Introduction to Cybernetics*, London: Chapman & Hall.
Ashby, W.R. (1962), 'Principles of the self-organizing system', in H. von Foerster and G.W. Zopf (eds), *Principles of Self-Organization*, New York: Pergamon, pp. 255–78.
Bénard, H. (1901), 'Les tourbillons cellulaires dans une nappe Liquide transportant de la chaleur par convection en régime permanent', *Annales de Chimie et de Physique*, **23**, 62–144.
Berlekamp, E., J.H. Conway and R.K. Guy (1982), *Winning Ways*, London: Academic Press.
Boisot, M. (1998), *Knowledge Assets*, New York: Oxford University Press.
Boisot, M. and B. McKelvey (2004), 'Counter-terrorism as neighborhood watch: a socio/computational approach for getting patterns from dots', working paper, The Sol Snider Center, The Wharton School, University of Pennsylvania, Philadelphia, PA.
Carley, K.M. (1996), 'A comparison of artificial and human organizations', *Journal of Economic Behavior and Organization*, **31**, 175–91.
Carley, K.M. and D.M. Svoboda (1996), 'Modelling organizational adaptation as a simulated annealing process', *Sociological Methods and Research*, **25**, 138–68.

Gell-Mann, M. (1994), *The Quark and the Jaguar*, Freeman, New York.

Gilbert, N. and K.G. Troitzsch (1999), *Simulation for the Social Scientist*, Philadelphia, PA: Open University Press.

Hassoun, M.H. (1995), *Fundamentals of Artificial Neural Networks*, Cambridge, MA: MIT/Bradford Press.

Kaplan, D. (2000), *Structural Equation Modelling: Foundations and Extensions*, Thousand Oaks, CA: Sage.

LeBaron, B. (2000), 'Volatility magnification and persistence in an agent based financial market', working paper, Graduate School of International Economics and Finance, Brandeis University, Waltham, MA.

McKelvey, B. (2001), 'Energizing order-creating networks of distributed intelligence', *International Journal of Innovation Management*, **5**, 181–212.

McKelvey, B. (2003), 'Emergent order in firms: complexity science vs. the entanglement trap', in E. Mitleton-Kelly (ed.), *Complex Systems and Evolutionary Perspectives on Organizations*, Amsterdam: Elsevier Science, pp. 99–125.

McKelvey, B. (2004), 'Toward a 0th law of thermodynamics: order-creation complexity dynamics from physics and biology to bioeconomics', *Journal of Bioeconomics*, **6**, 65–96.

McKelvey, B. (2005), 'Microstrategy from macroleadership: distributed intelligence via new science', in A.Y. Lewin and H.W. Volberda (eds), *Mobilizing the Self-Renewing Organization*, New York: Palgrave/Macmillan.

Mitchell, M. (1996), *An Introduction to Genetic Algorithms*, Boston, MA: MIT Press.

Omnès, R. (1999), *Understanding Quantum Mechanics*, Princeton, NJ: Princeton University Press.

Schelling, T.S. (1971), 'Dynamic models of segregation', *Journal of Mathematical Sociology*, **1**, 143–86.

Sklar, L. (1995), 'Philosophy of Science', in R. Audi (ed.), *The Cambridge Dictionary of Philosophy*, Cambridge, UK: Cambridge University Press, pp. 611–15.

Strathern, M. (2003), 'The symmetries and redundancies of terror – notes', working paper, Cranfield School of Management, Cranfield University, UK.

von Neumann, J. (1951), 'The general and logical theory of automata', in L.A. Jeffress (ed.), *Cerebral Mechanisms in Behavior – The Hixon Symposium*, New York: Wiley, pp. 1–41.

Wasserman, S. and K. Faust (1994), *Social Network Analysis: Methods and Applications*, New York: Cambridge University Press.

Zipf, G.K. (1949), *Human Behavior and the Principle of Least Effort: An Introduction to Human Ecology*, Cambridge, MA: Addison-Wesley.

PART II

Strategic Behavior

5. Terror incognito: international business in an era of heightened geopolitical risk

David A. Wernick

GEOPOLITICS AND THE INTERNATIONAL FIRM

Although it was not generally appreciated at the time, the balance of power between the great powers that prevailed during the post-World War II period provided a strong geopolitical framework for the growth of international business.[1] True, roughly half of the world's population resided in countries that were closed off to trade and foreign direct investment (FDI), periodic 'hot wars' erupted across the globe and the world on several occasions came perilously close to the brink of nuclear conflagration. Yet the rules of super-power engagement, enshrined in doctrine of 'mutually assured destruction', provided a modicum of stability in the international system and a solid foundation for the growth of industry, trade and foreign direct investment (Gray, 2004; Paul et al., 2004; Ikenberry, 2002).[2]

An even more favorable international business environment emerged during the late 1980s and early 1990s with the collapse of the Soviet Union and its Eastern European satellites and the embrace of market-oriented policies throughout much of the developing world (Friedman, 1999; Yergin and Stanislaw, 2002; Checa et al., 2003). Suddenly, international companies had many more markets with which to trade and invest.[3] Surveying the sudden transformation of the geopolitical map during the early 1990s, some Western analysts went so far as to proclaim the 'end of history' and the triumph of liberal market capitalism over all other ideological contenders (for example, Fukuyama, 1992).

Unfortunately, the celebrations were premature. As Beck (1992) observes, the fall of Communism did not mark the end of ideological struggle between nations nor the beginning of an era of peace and harmony in international affairs – at least not for long. Rather, it ushered in a 'risk society' marked by increasingly lethal transnational threats to the established global order.[4]

   The nature of the new risk society was dramatized by the 09/11 terrorist attacks on New York and Washington, DC, as well as the spate of nearly two dozen anthrax attacks in the months that followed.[5] The deadly Bali discotheque bombing of October 2002, the Madrid railway bombing of March 2004, and the bloody denouement of a hostage standoff at a primary school in the Russian city of Belsan later that year provided additional evidence, if any were needed, that the world had entered a new and more dangerous period,[6] where formerly unthinkable acts of savage terror were suddenly very real threats to governments, individuals and corporations.[7]

   In recent years international relations theorists have struggled to adapt their traditional models to what has variously been called the 'new threat paradigm' (Carter and Perry, 1999) and the 'new global anarchy' (Barber, 2003). Unfortunately, as Pearlstein (2004) observes, in the post-09/11 world the whole notion of polarity – long the linchpin of geostrategic thinking – has lost much of its relevance.[8] Instead, he contends that we are witnessing the emergence of a 'polyplex' global system, in which many different nation- and non-nation-state actors vie for power in an 'exceedingly difficult, unruly, congested, shrinking, non-polar, and swiftly evolving world'.[9] Among the most important of these non-state actors – particularly from the standpoint of the international firm – are transnational terrorist organizations.

TERRORISM: OLD AND NEW

Terrorism, loosely defined, has a long historical pedigree.[10] Political murder is mentioned in the Old Testament and featured prominently in the history of Ancient Greece and Rome.[11] Modern terrorism emerged in Russia in the 1880s and quickly spread to Western Europe, the Balkans and Asia. Dubbed the 'Golden Age of Assassination', the 1890s saw a wave of attacks by anarchists and revolutionaries against political figures and nobility. Terrorism crossed the Atlantic shortly thereafter, as European immigrants brought their political ideologies with them to the New World. In September 1901, a young anarchist of Polish extraction assassinated President McKinley at the Pan-American Exposition in Buffalo, prompting his successor, Theodore Roosevelt, to launch an ambitious international crusade to eliminate terrorism (Rapoport, 2003).[12]

   During the first half of the 20th century, terrorism was largely an anti-colonial enterprise, dominated by groups seeking nationhood. A new brand of left-wing terrorism arose during the 1960s, sponsored by the Soviet Union, East Germany and other members of the Communist bloc. These 'New Left' groups hijacked airplanes, kidnapped politicians and undertook other audacious stunts in an effort to publicize their grievances. Indeed, between 1960 and 1990, some 700 hijackings took place around the world (Rapoport, 2003). Left-wing terrorism enjoyed its heyday during the 1960s and 1970s, but declined during the 1980s and has virtually disappeared since the fall of Communism (Laqueur, 2003).

Although there is no universally accepted definition of terrorism, most observers agree that terrorist organizations share certain fundamental traits, such as the commitment to using violence or the threat of violence to attain political or ideological goals and the willingness to attack noncombatants.[13] Notwithstanding these commonalities, there is growing consensus that the new strain of terrorism that has emerged since the end of the Cold War is fundamentally different in character from past variants (Hoffman, 1998; Stern, 1999; Laqueur, 1999; Pearlstein, 2004).[14] Since these differences make the new terrorism potentially more threatening to the international firm, and society as a whole, they will be reviewed in detail.

Transnational Nature

The 'old terrorism' of the 1960s and 1970s, as Pearlstein (2004) observes, involved essentially two types of groups: those that operated exclusively within the boundaries of a single nation-state and did not receive external support (which he terms 'first generation intranational terrorist organizations'), and those that did conduct activities across borders, but did so with support and direction from an external sponsor (which he labels 'second generation international terrorist organizations').[15] What is unique about the new terrorism is it is conducted by independent, privately financed organizations, which, like transnational corporations, may shift their activities across borders as circumstances favorable to the organization dictate. Pearlstein refers to these organizations, of which al-Qaeda is the prototype, as 'third generation transnational terrorist organizations'.

Decentralized Structure

Whereas the old terrorism was generally conducted by rigidly centralized organizations with a clear command and control apparatus, the new terrorism is dominated by fluid, decentralized networks (Sageman 2004; US Department of State, 2005). Al-Qaeda, for example, is a loose organization of some three dozen Islamist groups scattered throughout more than 50 countries in Asia, the Middle East, the Caucasus and the Horn of Africa.[16] Its affiliates share a virulently anti-Western ideology and support the goal of establishing a network of fundamentalist theocracies stretching from Morocco to the Philippines. Since the destruction of its sanctuary in Afghanistan in 2001, al-Qaeda has assumed an even more decentralized, protean structure and is increasingly linking up with gangsters, drug traffickers, arms dealers and other transnational criminal organizations (Curtis, 2002; Stern, 2003; Sageman, 2004).[17]

Religious Rather than Political Orientation

Whereas the old terrorist groups were largely secular in orientation and motivated by political ideology or nationalism, the new terrorists tend to be driven by religion. Indeed, of the 11 international terrorist groups identified by the Rand Corp. in 1968, none were classified as religiously motivated (Hoffman, 1998). Thirty-five years later, nearly half of the 77 terrorist groups identified by the US State Department in its Global Patterns of Terrorism 2003 report were militant Islamic groups (US Department of State, 2004). Similarly, whereas the old groups tended to have well-defined and limited political objectives, which, if not justifiable, were at least understandable to external observers, the new terrorists appear to have no clear political agenda,[18] and are not particularly amenable to dialogue or negotiation (Laqueur, 2004, Juergensmeyer, 2002).[19] As former Central Intelligence Agency (CIA) Director James Woolsey puts it, 'Today's terrorists don't want a seat at the table, they want to destroy the table and everyone sitting at it' (National Commission on Terrorism, 2000).

Civilians as Targets

Whereas the old terrorist groups generally shied away from targeting noncombatants, presumably out of fear that indiscriminate killings might undermine their propaganda efforts or alienate financial backers, the new terrorist groups appear to have few qualms about launching such attacks, as demonstrated by 09/11 and recent attacks on international aid and humanitarian groups in Iraq and Afghanistan.[20] Indeed, some contend that killing large numbers of civilians is precisely the objective of groups like al-Qaeda since such mass casualty attacks (especially those involving multiple synchronous suicide bombers) cause severe trauma and anxiety, thereby increasing the psychological burden on its opponents (Nacos, 2003).[21]

Hard and Soft Targets

Whereas the old terrorist groups tended to direct their assaults against 'hard targets' such as embassies and military compounds, the new terrorist organizations are increasingly attacking 'soft targets', such as oil tankers, civilian aircraft, hotels, banks and other business facilities. The shift appears to be both strategic (to inflict maximum economic pain),[22] as well as tactical (these targets are generally more accessible). Among the soft targets attacked by al-Qaeda and its affiliates between 2002 and 2004 were three American hotel chains (the Sheraton in Karachi, the JW Marriott in Jakarta, and the Hilton in Cairo), a British bank (HSBC) in Istanbul, a discotheque in Bali, and a French oil tanker off the coast of Yemen.[23] There was also the near-miss surface-to-air missile attack on an Israeli passenger aircraft in Mombasa in November 2002, and scores of disrupted plots in the US, Europe and Asia, including one targeting Microsoft's operations in Singapore (Davies, 2002). Given the sharp increase in security around government and military installations since 09/11, terrorism experts believe the trend of attacking soft targets will continue for the foreseeable future.[24]

Global Fundraising

Unlike previous generations of terrorist organizations which tended to draw financial support from domestic sources, al-Qaeda funds its activities through private networks that are truly global in scope. In addition to receiving funds from wealthy patrons in the Middle East and siphoning resources from *hawalas* (Islamic charities), the group operates scores of front companies and legitimate enterprises around the world which facilitate the movement of money between its leadership and operational cells (National Commission on Terrorist Attacks Upon the United States Commission, 2004). Indeed, Osama bin Laden is reputed to have owned or controlled at one time some 80 companies throughout the Middle East and Africa, including construction, manufacturing, currency trading, import–export, and agricultural enterprises in the Sudan (Bergen, 2001).[25]

Global Recruitment

Whereas the old terrorist groups tended to select their foot-soldiers domestically, the new terrorists conduct their recruitment efforts on a global scale. In addition to its activities in countries with majority Muslim populations, al-Qaeda is increasingly targeting the Islamic diaspora in the West. Its favored recruitment channels include universities, cultural centers and prisons (Stern, 2003; Mueller, 2005). Indeed, Jose Padilla, the al-Qaeda suspect who was snared by the Federal Bureau of Investigation (FBI) on a flight from Pakistan to Chicago in May 2002, allegedly on a reconnaissance mission for a future radiological 'dirty bomb' attack, was a former member of an American-Latino gang who had converted to Islam in prison. Meanwhile, in October 2004, Spanish authorities announced that they had taken into custody more than a dozen Moroccans suspected of being members of a terrorist cell made up almost entirely of North African Muslims recruited in Spanish prisons.[26]

Global Logistics Infrastructure

Unlike previous generations of terrorist groups which tended to depend upon the logistics infrastructure of their state sponsors to transport operatives and weapons, the new terrorist groups increasingly own and operate their own conveyances. In the case of al-Qaeda, this infrastructure is believed to include a fleet of anywhere from a dozen to 50 hijacked merchant ships that have been repainted and renamed and ply the high seas under false documentation, manned by crews with fake passports and forged competency certificates (Robinson, 2003; Korin and Luft, 2004). One of these 'phantom ships' is believed to have delivered the explosives to Africa used in the 1998 bombings of the US embassies in Kenya and Tanzania that killed 220 people and injured more than 5,000 (Robinson, 2003; Langewiesche, 2004).

Technological Sophistication and Media Savvy

Whereas the old terrorist groups disseminated their propaganda (generally, crudely designed pamphlets) via underground networks, al-Qaeda produces slick, multimedia CD-ROMs and DVDs and has a major presence on the internet. Indeed, The Foreign Policy Research Institute estimates that the number of jihadist websites has grown from about a dozen in 2000 to more than 4,000 in 2005 (CSIS, 2005). In addition to posting recruitment materials such as streaming media clips of attacks and beheadings on these websites, the group has managed to load the 13-volume Encyclopedia of Jihad and one-volume Jihad Manual onto the World Wide Web (Hoffman, 2003).[27]

Likewise, al-Qaeda is much more adept at using the media for propaganda purposes than traditional terrorist groups. While terrorist groups have always sought media attention to help publicize their grievances, al-Qaeda, with the help of Al-Jazeera, CNN, Fox News and other global television networks has raised the bar considerably. As Nacos (2003) points out, 09/11 was a well choreographed 'global television spectacular' that opened a new chapter in the annals of terrorism as communication because of the choices planners made with respect to method, target, timing and scope.[28]

Commitment to Acquiring WMD

Finally, and perhaps most troubling, unlike the old terrorist groups which had little interest in acquiring non-conventional weapons, the new terrorist groups have made the acquisition of these deadly weapons a priority.[29] Indeed, al-Qaeda's quest for weapons of mass destruction dates back to the early 1990s when it dispatched an operative to Sudan to purchase highly enriched uranium (Lee, 2003). Since then the group has been aggressively recruiting rogue scientists, including nuclear physicists and microbiologists, to help them develop a nuclear, radiological and biochemical weapons capability. There are also credible reports that al-Qaeda has been hunting for 'loose nukes' on the black market (Bunn and Wier, 2005).[30]

THE NEW INTERNATIONAL BUSINESS ENVIRONMENT

Coupled with the change in the nature of the terrorist threat in recent years has been a fundamental restructuring of the way international firms do business. During the 1980s and 1990s, many US manufacturers, taking their cue from the Japanese, began outsourcing various facets of their value chains to the developing world and establishing global production systems, based on just-in-time (JIT) management practices. The result was dramatic gains in operational efficiency,[31] enhanced accountability, productivity, customer service and product quality (Sheffi, 2002).[32] As companies have trimmed the waste and integrated distant suppliers into their global production networks, however, they have also increased their exposure to supply disruptions – a lesson brought home to all by the 09/11 attacks.[33]

In the hours following the attacks on the World Trade Center and Pentagon, borders were sealed, air traffic was grounded and federal buildings were evacuated. This caused havoc for the logistics operations of scores of international firms doing business in North America. Toyota, for example, came within 15 hours of having to halt production of its Sequoia SUV plant in Princeton, Indiana because one of its suppliers did not have enough steering sensors on hand and could not airlift in additional inventory from Germany (Sheffi, 2002). The Ford Motor Company, meanwhile, was forced to idle five of its US plants because trucks filled with engines, drive trains and other critical components were snarled in traffic at the Canadian border. The result: 12,000 units of lost production and financial losses of $30 million (Shrader and McConnell, 2002).

The vulnerabilities exposed by the 11 September attacks will not go away any time soon, as firms continue to integrate their supply chains across borders to take advantage of low-cost, high-quality labor.[34] Indeed, the continuing shift of global manufacturing to China is expected to cause trans-Pacific container volumes to triple by 2020 (Mongelluzo, 2004).

Political Risk and the International Firm

Political risk has existed in one form or another for centuries. During the 1600s and 1700s, pirates posed ongoing risk for European merchants traveling to and from the New World (Jarvis, 2003). In modern times, the concept has been used primarily to describe the risk that political decisions or events in a country will cause foreign investors there either to lose money or fail to capture their expected returns.[35] These risks may result from the actions or inactions of governments (Wells, 1998) or subnational groups, including labor unions, students and human rights activists, as well as extortion by criminal mafias and guerrillas (Korbin, 1979).

During the 1950s through the mid-1980s, the chief political risk for most international firms operating in developing countries, particularly those involved in natural resource exploitation or manufacturing, was that of nation-alization of their assets by left-wing governments (as in Chile, Peru and Venezuela during the 1970s), or worse, confiscation by revolutionary regimes (as in Cuba in 1959 and Iran in 1979). Indeed, between the end of World War II and 1985, nearly 2,000 expropriations occurred around the globe, resulting in the loss of between 15 and 20 percent of all US FDI (Minor, 2002).

In recent years, these more overt forms of political risk have become less common, as developing countries have sought to encourage FDI in hopes of accelerating national development (Moran, 1998). Nevertheless, less overt forms of political risk, such as corruption and 'creeping expropriation' have become more widespread. Creeping expropriation takes place when govern-ments change the rules of the game after investments have been made (Jarvis, 2003). Examples include the sudden revocation of investment incentives, the alteration of tax regimes, the imposition of import or export duties, or abroga-tion of contracts. Such actions can jeopardize foreign operations, assets, income or the ability to service debt, and may destroy the business assump-tions under which the original investment was made (Bremer, 2001).

Terrorism and Political Risk

International business theory has traditionally viewed terrorism as a type of political risk (Suder, 2004). As Czinkota, Knight and Liesch (2004) observe, however, there are important differences between these concepts. Political risk, for example, tends to occur within individual countries at the primary and micro levels, whereas terrorism tends to have more macro-level consequences and its effects often transcend borders.[36] This was particularly true of the 09/11 attacks which caused little direct damage to firms outside of lower Manhattan, but had major consequences for international firms with opera-tions throughout North America and around the globe.

Likewise, political risk tends to principally affect the FDI mode of entry, whereas terrorism can affect all entry modes – from exporting to joint ventures. Political risk also tends to target specific objects such as firms and their managers, while the targets of terrorism are often symbolic and its victims random. Furthermore, political risk generally builds up gradually in a predictable fashion, whereas terrorism tends to strike suddenly and without warning. And finally, since it can potentially disrupt operations in multiple regions simultaneously and bring assembly lines to a standstill, terrorism raises the level of uncertainty for international business more than do traditional political risks (Czinkota et al., 2004).

While the classical conceptualization of terrorism as a form of political risk might have sufficed at one time, we contend that it is anachronistic in a world of decentralized, global networks of religiously-inspired terrorists. Unlike their more secular and politically-minded predecessors, these new terrorist groups have the intent and capability to mount catastrophic attacks that create disruption and chaos on a global scale.

Geopolitical Risk: A New Phenomenon?

So, if the new strain of terrorism is similar but distinct from political risk, what exactly is it, and more importantly, what, if anything, can international firms do to mitigate their exposure to it? Following Suder (2004), our view is that the act of terrorism itself, as well as the threat and its aftermath, can be classified under the label of 'geopolitical risk', which we define as follows: the potential for international political actors (including non-state actors) and events to directly or indirectly affect the operations of international firms or their key value chain partners, resulting in lost revenues or business opportunities.

This definition covers not only the direct consequences of terrorist attacks against companies in foreign countries (as does political risk), but the indirect consequences of attacks against the critical commercial infrastructure (for example, airlines, oil tankers, sea freighters and information networks) that sustain the global economy. For example, our definition would extend to a terrorist attack on a vessel or port in the Malacca Straits – the narrow waterway between Malaysia, Singapore, Thailand and Indonesia – through which roughly one-quarter of global trade and half of the world's oil passes. In addition to diverting as many as 500 vessels a day and causing logistical havoc for shippers, such an attack would likely send oil prices and cargo insurance premiums soaring to new heights, with profound ramifications for firms across a wide spectrum of industries.[37]

Our definition also covers the risk that might accrue to foreign footwear, apparel and consumer electronics manufacturers from a supply disruption caused by a flare up in nuclear tensions on the Korean peninsula, a sharp increase in tensions between China and Japan over the latter's bid for permanent membership on the United Nations Security Council and claims to natural gas beneath the East China Sea, or an escalation in nuclear tensions between India and Pakistan over Kashmir.

Furthermore, our definition covers the risk that might accrue to companies doing business in countries with large numbers of political extremists – particularly militant Islamists – as well as countries where governments have undertaken politically unpopular foreign policies such as sending troops to fight alongside US forces in Iraq.[38]

Corporate Response to Terrorism

Prior to 09/11, terrorism was not a central concern to most US multinationals, aside from those operating in areas prone to ethnic or political violence. In the language of operations management, it was seen as a low-risk, high-consequence phenomena – akin to being hit by an earthquake, hurricane or tsunami. As such, it made little sense to devote scarce resources to defending against such attacks.

Indeed, the conventional wisdom across corporate America was that these resources were better spent on research and development, marketing or other revenue-generating activities. After all, most shareholders cared primarily about profits – not whether a firm had building evacuation plans or redundant data systems in the unlikely event of an attack. In one of the few detailed surveys of corporate vulnerability to major unexpected disasters, Comdisco Inc. found in 1999 that 30 percent of 200 of the largest US companies had no business continuity plans in place (Rothfeder, 2001). As one observer quipped, industry was reluctant to get involved with what seemed to be the 'corporate equivalent of planning one's own funeral' (Peck, 2004).

Today, by contrast, terrorism is among the top concerns in the boardrooms of multinational companies. Indeed, in the 2004 PriceWaterhouseCoopers Global CEO Survey, chief executives ranked terrorism among the top five potential threats to business growth, with 36 percent identifying terrorism as a significant threat or 'one of the biggest threats' to their organization. Similarly, a recent survey by RAND Europe and Janusian Security Risk Management (2004) of security and risk managers at leading UK corporations found that 66 percent of respondents believe that terrorism is a 'significant threat' to their organizations and more than one third expect terrorists to deliberately target their organization and staff.[39]

Along with the increase in threat perception has been a sharp increase in corporate security spending for many international firms. The Business Roundtable (2005), a US association of large multinational companies, for example, reported in its 2004 CEO security survey that US firms have increased spending on security by an average of 10 percent since the 09/11 attacks, and the association expects security budgets to increase dramatically in the coming years in response to 'real and perceived threats to core business functions'. Likewise, more than half of the companies surveyed by the Yankee

Research Group in 2003 said they would increase their security budget over the next three years (Deloitte Research, 2004). Much of the increase in spending is going to defend against cyber attacks, which, according to one source, cost global businesses \$12.5 billion in 2003 (Hulme, 2004).[40]

In addition to allocating additional resources to secure their physical and human assets and information networks, a growing number of firms are centralizing their security activities under the aegis of a chief security officer (CSO).[41] The CSO's responsibilities typically include everything from overseeing access control and data security to crisis management and business continuity.

Security issues are also receiving fresh attention from corporate boards. According to the Institute of Chartered Accountants in England and Wales and The Risk Advisory Group, more than half of all companies now report that they review risks every board meeting or once a quarter (Murray, 2004).

What Else Can Be Done to Mitigate Risks?

Traditionally, firms have mitigated terrorism risk by purchasing insurance. However, given the post-09/11 decision of insurers to strip out acts of terrorism from 'all risk' policies and offer terrorism insurance as a separate policy with much higher premiums and deductibles, insurance is a costly option (Lloyd et al., 2005). As such, risk mitigation in the post-09/11 world must be dealt with at the operational level. Here is a list of ten measures that international firms could adopt to enhance their enterprise resilience.[42]

Incorporate new terrorism-related variables into existing risk models
When considering whether to invest in a particular country, firms usually consider the country's general sociopolitical climate as well as the presence of militant labor unions, guerrillas, non-governmental organizations, and other groups that could pose problems. Given the new risk environment, they should also consider whether the country is home to transnational terrorist groups and their sympathizers. Relevant considerations include the scale and frequency of past attacks, the number of past attacks prevented by authorities, and the counterterrorism capabilities of the country's security services. Other factors to consider include whether there have been recent protests or acts of vandalism by disaffected immigrant groups that could portend future trouble, and the presence of transnational criminal organizations that might link up with terrorists.

Whereas countries such as the United Kingdom and Germany would tend to rank low on traditional measures of political risk, the fact that both countries are home to large numbers of radical Islamists suggests they might be vulnerable to terrorism.[43] British Prime Minister Tony Blair's steadfast support for the US-led war against Iraq adds another risk element in the case of the UK.

Engage in geopolitical scenario development

Pioneered as a strategic tool in the 1950s at the RAND Corporation, physicist-turned-strategist Herman Kahn developed scenarios for analysing the relationship between weapons development and military strategy. The technique was adopted by Royal Dutch/Shell in the early 1970s, and 'the Shell method' is credited with helping the firm anticipate the OPEC oil price hikes later that decade (Frieswick, 2002). Unlike forecasting or market research, scenario planning relies on imagining the future rather than extrapolating current trends from the present or past. Based on these hypothetical scenarios, firms construct strategies that enable them to respond effectively. Given the increasingly volatile and fluid geopolitical environment, firms should engage in scenario development, following Suder (2004), especially those in capital-intensive industries and manufacturers with long product-cycle times.

Engage in stress testing exercises

Like scenario planning exercises, stress testing requires managers to question assumptions and imagine hypothetical situations (Chopra and Sodhi, 2004). Unlike the former, however, which focuses on events external to the company, stress testing seeks to identify vulnerabilities across the firm's internal value chain. For instance, a typical exercise might involve a manufacturer identifying key suppliers, customers, plant capacity, distribution centers and shipping lanes, and then surveying locations and amounts of inventory represented by components, work-in-progress and finished goods. After completing such an assessment, managers might then attempt to determine how to respond to a terrorist incident or other disruption which affected either the supply of critical components or demand for finished goods.

As Chopra and Sodhi (2004) observe, 'Through stress testing, managers should be able to identify risk-mitigation priorities for the near, medium and long term. They will have identified product families at risk, as well as individual plants, shipping lanes, suppliers or customers that could pose risks. Managers will also have a clear idea of what risks might have an impact on sales, procurement costs, revenues, prices or even reputation.'

Establish flexible sourcing and inventory management policies

In addition to adopting JIT practices, many firms in recent years have moved to core or single-source supply models. And while these models have allowed firms to reduce costs dramatically,[44] they have also left firms more vulnerable than ever to disruptions caused by natural disasters, political upheaval or terrorism. Given the new risk environment, firms should consider lining up alternative suppliers in different locations rather than relying on single sources, while increasing the amount of materials sourced domestically.[45] They should also consider selectively increasing inventory levels (that is, carrying buffer stock), and even establishing a 'strategic emergency stock' to be used only in the case of an extreme disruption. While most, if not all, of these measures will tend to raise operating costs, as Martha and Vratimos (2002) observe, 'Determining whether greater flexibility is worth the extra cost is part of the new [post-09/11] calculus.'

Prepare contingency transportation arrangements
One of the few US automobile producers that weathered the 09/11 crisis with minimal disruption was Daimler Chrysler, largely because it had contingency transportation plans in place for key inputs. In the hours following the terror-ist attacks, the firm's supply chain mangers realized they were running low on an updated steering gear unit for the redesigned Ram pickup truck. The part was normally sent by air from a TRW plant in Virginia to their Mexican assembly plant. But with the closure of US airspace, they needed an alterna-tive method. They thus turned to an expedited truck service which was able to get the parts to the factory without major delays (Martha and Vratimos, 2002). Given the new risk environment, manufacturers should broaden their shipping arrangements, looking to line up both alternative modes of transportation and ports of entry that could be utilized in an emergency.

Carefully choose a foreign entry mode
As Knight, Czinkota and Liesch (2003) note, exporting has historically been viewed by many business scholars the least optimal approach for entering foreign markets, since it does not permit a firm to acquire the same degree of local market knowledge as it would through a foreign direct investment (FDI). However, since exporting requires no equity investment, it also offers firms considerably more flexibility in responding to dynamic circumstances than do investments in bricks and mortar operations. Moreover, it gives firms the abil-ity to make a quick exit should circumstances require it. Given the new global risk environment, exporting may deserve a fresh look – especially for compa-nies doing business in politically volatile markets.

Strengthen alliances with overseas partners
Another viable alternative to FDI is establishing overseas alliances and joint ventures with local firms. In addition reducing a firm's equity exposure, such arrangements allow investors to establish linkages with local firms and governments that might reduce their risk of becoming a terrorist target. Furthermore, such arrangements provide firms with access to information that may help them anticipate a possible attack and deal more effectively with its

aftermath (Knight et al., 2003). Joint ventures may also save firms the cost and risk of having to deploy foreign managers overseas. As Shrader and McConnell (2002) observe, 'a network of alliances, appropriately managed, is potentially more resilient than a collection of global acquisitions. Alliance partners retain local management, eliminating the costs and risks of deploying employees around the globe.'

Relocate data centers or move to more distributed data processing or storage architecture

While this goes against the conventional cost-cutting wisdom of the 1990s, decentralizing data systems can help ensure business continuity in the event of a terrorist attack or other major disruption. One Phoenix, Arizona-based firm, for example, recently decided to mirror critical data at a center in Tempe, Arizona – ironically the same facility it once used a second data center which was shut down in a cost-cutting move. According to the company's chief technologist, 'I've seen it go in circles. Years ago, everyone was centralized on mainframes, then everyone decentralized, then centralized again to save money. Now we're decentralizing again for disaster recovery reasons' (CIO Insight, 2002).

Participate in voluntary public–private supply chain security programs

In early 2002, the US Customs Service (now Customs and Border Protection) introduced the Customs-Trade Partnership Against Terrorism (C-TPAT), a voluntary public–private supply chain security initiative. Established with the help of seven major multinational companies (BP America, Daimler Chrysler, the Ford Motor Company, General Motors Corp., Sara Lee Corp. and Target), the program requires that companies conduct comprehensive security audits and correct weaknesses that could be exploited by terrorists. In return, C-TPAT members receive expedited processing at US ports of entry. As of April 2005, 9,000 participants, including some 400 foreign manufacturers, had signed up for the program (Bonner, 2005). Future changes to the C-TPAT program, as envisioned by US CBP commissioner Robert Bonner, will make it even more valuable to companies dependent upon timely shipments from overseas suppliers.[46]

Invest in smart technology

In the aftermath of 09/11, many firms have turned to technology to manage documentation and comply with new governmental security mandates. But beyond compliance, there are additional reasons for investing in smart technologies, which include everything from RFID (radio frequency identification system) tags to electronic container seals (e-seals). By building visibility into supply chains, firms can better manage their inventory and avoid having to resort to costly expedited shipping arrangements for replenishments. Moreover, by helping curb maritime theft – which costs global firms some $40 billion annually – e-seals can help deliver a return on investment. Indeed, a study of the first phase of the industry-funded Smart and Secure Trade Lanes initiative[47] found that companies shipping goods from Asia to the US by sea could save $378 to $462 per container by employing a variety of information technology tools to secure and streamline shipping (Deloitte Research, 2004).

CONCLUSION

As Howell (2002) observes, there is both offense and defense in international investment. Offense involves having strong marketing, solid finances and savvy marketing. Defense involves, among other things, being able to maneuver in very complex and conflictual social, religious, cultural and political environments. The recent emergence of transnational terrorism and geopolitical conflict as major threats to international business makes this truer than ever. In the coming years, the firms that prosper will likely be those that view security as a possible source of competitive advantage, rather than simply a dead cost, and take steps to anticipate possible catastrophes and deal effectively with their aftermath. In this new high risk environment, as Mitroff (2004) puts it, managers of international firms must have the capacity to 'think like sociopaths', while 'acting like saints'.

NOTES

1. The term 'geopolitics' was coined in 1899 by the Swedish political scientist and conservative politician Rudolf Kjellen and is generally used to describe the broad relationship between geography, states and world power politics (O Tuathail, 2000).
2. This is not to minimize the very real physical, psychological and economic costs of the Cold War to the superpowers, its citizens, and the rest of the world. As Booth (1998) points out, these costs include: 'casualties in proxy wars, minds manipulated in hospitals, the secrecy that undermined democracy, the degradation of culture, the cult of force, and the missile men ready at a moment's notice to turn the keys that would unleash a nuclear hell on very faraway places about which they knew nothing'.
3. Notwithstanding numerous external shocks during the decade, including the Mexican peso crash, the Tequila Effect, the Asian financial crisis, and the Russian meltdown, global FDI flows grew fivefold during the 1990s, reaching an all-time high of $1.3 trillion in 2000 (Hill, 2005). Meanwhile, the number of multinational enterprises (MNEs) around the world grew to nearly 56,000 by the end of the decade with over 73 million employees and global sales in excess of $9.5 trillion (Stopford, 2000).
4. Beck contends that many of the new borderless threats germinated during the Cold War in US and Soviet weapons laboratories under the guise of 'national security'. Ironically, the proliferation of these deadly weapons and the diffusion of the knowledge and technology needed to produce them has become one of the chief sources of insecurity in the post-Cold War era. In a similar vein, Johnson (2000) argues that Washington's decision to provide

billions of dollars worth of sophisticated weaponry and training to Cold War allies such as the Afghan mujahedeen during the 1980s is now coming back to haunt the US since veterans of that country's wars are now turning their weapons against US forces – a phenomena which he refers to as 'blowback'.

5. As Barber (2003) observes, the anthrax itself killed fewer that half a dozen people and did minimal systemic damage. However, because the attacks were conducted via the US Postal Service they sparked 'a nationwide fear that devastated the country's collective sense of security'.

6. Not everyone agrees that the post-Cold War period is more dangerous than the era that preceded it. O'Neill (2004), for example, contends that a full-scale nuclear exchange between the US and Soviet Union would have resulted in anywhere from 50 to 100 million casualties, massive economic and social dislocation, if not complete collapse, the destruction of critical national infrastructure, and the likely disintegration of central government control. Moreover, millions would have died from the 'horrendous environmental aftereffects' including radiation sickness that would be passed on to the next generation in the form of debilitating birth defects. While an al-Qaeda attack using a weapon of mass destruction such as a radioactive dirty bomb against an American or European city would inflict tremendous human and physical damage, the casualties and destruction, he points out, would likely be of a much smaller order.

7. As Stern (1999) observes, the danger of macroterrorism – an act of terrorism which causes more than $1 billion in losses or 500 deaths – was discernable well before 09/11. Indeed, the FBI estimates that had the Islamist terrorists responsible for the 1993 World Trade Center bombing not committed a minor error in the placement of their truck bomb, some 50,000 people might have perished instead of only six. Moreover, as Parachini (2003) points out, the March 1995 sarin nerve gas attack by Japanese religious cult Aum Shinrikyo on the Tokyo subway system which killed 12 and injured more than 5,000 demonstrated that the new breed of terrorists were willing to do what once had been taboo: 'kill indiscriminately with large quantities of explosives or even use poison or disease as a weapon'.

8. Pearlstein's view on the demise of polarity is not universally accepted. Waltz (2002), for instance, argues that we are witnessing a 'unipolar moment' which will soon give way to a new balance of power, perhaps led by an emerging European Union, China or Japan. Likewise, Gray (2004) contends that while the West's central security challenge at present is confronting al-Qaeda and its affiliates, within the next five to 15 years, we will witness the 'return of old-fashioned, state-centric great power geopolitics and geostrategy'.

9. As Pearlstein (2004) notes, the term polyplex combines the notion of poly, or many, and plex, from the word complex, to suggest extreme complication and disorder.

10. The word 'terrorism' itself comes from the French Revolution's 'Reign of Terror' (1793–94), when Robespierre and his Jacobin gangs rounded up and executed some 12,000 people deemed enemies of the Revolution. Since the Jacobins ruled the French state, they would not be called terrorists under current definitions. Yet their vision of a violent purge in the name of remaking society provided a model for future insurgents (Greenberg, 2001).

11. Among the earliest terrorist organizations were the Zealots, a Jewish group active in the first century AD that hired assassins known as *sicarii* to kill their enemies (Romans and Roman sympathizers) in an effort to create a mass uprising against their occupiers. Their tactics succeeded, leading to a disastrous revolt that ended in their own mass suicide atop the mountain Masada (Hoffman, 1998a).

12. Rapoport (2003) notes with irony the similarities between Roosevelt's anti-terrorist crusade and George W. Bush's 'global war on terrorism' launched exactly 100 years later.

13. Stern (1999) argues that another defining characteristic of terrorism is that it deliberately attempts to evoke fear or dread in the target population, although there is no consensus on this point. Held (1991), for example, argues that terrorist objectives may include gaining concessions, obtaining publicity or provoking repression rather than instilling fear. The US State Department's definition of terrorism, meanwhile, describes terrorism as politically motivated violence 'usually intended to influence an audience', but does not elaborate on the nature of that influence (United States Department of State, 2004).

14. Kushner (1998) argues that the origins of the new terrorism predate the collapse of the Soviet Union and can be traced to the Iranian Revolution in 1979. After toppling the Shah,

the government of Ayatollah Khomeini embarked on a systematic campaign of supporting militant Islamic fundamentalist movements throughout the Muslim world – a campaign which bore fruit first in Sudan, and later in Afghanistan.

15. Examples of first generation intranational terrorist groups include the Symbionese Liberation Army (US), the Angry Brigade (Britain), and November 17 (Greece), while the Red Brigades (Italy), Red Army Faction (Germany), and Direct Action (France) are representative of second generation international terrorist groups – all of which are now dormant or defunct.

16. There is much debate about whether Al-Qaeda is an organization, a movement, a network, an insurgency, or all of the above. As Brzezinski (2004) observes, the public perception of al-Qaeda as a 'highly organized, tightly disciplined, globally pervasive underground army of technologically skilled terrorists directed from an efficient command and control center' surely exaggerates its coherence and capabilities. However, the notion that al-Qaeda is simply a bunch of autonomous terrorist groups and freelancers without any central direction – either strategic or tactical – is probably equally false. Perhaps the best description is put forth by Sageman (2004), who characterizes it as the vanguard of a much larger worldwide movement of like-minded militant Islamist groups that interact, share resources and work together to achieve shared goals.

17. According to Spanish court documents, the perpetrators of the 2004 March 11 Madrid train bombings included an unlikely assortment of drug dealers, religious extremists and veterans of al-Qaeda training camps in Afghanistan who came together almost by chance. These terrorists reportedly used the proceeds from drug sales to pay for an apartment hideout, a car and mobile phones and traded drugs for 440 pounds of dynamite which was used in the attack (Johnson, 2005; Center for Strategic and International Studies, October 2004).

18. Some observers contend otherwise. Lewis (1998), for example, contends that bin Laden and his deputy Aymin al Zawahiri laid out their objectives very clearly in their 1998 Declaration of the World Islamic Front for Jihad against Jews and Crusaders. The declaration, which included a fatwa to kill Americans and their allies, made three central demands: (1) the departure of US forces from the Arabian Peninsula; (2) the end of sanctions against the Iraqi regime; and (3) the end of US support for the State of Israel. Likewise, Michael Scheuer (2004), the former head of the Central Intelligence Agency's Osama Bin Laden unit, argues that al-Qaeda has been very forthright about its political objectives: 'America has never had an enemy who has been more clear and lucid about his grievances, about his intention to respond to those grievances, and has followed through with repeated military actions designed to get our attention and to cause casualties and economic damage'.

19. The notion that al-Qaeda and like-minded extremist movements are 'irrational actors' is not universally accepted. Lake (2002), for example, argues that extremists use terror to provoke the target into a disproportionate response that radicalizes moderates and drives them into the arms of terrorists, expanding the extremists' supporters and allies. Viewed in this way, terrorism is eminently rational, although still morally reprehensible.

20. As the National Commission on Terrorism (2000) observed, the terrorist groups of the 1970s and 1980s tended to calibrate their attacks to produce enough bloodshed to get attention for their cause, but not so much as to alienate public support. In the words of terrorism expert Brian Jenkins, the old terrorist groups wanted 'a lot of people watching, not a lot of people dead'. Such self-imposed restraints against gratuitous violence no longer seem to apply. Indeed, Khalid Shaikh Mohammed, the imprisoned former al-Qaeda operations chief, has suggested that the objective of the suicide mission was fairly straightforward: 'The attacks were designed to cause as many deaths as possible and havoc and to be a big slap for America on American soil' (Fouda and Fielding, 2003).

21. A useful distinction between the modus operandi of old and new terrorist groups is put forth by Stern (1999), who observes that the new terrorists tend to eschew instrumental violence for political ends in favor of expressive violence designed to make a statement or cause panic and dread in their target audience.

22. As Bergen (2004) points out, prior to 09/11, attacking economic targets was not part of al-Qaeda's 'cosmology'. Having seen the huge payoff of the World Trade Center and Pentagon attacks presumably changed their view. Indeed, those attacks, which cost less than $500,000

to orchestrate, inflicted upwards of $100 billion in direct damage to the US economy and caused nearly $1.5 trillion in stock declines the week after the bombings. Likewise, according to documents found in al-Qaeda safe houses in Kabul and Kandahar, the suicide attack on the USS Cole in 2000 cost the group a mere $10,000, and for that, they killed 17 US soldiers and immobilized a billion dollar warship for 14 months – a considerable return on investment (de Borchgrave, 2003).

23. The October 2002 suicide attack on the French oil tanker M/V Limburg off the coast of Yemen appears to have been a case of 'target substitution'. Al-Qaeda has admitted that its original aim had been to attack a US Navy frigate, but it settled for the tanker since it was more accessible and scheduled to supply the US Fifth Fleet (Risk Management Solutions, 2004). Following the attack bin Laden released an audiotape making clear the group's intention to target commercial assets. 'By God, the youths of God are preparing for you things that would fill your hearts with terror and target your economic lifeline until you stop your oppression and aggression' (Korin and Luft, 2004).

24. As Witschel (2004) observes, a successful attack on a soft target might well entail the same overall results as an attack on a hard target. It creates a climate of mass hysteria fanned by the international media, intimidating not only the local population or those geographically close to the scene of the attack, but also people thousands of miles away, deterring them from visiting or investing in the country where the attack took place.

25. Al-Qaeda is also believed to have raised money through ostrich and shrimp farming in Kenya and diamond trading in other African nations (Congressional Research Service, 2004). There is growing evidence that members of the jihadist network are turning to cyber fraud to fund their activities. Indeed, the confiscated laptop of Bali bomb mastermind Imam Samudra showed that he tried to finance the deadly attack through credit card fraud and money laundering conducted over the internet (Swartz, 2005).

26. The group, known as Martyrs for Morocco, included 18 others who had been jailed for relatively minor crimes (Center for Strategic and International Studies, 2004).

27. Al-Qaeda has also harnessed the power of advanced encryption technologies such as steganography, whereby a message is encoded inside a family picture or audio clip and transmitted over the internet, to link distant cells (McCullagh, 2001). As law enforcement and intelligence agencies have stepped up surveillance of the group's electronic communications, its techniques have evolved. The intellectual architect of the 2004 Madrid railway bombings, for example, reportedly communicated with his affiliates by leaving draft messages in email accounts and forwarding the account numbers so there would be no electronic paper trail (Johnson, 2005).

28. As Nacos (2003) points out, the 09/11 terrorists could have struck at night and thereby spared many lives, but instead they chose to attack during broad daylight in order to guarantee maximum carnage and the most spectacular visuals. As Luke (2003) wryly observes, al-Qaeda figured out long ago that the Western media will 'replay the images of deadly success over and over again in accord with the media's prime directive: "if it bleeds, it leads" '.

29. In the past, Osama bin Laden has called acquiring nuclear weapons a 'religious duty' and vowed to kill four million Americans as retribution for aggression against Muslim nations. In May 2003, the al-Qaeda leader reportedly received religious sanction to use such weapons against the West by radical Saudi cleric Hamid bin al-Fahd. In a fatwa on his website entitled 'A Treatise on the Legal Status of Using Weapons of Mass Destruction Against Infidels', al-Fahd affirmatively answered the question of whether it was permissible under the four schools of Sunni Islam for the *mujahideen* to use nuclear weapons against the United States. Bin al-Fahd concluded that each school did permit the use of such weapons and that the *mujahideen* would be justified in inflicting millions of casualties in the United States (Scheuer, 2005).

30. Analysts believe that the biggest challenge to al-Qaeda's nuclear ambitions is procuring fissile material, such as plutonium or highly enriched uranium that makes up a nuclear weapon's core. Only a small amount of fissile material (6 to 8 kg of plutonium or 15 to 25 kg of HEU) is needed to make an implosion-type nuclear bomb, and, according to one report, some 600 to 650 tons of former Soviet fissile material is scattered among 300 buildings at more than 50 nuclear facilities (Lee, 2003).

31. One source estimates that American automotive companies have saved more than $1 billion a year in inventory carrying costs by using JIT methods over the past decade (Martha and Vratimos, 2002).

32. As Sheffi (2002) notes, having large stocks of inventory on hand within a factory environment creates complacency which tends to mask quality problems in the fabrication process. Instead of fixing these problems, it used to be easy for workers to discard defective parts and substitute existing stock. Under JIT systems, by contrast, quality issues cannot be disguised and tend to be fixed immediately.

33. In recent years such disruptions have been caused by a host of natural and manmade calamities – not just terrorism. Indeed, the 2002 West Coast USA port strike cost companies anywhere from $11 billion to $22 billion in foregone sales, additional air freight expenses, spoiled perishable goods and underutilized capacity. Meanwhile, even after the ports reopened, it took weeks to process the backlog of freight (Kearney, 2003).

34. As Kearney (2003) observes, although suppliers in developing countries are often the lowest-cost producers, goods can pass through as many as 11 middlemen in transit, greatly increasing the risk of a disruption.

35. As Bouchet, Clark and Groslambert (2003) observe, the literature on political risk is divided between those who see it as potentially producing both positive and negative outcomes (for example, Korbin, 1979) and those who only recognize negative outcomes (for example, Brewer, 1981).

36. According to Czinkota, Knight, and Liesch (2004), the primary level refers to research conducted on terrorist threats at the level of the individual person or firm, including the firm's operations abroad. The macro level refers to the effects of a terrorist attack on the global environment, and the micro level looks at its impact on specific regions, industries or levels in international value chains.

37. As a point of reference, maritime insurance premiums were tripled for ships calling at ports in Yemen following the 2002 attack on the M/V Limburg off the Yemeni coast (Richardson, 2004).

38. Indeed, AON Corporation implicitly acknowledges the increasing geopolitical nature of country risk in its 2005 annual risk ratings. Among the countries receiving elevated scores (indicating higher risks) are the Netherlands, Germany, Belgium and Denmark because of 'increased Islamic extremist activity'. Likewise, Australia, Poland and Estonia received elevated scores owing to their governments' participation in the unpopular US-led Iraq war.

39. As Briggs (2003) observes, post-09/11 surveys of global companies have found strong regional disparities in attitudes toward security, with firms from Europe, the Middle East and Africa considerably less concerned about security than their counterparts in the Americas.

40. Not all companies, however, have turned on the spending spigots. In an August 2004 survey by the Conference Board, 39 percent of senior executives at mid-market companies (with revenues between $20 million and $1 billion) saw security simply as a cost that should be strictly controlled.

41. According to Deloitte Research (2004), more than half of US companies with sales over $1 billion now have CSOs.

42. The term resilience is widely used to refer to the ability of individuals or organizations to react to unexpected disruptions, such as those caused by terrorist attacks or natural disasters. See Coutu (2002).

43. According to one estimate, there are up to 10,000 active supporters of al-Qaeda in the UK; another source calculates that there are more than 30,000 Islamic extremists in Germany (Taarnby, 2004).

44. As Pochard (2003) observes, Xerox reduced its supplier base from 5,000 to 400 between 1981 and 1985, and reduced its product costs by almost 10 percent a year. Likewise, Merck reduced its suppliers from 40,000 in 1992 to just 10,000 in 1997, experiencing considerable cost savings.

45. One cost-effective way for manufacturers to reduce risks, as Sheffi (2002) observes, is to run dual procurement systems where the majority of a firm's inputs or final products are purchased from inexpensive and high quality offshore suppliers, while a portion of the business is given to a local supplier who can pick up the slack in the event of a disruption. HP has used this strategy successfully with its inkjet printers in the North American market.

46. These changes involve three different tiers of membership based on the firm's level of investment in security. Tier one, for example, would include companies that have met minimal standards and received CBP certification. Their freight would receive reduced scoring on the Automated Targeting System (ATS), thereby decreasing the likelihood of inspections. Tier two would comprise companies that have taken the extra effort to get a CBP validation. Their freight would received a further reduction in ATS scoring, and hence fewer inspections. Tier three would be reserved for companies that have not only been certified and validated, but have adopted CBP best practices. Their goods would receive a fast lane through Customs as well as expedited processing following a terrorist incident (Bonner, 2005).
47. Smart and Secure Trade Lanes is an industry initiative being driven by three port operating companies which together account for 70 percent of the world's container port operations. It includes the use of electronic data collection through RFID, GPS, sensors and scanning systems.

REFERENCES

Barber, B. (2003), *Fear's Empire*, New York: W.W. Norton & Company Inc.

Beck, U. (1992), *Risk Society: Towards a New Modernity*, translated by M. Ritter, London: Sage.

Behrendt, S. and P. Khanna (2003), 'Risky business: geopolitics and the global corporation', *Strategy + Business*, **32**.

Bergen, P. (2001), *Holy War, Inc: Inside the Secret World of Osama Bin Laden*, New York: Touchstone.

Bonner, R. (2005), 'Supply chain security in a new business environment', prepared remarks, Miami, FL, accessed at www.customs.gov/xp/cgov/newsroom/commissioner/ speeches_statements/apr21_2005_miami.xml, 21 April.

Booth, K. (1998), 'Cold wars of the mind', in K. Booth (ed.), *Statecraft and Security: The Cold War and Beyond*, Cambridge, UK: Cambridge University Press, pp. 29–55.

Bouchet, M., E. Clark and B. Groslambert (2003), *Country Risk Assessment: A Guide to Global Investment Strategy*, Chichester, UK: John Wiley & Sons Ltd.

Bremner III, Ambassador L. Paul (2001), 'New risks in international business', *Viewpoint*, **2**.

Brewer, T.L. (1981), 'Political risk assessment for foreign direct investment decisions: better methods for better results', *Columbia Journal of World Business*, **16**(1), 5–12.

Briggs, R. (2003), *Doing Business in a Dangerous World: Corporate Personnel Security in Emerging Markets*, London: The Foreign Policy Centre.

Brzezinzki, Z. (2004), *The Choice: Global Domination or Global Leadership*, New York: Basic Books.

Bunn, M. and A. Wier (2005), 'Securing the bomb 2005: the new global imperatives', project on Managing the Atom, Belfer Center for Science and International Affairs, John F. Kennedy School of Government, Harvard University.

The Business Roundtable (2005), *Committed to Protecting America: CEO Guide to Security Challenges*, February.

Carter, A., J. Deutch and P. Zelikow (1998), 'Catastrophic terrorism: tackling the new danger', *Foreign Affairs*, **77**(6): 80–94.

Carter, A. and W. Perry (1999), *Preventive Defense*, Washington, DC: Brookings Institution Press.

Center for Strategic and International Studies (2004), *Transnational Threats Update*, **2**(12), accessed at www.csis.org/tnt/ttu/ttu_0410.pdf, October.

Center for Strategic and International Studies (2005), *Transnational Threats Update*, **3**(3), accessed at www.csis.org/TNT/ttu/ttu_0501.pdf, January.

Checa, N., J. Maguire and J. Barney (2003), 'The new world disorder', *Harvard Business Review*, August, 71–9.

Chopra, S. and Sodhi, M. (2004), 'Managing risk to avoid supply-chain breakdown', *MIT Sloan Management Review*, **46** (1), 53–61.

CIO Insight (2002), 'Security 2002: rethinking risk', accessed at www.cioinsight.com/article2/0,1397,537635,00.asp, 16 September.

The Conference Board (2004), 'Security in mid-market companies: the view from the top', *Executive Action*, **102**.

Congressional Research Service (2004), 'Foreign terrorist organizations', order code RL32223, 6 February.

Coutu D.L. (2002), 'How resilience works', *Harvard Business Review*, **80**(5), 46–50, 52, 55.

Curtis, G. and T. Karacan (2002), *The Nexus Among Terrorists, Narcotics Traffickers, Weapons Proliferators, and Organized Crime Networks in Western Europe*, Washington, DC: The Library of Congress.

Czinkota, M. and G.A. Knight (2004), 'Managing the terrorist threat', *European Business Forum*, **20**, 42–5.

Czinkota, M., G.A. Knight and P.W. Liesch (2004), 'Terrorism and international business: conceptual foundations', in G.S. Suder (ed.), *Terrorism and the International Business Environment: The Security-Business Nexus*, Cheltenham, UK and Northampton, MA, USA: Edward Elgar.

Davies, R. (2002), 'An evolution of terror: extreme events and Al Qaida', in R. Briggs, (ed.), *The Unlikely Terrorists,* London: The Foreign Policy Centre.

de Borchgrave, A. (2003), 'Clash of civilizations – or new world disorder', lecture to the Foreign Policy Association, New York, 12 March, accessed at www.fpa.org/topics_ info2414/topics_info_show.htm?doc_id=156399.

Deloitte Research (2004), 'Prospering in the secure economy', accessed at www.deloitte.com/dtt/cda/doc/content/Prospering%20Australia%20-%20low %20res.pdf.

Friedman, T. (1999), *The Lexus and the Olive Tree*, New York: Farrar, Straus & Giroux.

Frieswick, K. (2002), 'The difficulties of thinking ahead: doing scenario planning requires some scenario planning of its own', *CFO Magazine*, accessed at www.cfo.com/printable/article.cfm/3003198?f=options, 5 February.

Fouda, Y. and N. Fielding (2003), *Masterminds of Terror: The Truth Behind the Most Devastating Terrorist Attack the World has Ever Seen*, New York: Mainstream Publishing.

Fukuyama, F. (1992), *The End of History and the Last Man*, New York: Avon Books.

Gray, C. (2004), *The Sheriff: America's Defense of the New World Order*, Lexington, KY: The University Press of Kentucky.

Gray, C. (2005), 'How has the war changed since the end of the cold war?', *Parameters, US Army War College Quarterly*, **35**(1), 14–26.

Greenberg, D. (2001), 'The changing face of terrorism: it's becoming something fundamentally different', *Slate*, accessed at www.slate.msn.com/id/115391, 13 September.

Gunaratna, R. (2004), 'The post Madrid face of Al Qaeda', *The Washington Quarterly*, **27**(3), 91–100.

Held, V. (1991), 'Terrorism, rights, and political goals', in R.G. Frey and Christopher W. Morris (eds), *Violence, Terrorism, and Justice*, New York: Cambridge University Press.

Hill, C.W. (2005), *International Business: Competing in the Global Marketplace*, New York: McGraw Hill.

Hoffman, B. (1998a), *Inside Terrorism*, New York: Columbia University Press.
Hoffman, B. (1998b), 'Revival of religious terrorism begs for broader US policy', *Rand Review*, accessed at www.rand.org/publications/randreview/issues/rr.winter98.9/methods.html, accessed April 1, 2005.
Hoffman, B. (2003), 'Al Qaeda, trends in terrorism, and future potentialities: an assessment', Washington, DC: The Rand Corporation, accessed at www.rand.org/publications/P/ P8078/P8078.pdf, accessed April 1, 2005.
Howell, L. (2002), 'Managing political risk in the age of terrorism', in J. Choi and M. Power (eds), *Global Risk Management: Financial, Operational, and Insurance Strategies*, Oxford: Elsevier Science.
Hulme, George V. (2004), 'Under attack', *Information Week*, accessed at www.informationweek. com/shared/printableArticle.jhtml?articleID=22103493, 5 July.
Ikenberry, J.G. (ed.) (2002), *America Unrivaled: The Future of the Balance of Power*, Ithaca, NY: Cornell University Press.
Jarvis, D. (2003), 'Political risk in international relations: empirical experiences and conceptual approaches', working papers, University of Sydney, School of Economics and Political Science.
Johnson, C. (2000), *Blowback: The Costs and Consequences of American Empire*, New York: Henry Holt.
Johnson, K. (2005), 'Terrorist threat shifts as groups mutate and merge', *The Wall Street Journal*, 14 February, p. A15.
Juergensmeyer, M. (2002), 'Religious terror and global war', paper 2, University of California Santa Barbara Global and International Studies Program, accessed April 1, 2005 at http://repositories.cdlib.org/gis/2.
Kearney, A.T. (2003), 'Supply chains in a volatile, vulnerable world', *Executive Agenda*, **6**(3), accessed at www.atkearney.com/shared_res/pdf/EA63_supply_chains_S.pdf.
Knight, G.A., M. Czinkota and P. Liesch (2003), 'Terrorism and international business', proceedings of the 2003 Annual Meeting, Academy of International Business, Honolulu, HI.
Korbin, S. (1979), 'Political risk: a review and reconsideration', *Journal of International Business Studies*, **10**, 67–80.
Korin, A. and G. Luft (2004), 'Terrorism goes to sea', *Foreign Affairs*, **83**(6) (November/December).
Kushner, H. (1998), 'The new terrorism', in H. Kushner (ed.), *The Future of Terrorism: Violence in the New Millennium*, Thousand Oaks, CA: Sage.
Lake, D. (2002), 'Rational extremism: Understanding terrorism in the twenty-first century', *Dialog I.Q.*, Spring, 15–29.
Langwiesche, W. (2004), *The Outlaw Sea*, New York: North Point Press.
Laqueur, W. (1998), 'Terror's new face', *Harvard International Review*, **20**(4), 48–51.
Laqueur, W. (1999), *The New Terrorism*, New York: Oxford University Press.
Laqueur, W. (2003), *No End to War: Terrorism in the Twenty-First Century*, New York: The Continuum International Publishing Group Inc.
Laqueur, W. (2004), 'The terrorism to come', *Policy Review*, **126**.
Lee, R. (2003), 'Nuclear smuggling: patterns and responses', *Parameters, US Army War College Quarterly*, **33**(1), 95–111.
Lewis, B. (1998), 'License to kill: Usama Bin Ladin's declaration of jihad', *Foreign Affairs*, **77**(6), 14–19.
Lloyd, D., J. Arlington, S. Carroll, D. Lakdawalla, R. Reville and D. Adamson (2005), *Issues and Options for Government Intervention in the Market for Terrorism Insurance*, Santa Monica, CA: Rand Center for Terrorism Risk Management Policy.

Luke, T. (2003), 'Post-modern geopolitics in the 21st century: lessons from the 9.11.01 terrorist attacks', occasional paper no 2, Center for Unconventional Security Affairs, University of California Irvine.

Martha, J. and E. Vratimos (2002), 'Creating a just-in-case supply chain for the inevitable next disaster', *Mercer Management Journal*, **14**.

McCullagh, D. (2001), 'Bin Laden: steganography master?', *Wired News*, 7 February.

Minor, J. (2002), 'Mapping the new political risk', *Risk Management Magazine*, accessed April 1, 2005 at www.rmmag.com/Magazine/PrintTemplate.cfm?AID= 1892.

Mitroff, I. (2004), 'Think like a sociopath, act like a saint', *Journal of Business Strategy*, **25**(5), 42–53.

Mongelluzzo, B. (2004), 'Report weighs cost-benefit of future port development', *Air Cargo World*, September.

Moran, T. (ed.) (1998), *Managing International Political Risk*, Malden: Blackwell Publishers.

Mueller, Robert S. III (2005), testimony before the US Senate Select Committee on Intelligence, 16 February.

Murray, S. (2004), 'Facing a new world of risk', *Financial Times Special Report: Understanding Corporate Security*, 14 July.

Nacos, B. (2003), 'The terrorist calculus behind 9-11: a model for future terrorism?', *Studies in Conflict and Terrorism*, **26**, 1–16.

National Commission on Terrorism (2000), 'Countering the changing threat of international terrorism: report of the national commission on terrorism', Washington, DC, accessed April 1, 2005 at www.fas.org/irp/threat/commission.htm.

National Commission on Terrorist Attacks Upon the United States (2004), *The 09/11 Commission Report: Final Report of the National Commission on Terrorist Attacks upon the United States*, New York: Norton.

O Tuathail, G. (2000), 'The post-modern geopolitical condition: states, statecraft, and security at the millennium', *Annals of the Association of American Geographers*, **90**(1), 166–78.

O'Neil, A. (2004), 'Keeping the contemporary threat environment in perspective', *The Drawing Board: An Australian Review of Public Affairs*, accessed 31 May at www.econ.usvd.edu.au/ drawingboard/digest/0405/oneil.html.

Parachini, J. (2003), 'Putting WMD terrorism into perspective', *The Washington Quarterly*, **26**(4), 37–50.

Paul, T.V., J. Wirtz and M. Fortmann (2004), *Balance of Power: Theory and Practice in the 21st Century*, Stanford, CA: Stanford University Press.

Pearlstein, R. (2004), *Fatal Future: Transnational Terrorism and the New Global Disorder*, Austin, TX: University of Texas Press.

Peck, Helen (2004) 'Resilence – surviving the unthinkable', *Logistics Manager*, accessed at www.som.cranfield.ac.uk/som/research/centres/lscm/downloads/logisticsmanager.pdf.

Pochard, S. (2003), 'Managing risks of supply-chain disruptions: dual sourcing as real option', Massachusetts Institute of Technology, August.

PriceWaterhouseCoopers 8th Annual Global CEO Survey, accessed April 1, 2005 at www.pwcglobal.com/ Extweb/insights.nsf/docid/48C44DA89CB0CC4185256 F7F0061C641/$file/8thAnnualGlobalCEOSurvey.pdf.

Rand Europe and Janusian Security Management Ltd (2004), *Terrorism and Business Survey 2004*, May.

Rapoport, D. (2003), 'Generations and waves: the keys to understanding rebel terror movements', unpublished manuscript, accessed April 1, 2005 at www.international. ucla.edu/cms/files/David_Rapoport_Waves_of_Terrorism.pdf.

Richardson, M. (2004), 'Growing vulnerability of seaports from terrorism', *Viewpoints*, Institute of South East Asian Studies, 5 March.

Risk Management Solutions (2004), 'Managing terrorism risk in 2004', accessed April 1, 2005 at www.rms.com/publications/terrorism_risk_modeling.pdf.

Robinson, C. (2003), 'Al Qaeda's navy – how much of threat?', Center for Defense Information, accessed at www.cdi.org/friendlyversion/printversion.cfm?document ID=1644, 20.

Rothfeder, J. (2001), 'Analysis: risk management', *CIO Insight*, accessed 1 November at www.cioinsight.com/ print_article2/0,2533,a=19062,00.asp.

Sageman, M. (2004), *Understanding Terror Networks*, Philadelphia, PA: University of Pennsylvania Press.

Scheuer, M. (2005), 'Al-Qaeda's completed warning cycle – ready to attack?', The Jamestown Foundation, accessed 3 March at www.jamestown.org/news_details. php?news_id=96.

Sheffi, Y. (2001), 'Supply chain management under the threat of international terrorism', *International Journal of Logistics Management*, 2(2), 1–11.

Sheffi, Y. (2002), 'Supply chains and terrorism', in E. Kausel (ed.), *The Towers Lost and Beyond*, Cambridge, MA: Massachusetts Institute of Technology.

Shrader, R. and M. McConnell (2002), 'Security and strategy in the age of discontinuity: a management framework for the post-09/11 world', *Strategy + Business*, 26, 1–12.

Stern, J. (1999), *The Ultimate Terrorists*, Cambridge, MA: Harvard University Press.

Stern, J. (2003), 'The protean enemy', *Foreign Affairs*, 82(4).

Stopford, J. (2000), 'Multinational corporations', *Foreign Policy*, 117, 13–14.

Suder, G.S. (ed.) (2004), *Terrorism and the International Business Environment: The Security-Business Nexus*, Cheltenham, UK and Northampton, MA, USA: Edward Elgar.

Swartz, J. (2005), 'Terrorists' use of internet spreads', *USA Today*, accessed 20 February at www.usatoday.com/ money/industries/technology/2005-02-20-cyber-terror-usat_x.htm.

Taarnby, M. (2004), *Terrorism Monitor: The European Battleground*, The Jamestown Foundation, 2 (23), accessed 2 December at www.jamestown.org/publications_ details.php?volume_id= 400&issue_id= 3161&article_id=2368947.

United States Department of State (2004), *Patterns of Global Terrorism 2003*, Washington, DC: US Department of State.

United States Department of State (2005), *Country Reports on Terrorism*, Washington, DC: US Department of State.

Waltz, K. (2002), 'Structural realism after the Cold War', in J.G. Ikenberry (ed.), *America Unrivaled: The Future of the Balance of Power*, Ithaca, NY: Cornell University Press, pp. 29–68.

Wells, L. (1998), 'Good and fair competition: does the foreign direct investor still face other risks in emerging markets', in T. Moran (ed.), *Managing International Political Risk*, Massachusetts, US and Oxford, UK: Blackwell Publishers.

Witschel, G. (2004), 'The legacy of September 11', in G.S. Suder (ed.), *Terrorism and the International Business Environment: The Security-Business Nexus*, Cheltenham, UK and Northampton, MA, USA: Edward Elgar.

Yergin, D. and J. Stanislaw (2002), *The Commanding Heights: The Battle for the World Economy*, New York: Touchstone.

6. Country risk spillovers in the Middle East: a prelude to the road map for peace and the war on terror

Ilan Alon and David L. McKee

INTRODUCTION

The Middle East is a geopolitical region, which is plagued by inter-political and intra-political conflicts and is of strategic importance to the most developed nations. Emery et al. (1986, p. 2) suggested that 'commercial relations with the Middle East are influenced strongly by political factors, perhaps more than in any other region of the non-industrial world'. According to the International Monetary Fund (IMF), the Middle East and North Africa region has 70 percent of the world's known oil reserves, and oil accounts for about 40 percent of the world's energy needs (IMF, 2003). The United States has increased its oil imports by 86 percent since OPEC's 1973 oil embargo, consumes 25 percent of the world's oil, imports 55 percent of the oil it uses, and, if present trends continue, will import more than 70 percent of its needed oil within 20 years (Global Exchange, 2003).

Investment flows to the Middle East have been moderate comparatively speaking. According to UNCTAD's (2002) World Investment Report, 'even with declining investment flows, the region least affected by globalization – the Muslim Middle East – remains most isolated, as FDI flows to the 22 Arab League members and Iran totaled only $5.5 billion, or less than 1 percent of world totals' Azzam (1999), Chief Economist and Managing Director of Middle East Capital Group, wrote that despite a phenomenal growth in FDI in the late 1990s, the Arab World was largely bypassed, ending 1998 with a FDI stock of $5.9 billion, less than 1 percent of the world's FDI. In contrast, China has attracted about $45 billion of FDI for the same year. The Middle East's share of world trade and investment is, relatively speaking, on the decline. Among the reasons cited by the Progressive Policy Institute (2002) are:

- the Arab-Israeli disputes;
- the lack of democracy and political frustration;

- shared cultural and historical resentment toward colonialism;
- high trade barriers and protectionism; and
- poverty, social frustration and low living standards.

In an article dating from 1998, Bernard Hoekman observed that Middle Eastern and North African countries faced two major trade policy issues. The first concerned electing trade policies fostering integration with the world economy, while the second was the setting up of institutions rendering the policies in question credible. Writing about the same region, John Page (1998) suggested that the restoration of long-run growth would require increasing investment and improving productivity. These investments, in turn, were influenced by political outbreaks and perceived instability in these countries as well as their neighbors. International capital flow into and out of the Middle East is thus dependent on the political and economic events that engulf the region.

The purpose of this study is to examine the political risk spillovers that exist between various countries of the Middle East. To achieve this, we review the reasons for the spillovers in country risk and follow the review with an examination of the correlations between country risk measures of selected countries.

WHY DO COUNTRY RISK SPILLOVERS OCCUR?

Political and country risks in one country may alter the risk perceptions in nearby countries; that is, country and political risks spill over inter-regionally. This is especially true in the Middle East where risk and volatility abounds and where events have global repercussions. We discuss geopolitical influences, a common economic space, cultural factors and investment sentiments as variables responsible for country risk spillovers.

Geopolitical Influences

Countries in the same region are affected by common geopolitical influences. This is manifested regionally in two ways, externally and internally. First, the Middle East is a high-priority region for US policy-makers who attempt to influence multiple countries' policies simultaneously to achieve international political goals. Such influences were illustrated recently via the debates over Iraq.

Second, internally, the sharing of borders allows the movement of people, special interest groups and terrorists who at the aggregate level can destabilize the region through their actions. The sharing of geographical space creates social and political conflicts that can spread through multiple countries regionally. The Syrian occupation of Lebanon is a case in point. Syrian forces have occupied Lebanon since the country's civil war began in 1975, and still had an estimated 35,000 Syrian soldiers there (ABC News, 2000). The occupation allowed Syria to control Lebanese politics, benefit from an uneven economic exchange and threaten Israel without a direct confrontation. Israel's multiple border disputes with its neighbors are additional illustrations that have led to a number of regional wars. Neighboring countries often share political risk factors, such as the possibility of war, exiled opposition groups, international terrorism and border conflicts (Alon and Martin, 1998).

Common Economic Space

Countries in the same region often share an economic space. In the case of the Middle East, this economic space is oil. Many of the countries in the Middle East adhere to the Sheiko-Capitalism economic model. This model is based on oil revenue supporting a socialist system of government coupled with a strong political ruler who determines the fate of market events. This system allows personal relationships to triumph over institutional policies. Business relationships continue as long as the ruler allows them. The ruling family behaves as a head of the clan using state resources to distribute favors to those who are loyal (Ali, 1995). Kassicieh and Nassar (1982) suggested that the oil-based economic dependency in the Middle East has destabilized their social and political structures. The Arab states in question, although authoritarian in varying degrees, have provided benefits in the form of housing, medical services, and in some instances employment to their citizens (McKee, Garner and McKee, 1999). This has generated destabilization risks. The oil-producing Arab countries have, on the one hand, benefited from the oil-based income flows for basic welfare services and, on the other hand, learned to depend on them. Therefore, changes in the value of oil, due to fluctuating demand or shocks in supply, have affected the welfare state of multiple economies in the Middle East, resulting in a disgruntled citizenry during times of hardship.

Other factors that need to be considered in the risk analysis of a country are the micro aspects of the investment. Investment in politically-sensitive industries is likely to promote a higher level of risk. As early as 1971, Robock suggested that foreign ownership of the extractive industries is often domestically controversial, raising the level of political risk facing the foreign owners.

Inter-regional trade and cooperation among various Arab states also increase the economic ties among them. Given their relative isolation from the global economy, many Arab states in the Middle East have had to cooperate with one another on issues of trade, energy, water, and defense.

Cultural Similarity/Difference

Culture affects how people in different countries interpret information and act under different scenarios. Due to its unique nature, the Middle East culture has been often misunderstood by the West. Parnell and Hatem (1999), for example, showed how cultural factors affect different behaviors in Egyptian and American managers. Religion is a source of contention inter-regionally in the Middle East. Mainstream Islamic beliefs, as seen by Arab populations in the Middle East, notwithstanding certain splinter groups, may have adopted specific interpretations on occasion which may be seen by non-Islamic elements as inflexible. Traditional religious values are central to life in Arabic societies and might be presumed to be pervasive influences in politics and economics, including the behavior of business organizations. However, these presumptions may be influenced and practiced by the day-to-day operations of dictatorships of various stripes and how they operate in the countries involved. Traditional Arab societies, dictatorships notwithstanding, have retained world views dating back centuries and such value systems are under study at time of writing in Islamic educational institutions on an ongoing basis.

Investors' Sentiment

Even if there are differing environments in selected emerging markets, investors and bankers in the West often group them together when categorizing country and political risks. When negative events in one developing country transpire, they scare international capital, causing flight to safety. The Asian contagion in 1997 is a good illustration. The Asian crisis spread quickly in the region collectively affecting the country risk ratings of the region and beyond (Alon and Kellerman, 1999).

The change in Iranian policy toward foreign investors that accompanied the fall of the Shah was unanticipated and caught many foreigners by surprise, resulting in major losses to foreign corporations operating in Iran. The revolution in both economic and political policies have sensitized investors of the potential dangers, not only in Iran, but also in other parts of the Arab world, the Middle East, and other Islamic countries. More recently, the World Trade incident of September 11 created a backlash against Muslim countries, and prevented foreign investors from risking their capital there.

In sum, it is obvious from the above economic, geopolitical and social reasons that countries in the same region share a common faith. As early as 1979, Haner wrote that political risk analysis should include an assessment of the hostility and the strength of neighboring countries. Political unrest, military confrontations and border disputes in neighboring countries are important factors in the host country's leadership and in the perceptions of foreign direct investors, especially when they relate to developing nations (Dassicieh and Nassar 1982, 1986). We, therefore, suggest that there is a regional country risk spillover, which will be reflected in high correlations among the country risk perceptions of bankers and potential investors.

METHOD

Institutional Investors' ratings are used to measure the foreign perceptions of country and political risk in the chosen countries for several reasons: these ratings are routinely used by international business and financial analysts in evaluating countries; multinational companies often use them to evaluate their risk exposure and adjust their companies' actions accordingly; they are publicly available through the magazine and, thus, available for future researchers; finally, they are used by international bankers who affect international business policy, international portfolio investment flows and the country's debt ratings and premiums.

The risk ratings range from zero to 100, with 100 representing the least amount of risk. The ratings are based on information compiled from 75 to 100 leading international banks and are weighed according to the banks' experience and stature in the international business community. Despite the widespread use of *Institutional Investor*'s country risk ratings in academic research (for example, Cosset and Roy, 1991; Lee, 1993; Somerville and Taffler, 1995), no known studies have examined the spillover effect.

The following countries are examined: Egypt, Iran, Iraq, Israel, Jordan, Kuwait and Saudi Arabia. These countries were chosen because they have experienced fluctuations in the political and economic environments, which may spillover to neighboring countries. Historically, these events included the Iranian revolution, the Iran–Iraq war, the Arab-Israeli conflict, the Gulf War, and the Desert Storm War.

We provide an historical analysis of the years 1980 to 1997, and consider the possibility that outside events may have changed the patterns of country and political risk spillovers within the region by dividing our sample into two parts. The year 1990 was chosen as the break point because this time frame represents the end to the Cold War, marked by the collapse of Communism and a reduction of Soviet influence in the region, and the beginning of the Gulf War, when the US directly intervened in the political economy of the region. This time period is also associated with a structural change in the country and political risk environment for many of the countries in the Middle East. Alon and Qi (2003) found that the years surrounding Iraq's invasion of Kuwait and the Gulf War have been marked by a structural change in the country risk ratings of eight of the fourteen Middle Eastern countries in their study, including four OPEC countries – Iraq, Qatar, Kuwait and United Arab Emirates – as well as four non-OPEC members – Israel, Egypt, Oman and Bahrain.

RESULTS

Table 6.1 shows the country risk correlations of institutional investor among the selected countries for the entire test period: 1980 to 1997. Pearson's correlations over 50 percent are bolded for emphasis.

Table 6.2 provides the correlations for the time period 1980 to 1989. This time period is associated with the two superpowers, the US and Russia, displaying their influence in the region. Howell (1992) cited the Middle East as a region that is linked into the international political system where superpowers tend to impose their control. The Soviets supplied various Arab nations with military assistance, while the US consistently helped Israel. This contributed to the power struggle and violent territorial disputes that resulted in numerous wars between the Arab nations and Israel. With the exception of

Table 6.1   Correlations of country risk, 1980–97

	Egypt	Iran	Iraq	Israel	Jordan	Kuwait	Saudi Arabia
Egypt	1.00						
Iran	–0.29	1.00					
Iraq	0.46	–0.25	1.00				
Israel	0.34	**0.52**	0.15	1.00			
Jordan	**0.54**	**–0.54**	**0.76**	–0.02	1.00		
Kuwait	**0.50**	–0.43	**0.87**	0.01	**0.91**	1.00	
Saudi Arabia	**0.50**	–0.31	**0.90**	–0.09	**0.80**	**0.92**	1.00

Table 6.2   Correlations of country risk, 1980–89

	Egypt	Iran	Iraq	Israel	Jordan	Kuwait	Saudi Arabia
Egypt	1.00						
Iran	**–0.75**	1.00					
Iraq	**0.69**	**–0.69**	1.00				
Israel	0.14	–0.32	**0.81**	1.00			
Jordan	**0.78**	**–0.61**	**0.78**	0.39	1.00		
Kuwait	**0.90**	**–0.78**	**0.93**	**0.55**	**0.82**	1.00	
Saudi Arabia	**0.96**	**–0.75**	**0.78**	0.28	**0.80**	**0.94**	1.00

Table 6.3   Correlations of country risk, 1990–97

	Egypt	Iran	Iraq	Israel	Jordan	Kuwait	Saudi Arabia
Egypt	1.00						
Iran	–0.33	1.00					
Iraq	**–0.63**	–0.43	1.00				
Israel	**0.96**	**–0.55**	–0.44	1.00			
Jordan	**0.72**	**–0.73**	0.07	**0.82**	1.00		
Kuwait	0.23	**–0.67**	0.43	0.39	**0.64**	1.00	
Saudi Arabia	**–0.63**	0.20	0.38	**–0.58**	**–0.50**	0.33	1.00

Iran, these conflicts created a general decrease in the credit ratings of most of the nations of the Middle East during the 1980s. Iran registered an increase in its credit rating for this time period because it started out in the lowest position after the revolution.

Table 6.3 presents the results from the more recent time period, 1990 to 1997. Israel, Egypt and Jordan have shown a reduction in political risk resulting in an increase in their credit ratings due to the peace agreements between them (see Figure 6.1). Table 6.3 shows a strong positive correlation in the credit ratings of these countries.

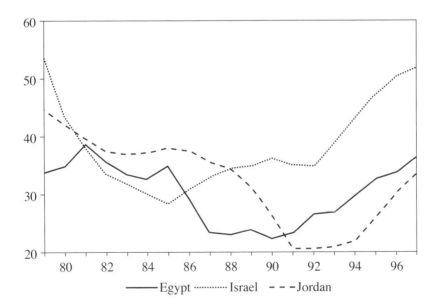

Figure 6.1   Country risk: Egypt, Israel and Jordan (years 1980–96)

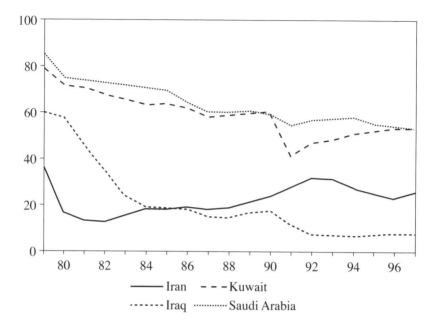

Figure 6.2   Country risk (years 1980–96)

The Gulf War has affected the political and financial institutions of Kuwait and Saudi Arabia. The invasion of Kuwait in August 1990 abruptly increased the political risk of that country, and mildly influenced the credit rating of Saudi Arabia (see Figure 6.2). US intervention in the war clearly diminished investment prospects in Iraq, but buffered the spillover effect of the war on Saudi Arabia. Iran's credit ratings seem to improve slightly immediately following the Gulf War.

CONCLUSIONS AND DISCUSSIONS

Given the high numbers of correlations in the country risk ratings of various Middle Eastern countries, this chapter gives support to the proposition that country and political risk spillovers exist. A closer examination of the data in the context of the Middle East experience is revealing.

First, comparing the two data periods (before the Gulf War and after the Gulf War) shows that the directions that some countries chose have changed their economic and political paths and their country risk ratings. Prior to the Gulf War, 17 correlations over 50 percent are noted (out of 21 possible permutations), while after the Gulf War only 11 are shown. Without an examination of the sign of the coefficient, this crude measure suggests that the magnitude of regional spillovers was reduced. This result may be attributed to a 'new world order' imposed by the United States on multiple countries in the region following the war. This result is counterintuitive because globalization over time usually results in higher integration and more economic interdependence.

Examining the factors responsible for country and political risk spillovers, we can address in turn a number of country groupings based on political, economic and social influences. Beginning in September 1980, the Iran–Iraq war ushered in a new era of political problems in the Middle East, sending shock waves throughout the region (Kassicieh and Nassar, 1986). While initially most of the countries in the region declared neutrality, by 1982 the Gulf Cooperation Council had openly expressed financial and logistical support for Iraq. Jordan, Saudi Arabia and Kuwait declared Iran an enemy of Arabism and Islam (Kassicieh and Nassar, 1986). Indeed, a strong spillover effect of political risk between Iraq and these Arab nations is evident in the data preceding the Gulf War.

The Gulf War is the single most powerful external influence affecting the countries' country and political risk ratings during the test time period. The Gulf War sent country risk shockwaves that spread beyond the borders of Iraq and Kuwait, perhaps starting a new era of regional political economy in the region. It was a turning point in Middle Eastern global politics: it is the first time in recent history that a regional Middle Eastern war had powerful repercussions on the global economy, culminating in the direct involvement of a superpower. Ironically, the overall country risk ratings of Saudi Arabia were not significantly affected by the Gulf War, despite the fact that so much Allied military activity was launched from within its borders. The military and financial support provided for Saudi Arabia has shielded its country risk ratings from deteriorating in the eyes of international bankers. Since Saudi Arabia is by far the largest producer of oil in OPEC, the international community had a large stake in preserving the stability of Saudi Arabia's borders.

Four out of the seven countries in our sample (Iran, Iraq, Saudi Arabia and Kuwait) are OPEC countries. Alon and Qi (2003) found that non-OPEC countries of the Middle East are more likely to exhibit unstable country risk ratings, in addition to being more likely to have less favorable country risk ratings, compared with their OPEC-member neighbors. Given their common economic denominator, one can expect a similar pattern in their country risk profile. Saudi Arabia exhibited very high positive correlations with Iraq and Kuwait and a negative correlation with Iran prior to the Gulf War, but not so afterwards. Iraq, Kuwait and Saudi Arabia exhibit a strong correlation among their credit over the entire time period under investigation. These countries comprise a major portion of the world's oil reserves and are therefore of monumental importance to the West. Political risk events transpiring in these countries can send shock waves in the economies of most industrial nations. Rossant and Crock (1996) suggested that terrorist activities directed at US military installations in Saudi Arabia, growing Islamic opposition groups, and internal political stability of the largest oil exporters in the world can have long-lasting impacts. These threats are still relevant today.

Both before and after the Gulf War, Iran shows idiosyncratic correlations with its OPEC counterparts. A closer examination of the Iranian case, therefore, may have merit. Iran's correlations show a negative relationship with the rest of the Arab world, and a positive relationship with the risk perceptions of Israel. One possible reason for the opposite movement of the political perceptions of Iran with most of the Middle East countries examined is the Iranian revolution, which took place in 1978. Kassicieh and Nassar (1982) found that the Islamic revolution in Iran did not influence multinational activities, such as sales, contracts and investments, in nearby countries. They ironically found that investments in Saudi Arabia actually increased after the Iranian revolution because of increased oil dependency in the West.

Iran was able to insulate itself from regional conflicts in the 1990s and has shown an increase in its credit ratings. Iran is a unique country in the sense that much of the US investors' sentiments toward it are based on memories of the late 1970s (Henze, 1996). Rossant and Crock (1996) suggested that Iran's natural gas deals with India and Turkey have undermined US efforts to economically isolate the country and to prevent it from participating in the global marketplace. Given US sanctions toward Iran, the country had to devise a variety of ways to cope with isolationist pressures and make alliances with other countries.

It has been suggested that Iran shares many of the dilemmas of the other Gulf states, in particular the reliance on oil as a source of most of its revenues (Sick, 1997). Nonetheless it is the only Gulf country in the region to have a somewhat diversified industrial base. 'In addition to its exports of carpets and agricultural products, it manufactures steel, assembles automobiles, builds ships and small aircraft, and produces most of its own pharmaceuticals, plastics and many other basic goods' (p. 22). Of course difficulties with the United States and the Iran–Iraq war have dramatically impacted its international political and economic linkages. It is too soon to say at this writing how the nation will be impacted by the ongoing situation in Iraq.

Another regional group worth isolating in our sample includes Israel, Jordan and Egypt. These countries have been engaged in direct wars and in making peace. The 1990s have shown that peace treaties can positively influence the perceptions of foreign investors, increasing their credit ratings vis-à-vis leading international banks. The data show concurrent variation in these countries' political risk ratings. Resolving the Arab-Israeli conflict can result in a reduction of violent confrontations and lead to significant increases in the investments of multinational corporations in the region.

Jordan may be somewhat of a special case, occupying an area that abuts both the Israel–Palestine situation and Iraq. Writing in 1995, Nazih N. Ayubi pointed out that the nation's royal family has had to provide substance to what he termed an otherwise artificial state, lacking any really distinct geographical or human base (p. 367). Ayubi observed that the need for Jordan to consolidate its socio-economic base grew more critical following events in the West Bank and a rapid increase in the Palestinian population in Jordan. Certainly resolving existing regional conflicts appears especially critical to the future potential of the Jordanian economy.

Of course ongoing events in Iraq render predictions concerning the future disposition of matters involving that nation difficult at best. Indeed, such matters may certainly impact Kuwait and Saudi Arabia, if not the entire region and beyond.

REFERENCES

ABC News (2000), 'Occupational hazards: Syria on brink of conflict over Lebanon', accessed 24 July at http://abcnews.go.com/sections/world/DailyNews/strat-for001006.html.

Ali, Abbas (1995), 'Management in a Sheiko-capitalism system', *International Studies of Management and Organization*, **25**(3), 3–6.

Alon, I. and E. Kellerman (1999), 'Internal antecedents to the 1997 Asian economic crisis', *Multinational Business Review*, **7**(2), 1–12.

Alon, I. and M. Martin (1998), 'A normative model of macro political risk assessment', *Multinational Business Review*, **6**(2), 10–19.

Alon, I. and Min Qi (2003), 'Do international banks' assessments of country risk follow a random walk? An empirical examination of the Middle East', *Journal of International Business Review*, forthcoming.

Ayubi, Nazih N. (1995), *Over-stating the Arab State: Politics and Society in the Middle East*, New York: I.B. Tauris Publishers.

Azzam, H.T. (1999), 'Foreign direct investment inflow to Arab countries on the decline', *Jordan Times*, accessed July 24 at www.jordanembassyus.org/120999007.htm.

Cosset, J.-C. and J. Roy (1991), 'The determinants of country risk ratings', *Journal of International Business Studies*, **22**, 135–42.

Emery, L.J., N.A. Graham and M.F. Oppenheimer (1986), *Technology Trade with the Middle East*, Boulder, CO: Westview Press.

Global Exchange (2003), 'America's freedom requires energy independence', accessed July 24 at www.globalexchange.org/campaigns/oil/743.html.

Henze, P.B. (1996), 'A new policy for a new Middle East', *Wall Street Journal*, 31 January, p. A18.

Hoekman, B. (1998), 'The World Trade Organization, the European Union, and the Arab world: trade policy priorities and pitfalls', in Shafik Nemat (ed.), *Prospects for Middle Eastern and North African Economies: From Boom to Bust and Back?* Oxford: MacMillan Press, pp. 96–129.

Howell, L.D. (1992), 'Political risk and political loss for foreign investment', *The International Executive*, **34**(6), 485–98.

Institutional Investor (1990–1997), 'Country risk ratings', March editions.

International Monetary Fund (2003), 'Middle East to dominate world's oil for many years', *Finance and Development*, accessed July 23 at www.imf.org/external/pubs/ft/fandd/2003/03/okog.htm.

Iqbal, M. (1960), *The Reconstruction of Religious Thought in Islam*, Lahore, Pakistan: Javid Iqbal.

Kassicieh, S.K. and J.R. Nassar (1982), 'Political risk and the multinational corporation: a study of the impact of the Iranian Revolution on Saudi Arabia, Kuwait and the United Arab Emirates', *Management International Review*, **22**(3), 22–32.

Kassicieh, S.K. and J.R. Nassar (1986), 'Political risk in the Gulf: the impact of the Iran–Iraq War on governments and multinational corporations', *California Management Review*, **28** (Winter), 69–86.

Lee, Suk Hun (1993), 'Relative importance of political instability and economic variables on perceived country creditworthiness', *Journal of International Business Studies*, 4th quarter: 801–12.

McKee, D.L., D.E. Garner and Y.A. McKee (1999), *Accounting Services, the Islamic Middle East, and the Global Economy*, Westport, CT: Quorum.

Nigh, D. (1986), 'Political events and the foreign direct investment decision: an empirical examination', *Managerial and Decision Economics*, **7**, 99–106.

Page, J. (1998), 'From boom to bust – and back? The crisis of growth in the Middle East and North Africa', in Shafik Nemat (ed.), *Prospects for Middle Eastern and North African Economies: From Boom to Bust and Back?*, Oxford: Macmillan Press, 133–58.

Parnell, J. and T. Hatem (1999), 'Cultural antecedents of behavioral differences between Egyptian and American managers', *The Journal of Management Studies*, **36**, 399–418

Progressive Policy Institute (2002), 'Draining the swamp: a Middle East trade policy to win the peace', accessed July 24 2003 at www.ppionline.org/ppi_ci.cfm?knlgAreaID=108&subsecID=127&contentID= 250059.

Rossant, J. and S. Crock (1996), 'Operation Desert Risk', *Business Week*, 16 September, pp. 42–4.

Sick, G.G. (1997), 'The coming crisis in the Persian Gulf', in G.G. Sick and L.G. Potter (eds), *The Persian Gulf at the Millennium*, New York: St. Martin's Press, pp. 11–30.

Somerville, R.A. and R.J. Taffler (1995), 'Banker judgment versus formal forecasting models – the case of country risk assessment', *Journal of Banking and Finance*, **19**(2), 281–97.

UNCTAD's World Investment Report (2002), accessed July 24 2003 at www.unctad.org/wir/index.htm.

7. Terrorism and financial management

Raj Aggarwal

INTRODUCTION

Terrorism is changing the nature of finance and the finance function in most businesses. In addition to the direct negative effects of terrorism on businesses that are impacted directly, all businesses now have to comply with a vastly expanded set of regulations – regulations regarding financial transactions and computer security that have resulted from recent terrorist activity. In addition, businesses also have raised the level of expenditures related to security and business continuity. This chapter reviews briefly the consequent changes in the finance function.

It is important to counter the negative effects of terrorism. In addition to negative social and political impacts, terrorism can also have negative economic consequences. Terrorist activity can increase the risks faced by investors. There is evidence that terrorism-related uncertainty raises discount rates and reduces the value of future benefits and, thus, the level of investment, future consumption and economic growth in an economy (Eckstein and Tsiddon, 2004).

Further, due to the increased likelihood of supply chain disruption and associated higher insurance and other costs in international supply chains, international trade and commerce may also be affected negatively by terrorism reducing the welfare and wealth-enhancing effects of international trade. The increase in these terrorism-related international trade transactions costs have been estimated to be between 0.5 and 3 percent *ad valorem* (Walkenhorst and Dihel, 2002). While this increase in transactions costs does not seem very large, it can have a significant negative impact on world trade (Nitsch and Schumacher, 2004).

Terrorism may also impact firm values negatively. The US stock market declined significantly in the days and weeks following the 11 September attacks on the New York World Trade towers. Similarly, the Spanish stock market also declined following the Madrid terrorist bombings. While most financial markets recover from the negative effects of terrorism, US markets seem particularly resilient (Chen and Sierns, 2004).

A recent study documents that shares of foreign companies that trade in the

US as American Depository Receipts (ADRs) also suffered price declines in the days following terrorist attacks in their home countries. While there seems to be some evidence that these terrorist activity-related stock price declines may mostly be temporary, it seems that security breaches at a firm have a long-term negative impact on the stock price and value of a business (Rapoport, 2005). Of course, even temporary declines in stock prices may increase the likelihood of a friendly or hostile takeover of a firm.

Terrorism is likely to impact different firms and industries differently. As an example, some firms may present particularly attractive or convenient targets for terrorists. Similarly, some industries may be impacted more heavily by terrorism, for example, transportation, travel and tourism related industries (for example, Carter and Simkins, 2004).

As this brief review indicates, it is economically important to counter the negative impacts of terrorism. Businesses need to explore and assess steps and procedures to fortify against the possible negative effects of terrorism on the continuity and value of the firm. The Chief Enterprise Risk Officer (CRO), Chief Information or Technology Officer (CIO or CTO) and the Chief Financial Officer (CFO) have important roles to play in this regard. However, these terrorism-related changes in the roles and functions of the CRO, CIO and CFO in a business must be understood in a wider context of other recent changes in the roles and functions of the executives in business firms.

RECENT CHANGES IN THE CFO/CRO/CIO POSITIONS

The Chief Financial Officer (CFO), the Chief Information Officer (CIO), and the Chief Enterprise Risk Officer (CRO) each have important roles to play in the fight against terrorism and in the efforts to ensure business continuity and maximize the value of a firm. There are many terrorism-related changes in the roles and functions of the CIOs, CROs and CFOs in a business and these changes must be understood in a wider context of other recent changes in the roles and functions of CIOs, CROs and CFOs in business firms.

The CFO: From Bean Counter to Strategic Partner to a Controllership Emphasis

The Chief Financial Officer in a business usually has two distinct sets of responsibilities. One set of responsibilities has to do with functions generally identified with the role of the Treasurer. These would include internal financial planning, analysis of capital expenditures, managing banking relationships, stewardship of working capital management, acquisition of short- and long-term debt and equity, dividend policy and other aspects of internal finance. Finally, the tasks included in the Treasurer-related CFO functions and responsibilities include the provision of strategic and analytic support for the various parts of a business unit such as sales or marketing. Most of these Treasurer-related functions of CFO responsibilities reflect the role of the CFO as a strategic partner for assisting the profitability and growth of business units.

The second set of functions are associated with the role of the Controller. These would generally include internal and external financial reporting, regulatory and tax compliance, and accounting, audit and other activities designed to ascertain the accuracy and integrity of financial information. Most of these Controller-related functions of a CFO reflect the CFO role as a 'bean counter' and 'policeman' in a business, perhaps as the senior manager providing a necessary 'reality check'.

While there has always been some tension between these strategic partner and bean counter/policeman roles of a CFO, in recent years the balance seems to have swung rather widely. In the late 1990s, with a frothy equity market, CFOs seemed to emphasize their role as strategic partners much more than their role as bean counters/policemen. The large number of accounting scandals in the early 2000s were very visible symptoms of the relative decline of the Controller function in many businesses. The passage of the Sarbanes-Oxley Act in the US and related legislation in the EU in 2002–2003 have served to re-emphasize once again the Controller role of the business CFO. Indeed, the finance-related provisions of the 2001 US Patriot Act in the US and related money laundering legislation in the EU have further emphasized the controller role of the business CFO.

New Regulations for the CFO: Sarbanes Oxley and Patriot Acts

The Sarbanes-Oxley Act (SOX) has greatly increased the responsibility of the CFO with regard to ensuring the integrity of the accounting data used to prepare financial reports, as now more extensive audit trails and controls are required. It has also greatly increased the independence of the external auditors and accountants so that they now report to the audit committee of the board of directors rather than to corporate management, and now auditors are highly limited in the non-audit work they can do for a company (mostly only tax work). Similarly, the Patriot Act (PA) now requires better identification of customers and more extensive reporting to the government of unusually large or suspicious transactions. While most companies are moving from a project approach to compliance with (at least the section 404 internal control aspects of) SOX to a process approach, many companies are still developing and implementing processes to comply with the Patriot Act.

The Evolving New Role of the CRO

The Chief Risk Officer (CRO) is a relatively new role in most non-financial organizations, and so it is still evolving and not yet well-established. There are a number of aspects of this ongoing evolution of the CRO function that must be considered before understanding the role of the CRO in fighting terrorism.

First, most non-financial organizations do not have a CRO. In most such organizations, the CRO function is often performed by the Chief Financial Officer (CFO). In other cases, the CRO generally reports to the CFO. Only in very rare cases does a CRO not report to the CFO. Some organizations question the need for a CRO – should not the risks faced by an organization be managed by the Chief Executive Officer (CEO) or its President and Chief Operating Officer (COO)? Thus, the organizational position of the CRO is yet undefined in most non-financial organizations.

Secondly, the functional role of the CRO is still evolving. In many companies the CRO is responsible just for insurance policies carried by a firm. In other cases, the CRO responsibilities also include the management of interest rate and other financial risks. The regulatory definition of the CRO responsibilities in financial institutions includes managing the market, credit, operational, legal and reputational risks of the firm. The new Basel II requirements mandate the establishment of CRO function, and integrated risk management in large international financial institutions. Finally, in a few non-financial organizations, the CRO role has been expanded to include other tactical (and in some cases even strategic) risks faced by a business. Thus, at present, the CRO function is not well developed.

Finally, the role and function of the CRO is also uncertain as the nature of the risks faced by an organization is not always well understood. Some risks are known and can be estimated, some are known but cannot be estimated, some risks are not known, and others are not even knowable. Risks faced by businesses that should be managed can arise from low probability and high loss events, high probability and high loss events, or from high probability and low loss events. Optimal procedures to manage each of these risk categories differ greatly. However, it is not always clear what specific risks fall into these categories and further, a business may not even be cognizant of some risks. Thus, risk analysis is not a well defined discipline and the evolving nature of the CRO function reflects this lack of clarity and definition of the risks faced by a business.

However, it is clear that the challenges created by terrorism and the related regulations that must be met have greatly enhanced the role and importance of the CRO. Indeed, the need to comply with numerous new regulations related to financial transactions has created at least a specific set of responsibilities for a possible CRO. The initial evidence seems to be that few non-financial organizations have created a CRO position in response to these regulations, with the responsibility for complying with these new regulations distributed among other existing officers in a business. It remains to be seen if these initial conclusions change over time.

Recent Changes in the Role of the CIO

In recent decades, ever larger types of corporate data are stored and managed electronically. For example, almost all businesses now use electronic means to store and process accounting data. It is no longer an exaggeration to say that all other areas and functions in a business now depend increasingly on electronic information systems. Thus, the security and integrity of financial and other critical corporate data has become increasingly important and, therefore, there has been a resultant rise in the importance of the Chief Information Officer (CIO) in any business.

The CIO function has grown to have at least three major areas of responsibility in a business. The first area of responsibility for the CIO is to provide appropriate operating and strategic information in a timely manner – information that can optimize the operating efficiency, speed of response, and competitive strengths of a business. In this function, the CIO must act as a strategic and operating partner for a firm's business units and understand how each business unit operates, as well as its needs for information.

The second major function of a CIO is to ensure the accuracy and integrity of corporate information. Reports in the media about domestic and international computer hackers breaching information security and accessing corporate and customer records have become almost daily occurrences. These break-ins not only compromise the integrity and accuracy of corporate information, but they also threaten corporate intellectual and other assets as well as the possible loss of competitive information. Some of these information system break-ins may also threaten a company's ability to operate and serve its customers through computer viruses that overwhelm information systems and result in denial of information services. Thus, the need for maintaining information system security has increased greatly in recent years. This part of the CIO's job has taken on greatly increased importance in recent years.

Finally, the job of the CIO has be expanded to reflect the many forms of electronic reporting (for example, to the Securities and Exchange Commission, SEC) and regulatory compliance such as the data security and reporting required to safeguard customer privacy (and other regulatory requirements). Consistent with the rise of business information systems and because of the increased accuracy and efficiency of electronic reporting, most regulatory agencies now require electronic reporting by the companies that they regulate.

Thus, this brief review of the major changes and evolution in the roles and functions of the CFO, CRO and CIO indicates that all three functions in a business have undergone significant increases in importance in recent years. Interestingly, these changes seem, as explained below, consistent with the changes required to fight terrorism, which go well beyond those required just for the efficient and effective operation of a business.

RISE OF TERRORISM

Terrorism has been a weapon of choice for non-governmental combatants for hundreds of years. In many cases, terrorism has also been used as a weapon by militarily weak states and in some cases even by militarily strong combatants, especially when they wish to remain anonymous. However, the use of terrorism has risen greatly in recent decades. There is some evidence that terrorist activity is related to political freedom and poverty levels (Abadie, 2004). The need to fight terrorism took on a particular importance after the events of 11 September 2001, when a number of Islamic extremists hijacked four large commercial airplanes in the US in a successful bid to crash them into symbolic civilian and military targets with the largest ever loss of life on US soil caused by a hostile military action.

Terrorist activity globally has been going on for decades, with significant periods of quiet and significant periods of heightened activity (Enders and Sandler, 2002). A heightened level of terrorism has continued since 09/11 with targets attacked successfully in Europe, Asia, Africa and the Americas. There have been particularly spectacular attacks in Indonesia, Russia, Spain and the Middle East. There have been numerous instances of elevated alert levels in North America as well (US State Department, 2004). Terrorism has become a truly global phenomenon.

The fight against terrorism has involved a number of activities including overt and covert military action, formation of domestic agencies and government departments to better coordinate various civilian anti-terrorism activities, and the passage of enabling legislation to mandate the assistance of the private sector in the fight against terrorism. As the appropriate government agencies get organized, they are asking for ever larger budgets to enhance security against terrorism. As an example, in the United States, fiscal 2005 appropriations request for homeland security was $47.4 billion, a 14.7 percent increase from $41.3 billion requested in 2004.

THE DIRECT BUSINESS EFFECTS OF TERRORISM

Terrorism has impacted business directly in a number of ways. Terrorism can reduce expected returns due to higher costs and further reduce the value of a business by raising the discount rate to reflect increased risk. Terrorism-related risk may also act as a damper to reduce the appetite for risk among private businesses. As an example, it has been documented that the terrorist attacks of 11 September 2001 had a disastrous effect on share prices of airline industry stocks (Carter and Simkins, 2004; Marlett et al., 2004).

There are at least three major categories of anti-terrorism costs faced by private businesses. First, business continuity insurance is now more expensive, not only because all insurance rates went up after 09/11, but also because business now must guard against many more threats. For example, businesses must now buy terrorism insurance backed by the Federal government as terrorist acts are not covered by other insurance. However, only about one half of the 2,400 companies surveyed by Marsh in mid-2004 had purchased terrorism insurance (Hansen, 2004). TRIA (Terrorism Risk Insurance Act) provides that the government pay up to 90 percent of losses caused by terrorist attacks, up to $100 billion per year, above specified deductibles paid by insurers. But, TRIA is scheduled to expire in 2005 even though al-Qaeda is still very much in business (Banham, 2004).

Because of the terrorism threat, private businesses also now have to spend more on computer and other security to ensure business continuity, especially since it is widely contended that the next terrorist attack is likely to be a cyber attack rather than a physical attack (Doll, Rai and Granado, 2003). Just as computer viruses originate from anywhere in the world to infect US computer systems, cyber attacks by terrorists can originate with terrorists based and operating out of any country or location with access to the internet. As noted earlier, reports in the media about domestic and international computer hackers breaching information security and accessing corporate and customer records have become almost daily occurrences. Automated control systems that run most of US electric, water, gas and other supply systems are vulnerable and clearly need to be protected (Lenzner and Vardi, 2004).

Secondly, terrorism has raised the costs of international trade and investment. There is evidence that terrorism-related costs have increased international supply chain costs and depressed global trade. Terrorism has reduced the number of people coming to the US, especially from some countries, increasing personnel costs for many companies. Terrorism has also raised business travel costs.

In addition, terrorism has also raised due diligence costs of cross-border mergers and acquisitions and slowed down international investment. As an example, Citicorp was forced to sell its ownership (20 percent) of Saudi-American bank (Samba) to the Saudi government in May 2004 (for $760 million after tax gain) mainly because of account mishandling. It seems that account 98 at Samba was used to funnel money to some of the people associated with the

09/11 attacks. Citicorp and other foreign (for example, HSBC, ABN-Amro, Credit Agricol) owners of the Saudi-American Bank of Riyadh now face multiple lawsuits from 09/11 victims (Lenzner and Vardi, 2004).

Finally, the social and economic impacts of terrorism are not confined to a single firm and countering the effects of terrorism involves addressing many externalities and market failures. Unfortunately, there is very little incentive for private businesses to spend to improve national defenses against terrorism. Indeed, such spending would be a competitive disadvantage unless required for all competing firms. In fact, very few executives report spending to prevent terrorist attacks, for example, see the Council on Competitiveness survey in 2002 and Deloitte and Touche's survey of trucking executives in 2004 (as cited in Flynn, 2004).

However, private businesses are an important resource in fighting terrorism. One of the main focal points in this fight is to stop or make more difficult the financing of terrorist activity and private financial institutions play the most important role in this process. Nevertheless, it has been documented that fighting terrorism involves many externalities and market failures (Sandler, 2004).

Thus, the need for national regulation and coordinated transnational policy formation to efficiently counter the negative effects of terrorism (Sandler and Enders, 2004; Flynn, 2004). One example of this coordinated governmental activity is promoting insurance coverage against terrorism-related losses. The US Congress passed the Terrorism Risk Insurance Act in 2002 under which the US government would cover 90 percent of terrorism-related losses above a certain amount. The TRIA greatly helped private insurance companies provide terrorism insurance to their business clients.

Similarly, because of the 'tragedy of the commons', explicit governmental regulations on terrorism prevention that apply to every private company are necessary to fight terrorism. New regulations for the finance and money transfer industry have come from the Department of Treasury, Financial Crimes Enforcement Network. Thus, there has been a great increase in terrorism-related regulation in recent years and terrorism has greatly increased regulatory and compliance costs for businesses. Many of these regulations and compliance requirements are focused on the financial activities of firms – including such activities at non-financial firms. The next section describes some of these new financial regulations faced by businesses.

TERRORISM AND THE REGULATION OF FINANCIAL TRANSACTIONS

Anti-money-laundering regulations have been around for a long time. In 1990 the US Treasury came up with 40 recommendations in this area that were endorsed by 130 countries in 1996 and were adopted as an international standard. Following the attacks of 11 September 2001, there have been a number of reviews of the anti-money-laundering procedures and some additional requirements added by the US Patriot Act. These anti-money-laundering regulations are developed and enforced by the Financial Action Task Force (FATF), a part of the US Treasury department that was created in 1989.

The US Patriot Act (through the Treasury Department's Office of Foreign Assets Control (OFAC)) requires a number of actions by business, including requirements for enhanced internal control, customer identification and periodic assessments and reporting. These requirements are generally known as the Anti-money-Laundering and Customer Identification Program (ALCIP). Details of these requirements are available on the website: www. treas.gov/ofac). The European Union has passed similar legislation (Buck, 2005).

According to these regulations, a specific compliance officer is to be designated and identified in each firm that engages in external financial transactions. Such compliance officers are to maintain US Treasury lists of blocked property and blocked transactions, report suspicious transactions, and ensure compliance and reporting consistent with the requirements of the anti-money-laundering laws and regulations. An annual internal review and external audit of the ALCIP policies and procedures is to be conducted at least once a year and reported to the appropriate government agency.

Firms engaging in significant financial transactions are required to respond within 120 hours to requests for information on accounts and for requests for monitoring and blocking appropriate accounts. Currently, US government regulations generally consider transactions of $10,000 or more to be significant enough to warrant special attention. These firms are also required to report any suspicious account activity, and to collect, verify, and maintain identification information provided by new and existing customers under the Anti-money-Laundering Customer Identification Program. All of this clearly indicates a need for sophisticated monitoring systems and the education of selected employees regarding the requirements of ALCIP regulations. Unfortunately, due to market externalities, the best way to ensure that financial institutions disclose the identities of counterparties, especially when they originate through domestic and foreign correspondent banking relationships, may be through private incentives rather than through regulation (Fitzgerald, 2004).

However, learning to live with these new regulations may take some time. Western Union and First Data are the biggest US money transfer companies. Both operate through independent agents overseas and in the US – agents that are hard to police. Western Union paid fines of about $11 million since 09/11 for violations and had to sever relations with its partner in Syria, a government-owned bank, after that partner was accused of involvement in terrorism and money laundering (Simpson, 2004).

Banks and other financial institutions have many new regulations that require them to verify the identity of their customers and report large cash transactions and any other suspicious activity to the government. However, as this example of the money transfer companies shows, most banks and other financial institutions and companies have a huge learning curve facing them as they train their staff to comply with these new anti-terrorism regulations. Critics have contended that these new anti-terrorism regulations are unlikely to be effective (for example, *The Economist*, 2002). Fortunately, much has already been written elsewhere on the role of financial institutions in fighting terrorism. Thus, the rest of this chapter focuses on non-financial corporations' corporate anti-terrorism security activities.

FINANCIAL MANAGEMENT CHALLENGES IN FIGHTING TERRORISM

Computer Information System and Data Integrity

In this post-SOX and post-PA era, CFO responsibilities regarding accounting integrity, identification of counter-parties and reporting transactional activity has increased greatly. The CFO must ensure against unintended possible assistance to money-laundering activities or unintended transactions with inadequately identified counterparties. In addition, the CFO must also discharge other normal responsibilities safeguarding assets and ensuring financial support for the smooth functioning of a business. In addition to the need to comply with appropriate regulations, information system security is important for business reasons (see Doll, Rai and Granado, 2003 for details). Indeed, it seems that breaches in computer security at a business are likely to be punished by investors with a loss in market value for the breached firms (Rapoport, 2005).

As this brief discussion indicates, a typical CFO faces many challenges in ensuring accounting data integrity and in meeting regulatory requirements to fight terrorism. Some of these challenges are strategic in nature, focusing on the training and deployment of appropriate personnel and the design of secure systems of detecting and reporting appropriate transactions. Other challenges are more tactical and may involve ensuring that these systems do indeed work.

Challenges in Implementing XBRL Reporting

The CFO also faces many other continuing challenges in ensuring financial and accounting security. For example, there is now a continuing push to make financial data more widely and more easily available to investors over the internet even though such availability might pose additional security risks. Recently, the Extensible Business Reporting Language XBRL standard has been developed – a standard that will facilitate the dissemination of financial data in standardized formats over the internet.

The XBRL standard enables various systems and software anywhere in the financial reporting supply chain to exchange financial information using common universal standardized terminology. While present technologies allow such exchanges with varying degrees of ease and facility, the use of the XBRL standard reduces errors and financial information is transmitted effortlessly across differing applications and software. In doing so, XBRL enhances many financial processes. As an example, credit risk analysis is more accurate and it is easier (and cheaper) to compare various companies and credit counter-parties, especially since intra-industry comparisons is an essential and critical part of credit risk analysis. Such improvements in credit risk analysis may lower a company's cost of capital and increase its access to external capital. Further, as credit risk analysis is an important part of the finance function, the use of the XBRL standard is likely to have a significant positive impact on the efficiency and effectiveness of the finance function in a company.

The use of the XBRL financial standard also has a major positive impact on the management and efficiency of a company's supply chain for its physical products, as it facilitates and reduces errors in data transfers between various parts of a supply chain. This allows a tighter level of integration in the supply chain, reducing investment in inventories and working capital.

Thus, as this brief review of the advantages of XBRL indicates, the use of the XBRL standard promises to be highly beneficial for implementing companies. However, easier access to financial information facilitated by the XBRL standard may pose additional information system security challenges. XBRL is an internet message exchange protocol and many of the security issues surrounding the implementation of the XBRL standard have not yet been completely developed or worked out. For example, point-to-point security used in internet exchanges is not likely to be sufficient for securing information that travels between several intermediaries (Boritz and No, 2005).

Role of the Board of Directors Audit Committee

The Sarbanes-Oxley Act greatly increased the role and responsibility of Boards of Directors. In particular, the audit committee of the board is now responsible for more directly overseeing the audit and risk management functions in a firm. However, terrorist activity is not generally regarded as a source of significant risk at most companies. For example, a 2004 FM Global survey of the Global 1,000 executives indicated that less than 1 percent regard terrorism as a serious threat to their businesses (Ernst and Young, 2004).

However, the US Department of Homeland Security has endorsed the 09/11 Commission's recommendations that companies comply with the Emergency Preparedness and Business Continuity Standard (NFPA 1600) developed by the National Fire Protection Association and endorsed by the American National Standards Institute (ANSI). This standard seems to be an important guideline for many companies and is reflected in many changing corporate practices in this area. Audit committees and Boards of Directors may face additional liabilities if they ignore this standard and there is some evidence that many audit committees are now integrating their work with risk management and crises planning efforts in their companies (Ernst & Young, 2004). Clearly, after 09/11 there is a need for a more holistic approach to corporate risk management (Baranoff, 2004).

Changes in Financial Markets

The major financial markets have proven to be fairly resilient to shocks, including terrorist activity. Indeed, financial markets have developed a demonstrated ability to handle many financial crises in recent years (for example, the Asian Crises of 1997, the Russian and Latin American crises of the late 1990s, and the terrorism of the early 21st century). So far, financial markets and their regulators have been able to manage major crises, including major terrorist attacks, without breakdown. However, that does not mean that terrorism does not have any effects on a firm's financial activities.

For example, as discussed above, it seems clear that terrorism changes the perception of risk and financial markets reflect that increased level of risk aversion. Thus, terrorism can lead to at least a temporary widening of risk spreads and reduction in equity values. In many cases such changes are also associated with rationing of capital, where the smaller firms and weaker credits may be denied access to capital markets. For most business firms and financial institutions, these changes seem to argue for somewhat larger levels of safety stock and financial slack, that is, higher levels of net working capital and more conservative capital structures with lower debt ratios.

Financial Organization for Fighting Terrorism

Terrorism poses many direct and indirect challenges for a business firm. Not only does it have to assess and respond to new risks, it also has to comply with many complex new regulations. The organizational structure and the finance function in a firm must reflect these changes. For example, as discussed above, the role and function of the Chief Risk Officer (CRO) has expanded greatly.

In addition, the finance function must identify individuals responsible for managing the various compliance tasks resulting from the new terrorism-related regulations. The finance organization must also increase its efforts and involvement in computer and accounting information system security, and educate appropriate managers and staff about these changes in the finance organization and its functions.

CONCLUSIONS

While terrorism has been around for a long time, it has been receiving greatly increased attention in recent years. The events of 11 September 2001 were very significant in this regard and represent a turning point in the business impact of terrorism. There was a great increase in regulatory requirements facing companies that have large transactions with customers. In addition, concurrent regulatory changes unrelated to terrorism, such as the Sarbanes-Oxley Act in the US and similar legislation elsewhere, have further compounded the tasks of risk management and regulatory compliance facing most companies, their boards of directors, senior executives and their financial staff.

Among the changes facing the audit committees of corporate boards, the typical CFO, and financial and information systems staff originating in terrorism include an enhanced enterprise risk management function, greater emphasis on computer and information system security, including challenges related to the implementation of the XBRL standard for exchange of financial information, the need for allocating resources to meet the enhanced compliance requirements, the need to fortify defenses against the friendly or hostile takeover of the firm, and perhaps also the development of strategies to operate with somewhat higher levels of working capital and to reduce the company's level of financial leverage. These are all significant and important changes.

Thus, this chapter shows that terrorism has resulted in many changes in how companies are managed. The company's Board of Directors, senior executives, and its financial and risk management staff face the most critical changes. While many of the changes will result in better management, other changes will be increased deadweight costs of doing business in this post-09/11 era.

REFERENCES

Abadie, A. (2004), 'Poverty, political freedom, and the roots of terrorism', National Bureau of Economic Research working paper 10859.

Banham, R. (2004), 'Living with risk', *Treasury and Risk Management*, September, 22–8.

Baranoff, E.G. (2004), 'Risk management: a focus on a more holistic approach three years after September 11', *Journal of Insurance Regulation*, **22**(4), 71–81.

Boritz, E. and Won No (forthcoming), 'Security in XML-based financial reporting services on the internet', *Journal of Accounting and Public Policy*.

Buck, T. (2005), 'New money laundering legislation puts extra onus on EU professions', *Financial Times* 27 May, p. 4.

Carter, D.A. and B.J. Simkins (2004), 'The market's reaction to unexpected, catastrophic events: the case of airline stock returns and the September 11th attacks', *Quarterly Review of Economics and Finance*, **44**(4), 539–58.

Chen, A.H. and T.F. Sierns (2004), 'The effects of terrorism on global capital markets', *European Journal of Political Economy*, **20**(2), 349–66.

Council on Competitiveness (COC) (2003), *Competitiveness and Security Survey: Creating a Business Case for Corporate Security*, Washington, DC: COC.

Doll, M.W., S. Rai and J. Granado (2003), *Defending the Digital Frontier*, New York: John Wiley.

The Economist (2002), 'The needle in the haystack', 14 December, p. 69.

Ernst and Young (2004), 'Audit committees and the war on terror', *Board Matters Quarterly*, December, 7–8.

Eckstein, Z. and D. Tsiddon (2004), 'Macroeconomic consequences of terror: theory and the case of Israel', *Journal of Monetary Economics*, **57**, 971–1002.

Enders, W. and T. Sandler (2002), 'Patterns of transnational terror: alternative time-series estimates', *International Studies Quarterly*, **46**, 145–65.

Fitzgerald, V. (2004), 'Global financial information, compliance incentives and terrorist funding', *European Journal of Political Economy*, **20**(2), 387–401.

Flynn, S.F. (2004), 'Terrorism and the bottom line', *Forbes*, 4 October, p.48.

Hansen, F. (2004), 'Insuring against terrorism', *Business Finance*, October.

Jackson, D. and A. Dania (2005), 'The impact of terrorism on ADR valuation', working paper, University of Texas-Pan American, Edinburgh, TX.

Janczewski, L.J. and A. Colarik (2005), *Managerial Guide for Handling Cyber-Terrorism and Information Warfare*, Hershey, PA: Idea Group Publishing.

Lenzner, R. and N. Vardi (2004), 'Terror Inc.', *Forbes*, 18 October, pp. 52–4.

Marlett, D.C., J. Griffith, C. Pacini and R.E. Hoyt (2004), 'Terrorism insurance coverage: the market impact on insurers and other exposed industries', *Journal of Insurance Regulation*, **22**(2), 41–62.

Nitsch, V. and D. Schumacher (2004), 'Terrorism and international trade: an empirical investigation', *European Journal of Political Economy*, **20**(2), 423–33.

Rapoport, M. (2005), 'Companies pay a price for security breaches', *Wall Street Journal*, 15 June, p. C3.

Sandler, T. and W. Enders (2004), 'An economic perspective on transnational terrorism', *European Journal of Political Economy*, **20**(2), 301–16.

Simpson, G.A. (2004), 'Expanding in an age of terror: Western Union faces scrutiny', *Wall Street Journal*, 20 October, pp. A1, A14.

Walkenhorst, P. and N. Dihel (2002), 'Trade impacts of the terrorist attacks of 11 September 2001: a quantitative assessment', prepared for the International Conference on the Economic Consequences of the New Global Terrorism, Berlin, June 14–15.

United States Department of State (2004), 'Patterns of Terrorism', annual report on terrorism, accessed 22 June at www.state.gov/ct/rls/pgtrpt.

PART III

Corporate Management and Performance

8. Location decisions, or: modelling operational risk management under international terrorism

Gabriele G.S. Suder

Operational risk management is situated at the core of both event and business risk. It implies direct or indirect gains or losses in regard to comparative advantages such as those sought in investing abroad. Hymer, Vernon, Dunning and many others have helped us understand why and what drives a firm to become international or trans-national, with different degrees of host economy integration and linkages across borders. Locations and modes of internationalization are defined by management on the basis of the particular advantages that the firm gain from international operations. These advantages may be defined in terms of ownership, certain degrees of internalization and those based on location. The interplay between these factors will determine whether the company works on a local, regional, national or global scale.

International terrorism adds an important determinant to the definition of a firm's strategy. It is an external event that may lead to direct (mainly physical) or indirect (for instance, supply chain or consumer behavior) disruptions, that may hinder the internalization capacities of the firm in a given location, and its ability to profit of location-specific advantages. The investment decision of firms, or the decision to disinvest or to switch from particular locations, draws and re-draws the cartography of foreign direct investment flows.

With the trend of internationalization of business, international business (IB) research has attracted great attention. Location decisions are a branch of this field, and in particular of IB strategy (Ricart et al., 2004). As part of the internationalization process, choosing an international location is a crucial decision for a company. At the same time, dclocalization is also a crucial issue to home and receptor markets. This issue is treated within the framework of Krugman's (1994), Krugman and Vanables (1995) and Martin and Ottaviano's (1996) work. Location decisions have historically had to be adapted to fluctuations in the business environment of multinational enterprises, throughout the 'millennia-old' phenomenon of operations abroad (Moore and Lewis, 1999; Shenkar, 2004). Shenkar found that, nevertheless, few contributions have been made to IB research that attempt to analyse the modus operandi (the 'how' as an extension of the 'why'): what is the expertise and knowledge of a foreign business environment in terms of its structure? Some exceptions are made in studies in which, in particular, business strategy in regions is analysed, for example, in China.

Corporations possess geographic organizations that are shaped into international divisions (for example, Wal-Mart), geographically structured with a matrix structure combining functions and business units to regions (for example, Microsoft), and with different degrees of what is known as 'transnationality' (Bartlett and Goshal, 1989). It appears that the particular advantage of the transnational corporation lies in the efficient and effective transfer of explicit – geographical proximity, logistical ease, risk diversification motivations for location decisions – and tacit – experience, accumulated tacit knowledge, networking motivations – knowledge about global and local conditions. Management also decides which knowledge and competence is transferred to that location towards external parties, and which knowledge is to remain internal.

Location decisions require strategic decision-making for a first experience in going cross-border, or to make a decision of adding or changing a location to earlier internationalization stages. In both cases, decisions are made on the basis of existing alternatives. In the latter case, decisions emerge also from previous experience. Motives for location change are often local externalities, research and development spillovers, costs of knowledge transfer, and/or transport costs (Krugman and Venables, 1995). Transaction costs (Eden and Miller, 2001; Buckley and Casson, 1976) are cause to firms that relocate to benefit both from cost benefits and from entering foreign markets and these markets' resources potential, leading to location change.

If costs of a market are more important than the returns, a firm will typically consider relocation. This also applies in terms of security and safety costs. But a firm may also adapt its cost/return ratio by shifting to a different mode of operation with differently adapted levels of internalization. For both cases of initial internationalization and relocation – of outsourcing or offshoring; or of intra- or inter-firm trade of goods or services – the foreign business environment always needs to undergo severe scrutiny, and decisions along more than microeconomic criteria. The annual Competitiveness and Security Survey is one of the main sources that demonstrate the evolution of corporate awareness in the field of terrorism and its evaluation mechanisms; the 2003 survey illustrates clearly the concerns that corporations place into the framework of internationalization and its long-term challenges. Seventy-one percent of surveyed companies agree that there is a long-term positive return on investment for security, and that this security requires not only guarding of physical property and staff, but also of networks and operability. Yet 'business leaders are unsure what constitutes best practice' (Council on Competitiveness/ WRS, 2003, p. 1). This is where academia and IB research have an important role to play.

The rationales for multinational firms' motives and returns (as based on Vernon, 1966; Hymer, 1976; Buckley and Casson, 1976; Kogut and Zander, 1993) have been treated in depth by the contributions in regard to the process of internationalization (Johanson and Vahine, 1977, 1990), its impact on firm performance (Carpano et al., 1994), foreign entry modes and their impact on firm performance (Hennart, 1982; Root, 1987; Buckley and Casson, 1996, 1998) and the shape of organizational structures within this internationalization. They have been presented in the important literature reviews filed by Werner (2002), who classified international management research from 1996 to 2000 of the top ranked IB journals, and by the perspectives article by Ricart et al. (2004) in regard to IB research streams. Ricart et al.'s argument developing from this literature states that firms need to find efficient and effective models that take the 'ecology of places and firms' into account. The location selection is highly strategic for global companies: economic theory has long shown that internationalization appears to be crucial if companies want to obtain or maintain competitiveness. While gains and losses are intrinsic to any business operation, choosing the right international location represents an efficient solution to obtain competitive advantage that will make a difference by:

- optimizing or reducing costs;
- getting new opportunities for growth; or
- developing new strategic strengths.

Globalization has been detrimental to those firms that have not been capable of responsiveness to international integration (Prahalad and Doz, 1987; Bartlett and Goshal, 1989) and to those firms that are not taking into account that shareholder values exceed the expectations of profit maximization. In the face of global shifts (Dicken, 2003) and of the 'globalisation gap' (Isaak, 2005), we can forward the hypothesis that globalization is the compression of time and space that increases the frequency and duration of linkages between any given actor in the international environment – not only between corporate business relations. Only actors of the international environment who recognize the challenges of diversity can react to the risk terrorism entails.

LOCATING IN HOT SPOTS?

This compression, integration and quasi-convergence of time and space is the corporations' dilemma. Locate in high risk areas? And if so, how?

Corporations need to assess the potential benefits of operating in 'hot spots' or preferring a risk aversion behavior. This enhances the importance of operational risk management. 'Hot spots' in this context are:

*   locations with high terrorist risk (indicating direct impact on the firm, mostly meaning physical damage), which may include places like Iraq or Colombia;
*   locations that are particularly vulnerable to market disequilibrium (indirect impact, mostly measured via loss of consumer confidence, downturn of currency, infrastructural or logistical setbacks, factors that may cause the disruption of supply chains as analysed in Suder (2004) with an attempt to elaborate a geopolitical cartography), which may include places like the US and the EU.

Asymmetric international terrorism is an adversity in which a low degree of tools (in numbers and sophistication) and a low number of people have a high degree of impact – as in the 09/11 attacks. It illustrates that the tools developed in Information and Communication Technology (ICT) and transport for global integration and corporate internationalization become also the drivers of threat. They have in the past opened up places to the infiltration of a diaspora community of potential 'sleepers' (terrorists inactive for a period of time and living under a different but normal civil identity) worldwide. This phenomenon increases terrorism risk in locations that had yet been unaffected of such political risk factors in the pre-09/11 world. A consequential adaptation of location decisions is hence detached from the location in which a terrorism threat or attack is actually happening – a rather new phenomenon for political risk management.

The objective here is not to analyse the motivations or modalities of going international, nor the contribution that corporations may make to conflict and threat prevention strategies with or for governments in the long run. It is rather to explore whether and how post-09/11 international terrorism risk has an impact on location decisions framed by risk assessments of transnational companies (TNCs) within political risk evaluations that are traditionally limited to local or national terrorist assessment. Ricard et al. (2004) argue that 'to face the realities of the 21st century, a different paradigm is needed for relating IB and international strategy: a view that goes beyond the tension between globalization and localization controlled by [multinational companies]' (p. 179). Why should we study transnational companies in particular? In literature, a TNC is characterized as a firm that 'has the power to coordinate and control operations in more than one country, even if it does not own them' (Dicken, 2003, p. 198). These firms hence have the potential to adapt their structure and strategy to the changing external business environment, and to evaluate the particular advantages of locations at any given time.

In this case, how should TNCs build a strategic framework? In other words, how can we find a balance between 'hot spot' benefits – exploiting comparative advantages and gain of returns – on one hand and, on the other, the uncertainties that a firm takes on when adopting risk aversion behaviors, all in an exercise of drawing a model that allows for a generalization despite the companies' industry distinction, sector specificities and positioning and sustainability in relation to risk specifically? Tacit knowledge of markets and their risk levels is based on experience, accumulated tacit knowledge and networking, all studied for Taiwan by Chen et al. (2004) within the analysis of local linkages. Explicit knowledge comprises geographical proximity, logistical ease and risk diversification. If we take into account that both tacit and explicit motivations define important preferences in terms of location decisions, then each firm may model its specific location strategy using the simple framework as developed below from operational risk studies, and relate it to the ownership-, internalization- and location-specific advantages sought.

A LOCATION MODEL

Using conceptual and empirical methodologies, it is possible to come to initial assumptions that may serve to highlight certain current alterations in the perception of IB strategy in regard to risk assessment and management criteria in the contemporary world. Empirical research for this chapter included a sample of European transnational companies, through interviews and research data made available by the corporations. In addition, the available data from sources such as the World Investment Report, the World Competitiveness Report and diverse United Nations and World Bank publications proved useful for the study of TNC investment patterns after the events of 09/11 in New York and 03/11 in Madrid.

The model that is developed herein is based on the assumption that there is a rationale following the risk–return evaluation that involves the search of multinationals for tacit and explicit information depending on the mode of entry that it engages, or has engaged, into in its internationalization phase, and that may be altered through a shock scenario. In terms of operational risks, the firm takes most of the following elements of its value chain into account:

- procurement;
- orders, invoicing;
- manufacturing and inventory management;
- service provision;
- shipping, integrated logistics, and order fulfillment; and
- a full set of planning and time management.

These elements finally involve all aspects of management, reaching from human resources management to marketing and sales orientations. We can expect that explicit information on these elements can more easily be accumulated by the firm over distance than tacit information, and that this goes also for terrorism risk perceptions. Interestingly, in this context, the 2004 Ernst & Young survey indicates that firms operating across borders place greater importance on the proximity of markets (60 percent compared to an average of 48 percent in the preceding period) than on obtaining gains on productivity (37 percent compared to 52 percent) or flexibility of labor law (24 percent compared to 42 percent). In practical terms, international corporate executives generally use four main criteria for choosing locations – operational, financial, location and risk. The operational criteria deals with all that relating to the project activities, that is, the quality of transport and logistic infrastructures, of telecommunications infrastructures, the level of local labor skills, and the proximity of a target market (competition). It was found that, comparatively to other factors, corporate executives consider these criteria very important for assessing a potential location. The quality of operational resources is seen as being more important than the potential of target markets.

The financial criteria directly concern the finances of the company and the management of its revenue. In particular, they concern potential gains in productivity, tax burdens and costs of labor, but also public aid and the proximity of financial markets. They deal with potential productivity gains, labor costs, tax burden, flexibility of labor law, special treatment of foreign investments, public aid, grants and subsidies availability, access to financial investors, and the integration of a particular monetary zone. These criteria mainly rank second in international location decisions but remain essential, knowing that labor costs and social charges and the level of tax burden are omnipresent criteria.

The location or local criteria concern the operating environment of the company of a given country or region and the extent to which they offer the necessary means to develop to the firm. This includes the availability of sites, cost of lands and regulations, specific skills developed in the region, availability of specific expertise, local language, values and culture, the proximity of centres of innovation and research, as well as quality of life. In addition to these criteria, often we can also notice the bandwagon effect that Knickerbocker explored in 1973: competitors follow firms into emerging markets; this move is illustrated through an investment en bloc into a specific region.

Corporations define the different modes of location on the global scale following a certain categorization.

Production in the home market
Indirect exporting: A partner in the manufacturer's home country takes over all activities related to the foreign markets.

Direct exporting: Organization of distribution into foreign markets. Direct market representation and independent representation.

Production abroad

Licensing: Contractual arrangement whereby one company, the licensor, makes an asset available to another company, the licensee, in exchange for royalties, license fees, or some other form of compensation.

Franchising: Special form of licensing, more extensive in the transfer of know-how.

Joint ventures: Working with a local partner. Sharing of risk and the ability to combine different value chain strengths.

Strategic alliances: Collaborative ventures between international firms.

Acquisition/merger: Control and ownership of operations outside the home country for corporate growth.

Greenfield: Building your own facilities.

For our purposes, we categorize these modes into low, medium and high location levels, from top to bottom of the above list, and illustrated in Figure 8.1. An important body of literature focuses on foreign direct investment (FDI) and entry modes, contrasting the performance of firms that enter international markets in diverse fashions (amongst them Carpano et al., 1994; Buckley and Casson, 1996, 1998; Ruigrok and Wagner, 2003). Some focus on sectorial studies on internalizing transaction costs through ownership, joint venture and non-equity alliance (Jones et al., 1990 on car industry, or Sako, 1997 on microelectronic).

Causes and consequences of international production and sources of relative success were the emphasis of Porter's work, and took an activity-based approach on the coordination of critical TNC activities (Porter, 1985; Yip, 1995). Location-based advantages of TNCs are assessed by Eden and Potter (1993) as:

- resource-seeking investments (low cost input);
- cost-reducing investment (for example, labor cheaply used for semi-finishing and re-export); and
- market access investment (overcoming trade barriers).

The eclectic (oli) paradigm, explaining patterns and level of TNC activity (the oli paradigm), had already set out three advantages of international firms as ownership, location and internalization advantages, with transaction market failures causing multinational company (MNC) structures (Dunning 1988). Vernon (1992) and Dunning (1993) argued also that these firms can leverage resources through FDI, taking a resources-based perspective. Birkinshaw and

Hood (1998) added that strategy of TNCs is as much market-serving as it is resource-seeking. The model developed throughout this chapter attempts to classify both resources – as well as market-seeking criteria as motivations or 'returns' of investment. Also, it is taken into account that TNCs may reach scale economies of knowledge through its transfer across borders (Buckley and Casson, 1976; Kogut and Zander, 1993), and link these approaches on a global or regional level. Imagine a TNC that is faced with socio-cultural problems due to the impact that terrorism has on the public opinion and on consumer behavior. It will continue to be sensitive to local advantages such as currency or fiscal values, but will need to react to the socio-cultural disadvantages through image- or location-adaptations. It may also consequently be facing changing company laws and see its mode of entry and operation limited or forbidden.

Hence, the mode of entry that a TNC chooses reflects the answer to a multitude of variables that were analysed in the most relevant publications, and are priorities for the TNC:

- local advantages, including the above mentioned currency, resources, fiscalities, market-related needs or cultures, knowledge management (KM)
- government policies
- company taxation
- company law and legal issues
- regional policies
- infrastructure
- socio-cultural forces
- transaction costs
- organizational structure
- product life cycles
- knowledge transfer options
- risk – diversification possibilities
- decomposition abilities of activities
- 'ecology of firms and places'
- cross-border factor mobility
- 'herd' behavior

These priorities are set in a high level of complexity that contains strong uncertainties and risks that have become global issues. A first assumption that can be formulated on the basis of the above is that the TNC will adapt its mode of entry to certain 'return' expectations that can be illustrated in Figure 8.1.

Terrorism is a phenomenon that is traditionally taken into account in the IB stream of works about political risk. Part II of this volume dealt with the challenges to this classification.

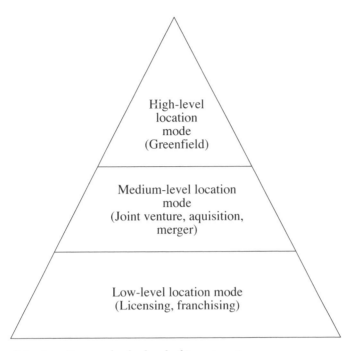

Figure 8.1   Location modes by level of investment

In 2004 in Europe, the criterion of clarity and stability of the political environment (which 50 percent of firms in the Ernst & Young survey consider very important) globally joined the other top priority criteria and has given 9 extra percentage points than 2003. Against the backdrop of a year full of uncertainties, a culture of risk awareness has emerged; it places priority on transparency, stability and clarity in the countries chosen for investment projects (Ernst & Young, 2004).

An event of the 09/11-type shows that event and business risk are linked to each other within the discipline of Operational Risk Management (Lam, 2003), in which 'operational risk is the risk of direct or indirect loss resulting from inadequate or failed internal process, people, and systems or from external events" (p. 210) excluding risks by credit or market risks. Indeed, decline in FDI in 2002 was uneven across regions, countries and sectors (UNTAD World Investment Report, 2004). The Report noted the following trends:

- flows into manufacturing and services declined;
- flows into primary sector rose; and
- FDI entering host economies through M&A declined.

Also at this period the declines of inflow to 16 of 26 developed countries were accompanied by:

- slowdown in corporate investment;
- declining stock prices;
- slowdown in consolidation in certain industries;
- weak economic conditions; and
- declining outflows.

Why do we identify these particular developments? The assumption is that, due to the complexity of the international business environment and the scope of operational risk, a terrorism attack of the breadth of 09/11 and 03/11 leads to an impact in location decisions that are not limited to the geographic proximity of the event, but will also concern other regions – for example, that in which the origin of the plan for the attack is assumed to come from. For instance, what was the impact of the above-mentioned terrorist acts on FDI on Pakistan, neighbouring Afghanistan, instead of any of the actual locations of attack, New York or Madrid? It is naturally impossible to clear the available FDI data from the impact of such events as economic downturns, a weak dollar, or local crises.

WHEN, WHERE AND HOW?

Operational risk management can limit potential loss through the mapping of entry and exit strategies or modes of adaptation to market situations, given the intra-firm risk assessment of locations on the basis of tacit and explicit knowledge criteria. In this case, it is useful for the TNC to have access to a model that provides a sound basis for this mapping, in which low-level location modes consist of licensing and franchising strategies. Medium-level ones include joint venture and international strategic alliance strategies, while high-level strategies involve international acquisition and merger as well as Greenfield modes of direct investment.

Return on investment is also classified into a low, medium and high level. These returns are calculated and classified by each firm – on the basis of firm-specific qualitative and qualitative data in response to the advantage sought in the location.

Finally, it is essential to determine the risks that 09/11-type terrorism have on these advantages per international location. It is useful to take advantage of assessment mechanisms used by security management and insurance organizations such as Swiss Re (Swiss Re, 2003) and those elaborated in Suder (2004) to define hot spots: having assessed risk (R) as the probability (P) multiplied by the impact (I), R = P x I. Impact is defined as the amount of money the firm will lose, whether directly or indirectly, and the probability of operational resilience. These assessment mechanisms allow a firm to decide how to:

- specify actors and assets in terms of vulnerability to risk (terrorism threat, act, and/or aftermath);
- devise continuity and resilience strategies; and
- make cost/benefit and risk–return assumptions.

On the basis of this data, management is able to focus its attention on questions regarding business, product and location diversification. Setting out these considerations results in the structure shown in Figure 8.2. From these relations, a model (like Figure 8.3) can then be constructed and applied:

From these relations results the probability (in terms of operational risk management) with which each location receives a certain type of investment. This is in accordance with location modes and strategies as discussed above, and should be the basis for a corporate mapping, or scenario planning as proposed in Suder 2004. While scenario-planning may be less objective than corporate mappings along the above model, the approach has the merit of

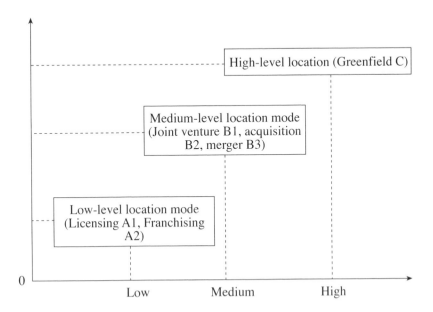

Figure 8.2   Determinants of location strategy

High		A1	B3, C
Medium	→ A2	A1 → A2	C
Low	→ A2	A2 → B3	C
	Low	Medium	High

Risk of terrorism impact on location

Return on investment

Figure 8.3   Model of location strategy by return on investment

including the very important tacit knowledge that is specific to each company or each activity within that firm, and that is essential to internalization decisions of knowledge and competences in balance to the factual risk–return evaluation.

Both approaches best lead to a cartography exercise that allows for a strategy away from highly concentrated operations, and towards a certain flexibility and diversification of risk. For certain operations, for example, a semi-globalization in stages of multidimensional intermediate stages of localization and integration may allow a respect of the 'ecology of places' (Ghemawat, 2003). In any case, the simplified model developed here allows an easy classification of location categories along return aspects, in order, on a business level, to 'take decisive action to eliminate the threat they [the terrorists] pose' (Bush, 2002). It also helps firms to anticipate threat in terms of the flexibility necessary when applying entry, adaptation or exit strategies, for example when turning to risk aversion if the risk–return evaluation is not conclusive.

In operational terms, we conceive that, in a 'hot spot', if the firm counts on significant returns and its decision-making is based on tacit and explicit knowledge about possible risks in the described framework, then a TNC will generally have high direct location motivations and hence opt for high location modes. The reverse situation with low tacit knowledge makes it difficult to opt for the economic theory's ideal of a perfect firm integration into the host country due to the remaining uncertainties about potential adversity.

RISK-TAKING AND INTERNALIZATION

As the global economy recovers from the downturn of 2001–2002, there is an increased focus on how corporations and decision-makers select international locations and undertake investment decisions. Corporate leaders expect a surge of investment in growth for the second half of the years 2005–2010. The World Economic Forum voiced opinions indicating that, 'it takes investment in competitiveness and a willingness to invest in innovation and risk-taking. When a company grows, it begins to turn its attention away from investing in businesses of the past and begins to invest in businesses and regions of the future. The primary requirements for growth, it was suggested in Davos, are entrepreneurship, skill and risk-taking' (WEF, Davos, 2005) Will this result in FDI patterns be characterized by a geographically broader diversification of locations, with more suppliers and sourcing, and with lower levels of internalization of operations for the sake of risk aversion?

At the same time, without doubt, 09/11 and – reinforcing the seriousness and globality of the phenomenon – 03/11, have been the principal events increasing the business world's attention to terrorism. While terrorism was not a main issue for business in the pre-09/11 TNC surveys, it became so with the attacks on America, and those of Bali and Madrid, reinforcing the concerns expressed in the Pinkerton survey, Security Magazine, Gartner's Symposium (2003) and the National Association for Business Economics. The RAND–*Financial Times*–Janusian (2004) survey indicated that across the world – in North America, East/Southeast Asia, sub-Saharan Africa, the Middle East and North Africa region and Western Europe, al-Qaeda is perceived to be the biggest threat. The Middle East, at 71 percent, represented the region of greatest terrorism threat to businesses and the region where (by 61 percent) companies would now reconsider sending their employees on business travel, while almost 80 percent consider additional protective measures for their employees in that region. It is similarly noteworthy that Western Europe was second in threat perception (at 52 percent) and employee protection (at 42 percent roughly matching Central, East, South and Southeast Asia, as well as sub-Saharan Africa), while Latin America – a region that traditionally has held high terrorism concern for businesses – was pushed to the bottom of the ladder (at only 18 percent threat perception and 21 percent concern over employees in the region) in terms of regions of concern. Yes, perceptions have indeed changed.

Although a majority (52 percent) of respondents did not feel that terrorists would deliberately target their business, 65 percent regarded terrorism as a 'significant threat' to their organization. While most companies spend less than 2 percent of their budget on security globally or domestically – with less than one-tenth of respondents spending more than 5 percent of their budget on security – very similar percentages of these security budgets (that is, 54 percent globally and 53 percent domestically) are spent in countering terrorism through various means. Interestingly, however, a significant percentage (29 percent globally and 26 percent domestically) spend more than 20 percent of their security budget to counter terrorism (RAND–Janusian–FT, 2004).

Also, the risk of chemical and biological terrorism is perceived, with 30 percent believing that it would affect their organization in the future (up from only 18 percent in 2003). While nuclear terrorism was seen as a low probability threat, more than 21 percent (up from only 12 percent in 2003) felt that they were threatened by radiological ('dirty bomb') terrorism – indicating that more than 50 percent of respondents felt that a weapons-of-mass-destruction terrorist attack was likely. This was a massive increase on the 2003 results, which had at the time indicated that cyber-threats were considered more likely than a WMD terrorist attack (RAND–Janusian–FT, 2004). Finally, Gartner (2003) demonstrates that cyberterrorism is a threat of utmost importance to business and its environment.

OPERATIONAL RISK AND LOCATION DECISIONS: CONCLUSIONS

Because the 'know your customer's customer' principle is impracticable (Höche 2005, p. 13) for most corporations, operational risk can only be limited to the desired extent if it is managed within a framework of diversification of sourcing and suppliers, a flexibility in entry and exit strategies, and on the basis of a firm-specific set of location modes.

The economy (Gudeman, 1986; Rosser, 1996) revolves around making, holding, using, sharing, exchanging and accumulating valued objects and services. It consists of two realms – the market, which has an instrumental purpose and is guided by competition as well as the accumulation of gains (that is, profit maximization), and the community, which gains its motivation by social fulfillment, curiosity or the pleasure of mastery. The base of exchange is then the convergence of shared interests, including lasting resources, produced items and services, ideological constructs (that is, knowledge, technology, laws, practices, skills, customs), but also cultural agreements, beliefs. Locally defined values express identity; they are embodied in goods, services, ideologies. These constitute values that are tacit or explicit, and heterogeneous. This is where knowledge becomes an important factor next to factual risk–return assessments when taking location decisions. The logic of this is that, as Dicken (2003) found, international trade is predominated by a high degree of cross-investment between the highly developed economies, although foreign direct investment into developing countries rises because firms are aware of the importance of this knowledge for their international mapping. The core elements of prevention, that is, collaboration, information-sharing, threat recognition, risk management and intervention (Office for Domestic Preparedness, 2003) are valid for both homeland and business decisions: limiting or preventing the impact of terrorism through anticipation are key. Amongst other factors, we can argue that a new type of risk – the one that we identified as 09/11-type terrorism – has a potentially global impact on operations. While formerly, location decisions were predominated by homogeneity and convergence criteria, today formerly 'low risk' places have become hot spots in terms of operational risk of locations. Hymer, Vernon, Dunning and many others had helped us understand why and what drives a firm to operate across borders. Operational risk management helps to model location strategies and modes of internationalization that are defined by management on the basis of particular advantages the firm may gain from international operations: the ownership-specific advantages, internalization advantages of specific defined degrees, and location-specific advantages that define whether a corporation works on a local, regional, national or global scale – defining thus its entry, adaptation and exit strategies.

REFERENCES

Bartlett, C.A. and S. Goshal (1992), *Transnational Management*, Homewood, IL: Irwin.
Ball, D.A., H. Wendell and J.R. McCulloch (1996), *International Business*, 6th edn, Homewood, IL: Irwin.
Bartlett, C.A. and S. Goshal (1989), *Managing Across Borders: The Transnational Solution*, Boston, MA: Harvard Business School Press.
Birkinshaw, J. and N. Hood (1998), 'Multinational subsidiary evolution: capability and charterchange in foreign-owned subsidiary companies', *Academy of Management Review*, **23**(4), 773–95.
Buckley, P.J. and M.C. Casson (1976), *The Future of the Multinational Enterprise*, New York: Holmes and Meier Publishers.
Buckley, P.J. and M.C. Casson (1996), 'An economic model of international joint venture strategy', *Journal of International Business Studies*, **27**(5), 849–76.
Buckley, P.J. and M.C. Casson (1998), 'Analyzing foreign market entry strategies: extending the internalization approach', *Journal of International Business Studies*, **29**, 539–61.
Bush, G.W. (2002), *The National Strategy for Homeland Security*, Washington, DC: Office of Homeland Security.
Carpano, C., J.J. Chrisman and K. Roth (1994), 'International strategy and environment: an assessment of the performance relationship', *Journal of International Business Studies*, **25**(3), 639–56.
Chen, T.-J., H. Chen and K. Ying-Hua (2004), 'Foreign direct investment and local linkages', *Journal of International Business Studies*, **35**, 320–33.
Council on Competitiveness/Wilson Research Strategies (2003 and yearly reports), *Competitiveness and Security Survey*, Washington, DC and McLean, VA.

Dicken, Peter (2003), *Global Shift*, London: Sage.

Dunning, J.H. (1988), 'The eclectic paradigm of international production: a restatement and some possible extensions', *Journal of International Business Studies*, **19**, 1–31

Dunning, J.H. (1993), *Multinational Enterprises and the Global Economy*, Reading, MA: Addison-Wesley Publishing Company.

Ernst & Young (2004), 'Attractiveness of Europe survey 2004: international executives assess Europe', working paper.

Eden, L. and S. Miller (2001), 'Opening the black box: multinationals and the cost of doing business abroad', paper presented at Academy of Management Conference, Washington DC.

Eden, L. and E. Potter (1993), *Multinationals in the Global Political Economy*, New York: St. Martin's Press.

Gartner Symposium (2003), *The Effect of Global Unrest on Business and IT*, http://symposium.gartner.com/story.php.id.3495.s.5.html.

Ghemawat, P. (2003), 'Semi-globalization and the international business strategy', *Journal of International Business Studies*, **34**(2), 138–52.

Gudeman, S. (1978), 'Anthropological economics: the question of distribution', *Annual Review of Anthropology*, **7**, 347–77.

Gudeman, S. (1986), *Economics as Culture: Models and Metaphors of Livelihood*, London: Routledge and Kegan Paul.

Hennart, J.-F. (1982), *Theory of Multinational Enterprise*, Ann Arbor, MI: University of Michigan Press.

Höche, T. (2005), 'Der Entwurf einer dritten EU – Richtlinie zur Verhinderung der Nutzung des Finanzsystems zu Zwecken der Geldwäsche und der Finanzierung des Terrorismus 2005', Wertpapier, Mitteilungen 4, Bd. 59, 1.

Hymer, S.H. (1976), 'The international operations of national firms: a study of direct investment', PhD thesis 1960, Cambridge, MA: MIT Press.

Isaak, Robert A. (2005), *The Globalization Gap: How the Rich Get Richer and the Poor Get Left Further Behind*, Upper Saddle River, NJ: Financial Times Prentice Hall.

Johanson, J. and J.E. Vahine (1977), 'The internationalisation process of the firm – a model of knowledge development and increasing market commitments', *Journal of International Business*, **8**, 23–32.

Jones, D.T., D. Roos and J. Womack (1990), *The Machine that Changed the World: Based on the Massachusetts Institute of Technology $5 million 5-year Study on the Future of the Automobile*, New York: Rawson.

Knickerbocker, F.T. (1973), *Oligopolistic Reaction and the Multinational Enterprise*, Cambridge, MA: Harvard University Press.

Kogut, B. and U. Zander (1993), 'Knowledge of the firm and the evolutionary theory of the MNC', *Journal of International Business Studies*, **24**(4), 625–45.

Krugman, P. (1994), 'Competitiveness: a dangerous obsession', *Foreign Affairs*, March–April.

Krugman, P. and A.J. Vanables (1995), 'Globalization and the inequalities of nations', *Quarterly Journal of Economics*, **110**(4), 857–80.

Lam, J. (2003), *Enterprise Risk Management: From Incentives to Controls*, Hoboken, NJ: John Wiley & Sons.

Martin, P. and G. Ottaviano (1996), 'Growing locations: industry location in a model of endogenous growth', *European Economic Review*, **43**(2), 218–302.

Moore, K. and D. Lewis (1999), *Birth of the Multinational*, Copenhagen: Copenhagen Business School Press.

Office for Domestic Preparedness (2003), *Guidelines for Homeland Security: Prevention and Deterrence*, Washington, DC: US Department for Homeland Security.

Piggott, J. and M. Cook (1999), *International Business Economics: A European Perspective*, 2nd edn, Harlow: Addison Wesley Longman.

Porter, M.E. (1985), *Competitive Advantage: Creating and Sustaining Superior Performance*, New York: Free Press.

Prahalad, C.K. and Y. Doz (1987), *The Multinational Mission: Balancing Local Demands and Global Vision*, New York: Free Press.

RAND Corporation, *Financial Times* and Janusian Security Risk Management (2004), *Terrorism and Business Continuity Survey 2004*, accessed 8 May at www.janusian.com/survey.

Ricart, J.R., M.J. Enright, S. Ghemawat and Tarun Khanna (2004), 'New frontiers in international strategy', *Journal of International Business Studies*, **35**, 175–200.

Root, F.R. (1987), *Entry Strategies for International Markets*, Lexington, MA: Lexington Books.

Rosser, J.B. Jr. and M.V. Rosser (1996), *Comparative Economics in a Transforming World Economy*, Homewood, IL: Irwin.

Ruigrok, W. and H. Wagner (2003), 'Internationalisation and performance: an organizational learning perspective', *Management International Review*, **43**(1), 63–84.

Sako, M. (1997). 'Shunto: the role of employer and union coordination at the industry and inter-sectoral levels' in Mari Sako and Hiroki Sato (eds), *Japanese Labour and Management in Transition*, London: Routledge.

Shenkar, O. (2004), 'One more time: international business in a global economy', *Journal of International Business Studies*, **35**, 161–71.

Suder, G. (ed.) (2004), *Terrorism and the International Business Environment: The Security–Business Nexus*. Cheltenham, UK and Northampton, MA, USA: Edward Elgar.

Swiss Re (2003), *Terrorism Risks in Property Insurance and Their Insurability After 11 September 2001*, Zurich: Swiss Reinsurance Company.

United Nations Conference on Trade and Development (UNCTAD) (2003), *World Investment Report: FDI Policies for Development: National and International Perspectives – Overview*, New York and Geneva: United Nations.

Vernon, R. (1966), 'International investment and international trade in the product life cycle', *Quarterly Journal of Economics*, **80**, 190–207.

Vernon, R. (1992), 'Transnational corporations: where are they coming from, where are they heading to?', *Transnational Corporations*, **1**(2), 7–35.

Werner, S. (2002), 'Recent developments in international management research: a review of 20 top management journals', *Journal of Management*, **28**, 277–305.

World Economic Forum (2005), 'Corporate leaders expect surge of investment growth for 2005', Davos meeting press release, 29 January.

Yip, G.S. (1995), *Total Global Strategy: Managing for Worldwide Competitive Advantage*, business school edn, Englewood Cliffs, NJ: Prentice-Hall.

9. Global supply chain under conditions of uncertainty: economic impacts, corporate responses, strategic lessons

John R. McIntyre and Eric Ford Travis

Here is a harbour without ships, a port without trade, a fishery without nets, a people without business; and that which is worse than all ... much less do they understand it.

Daniel Defoe, *A Tour Thro the Whole Island of Great Britain*, letter 12, 1747

INTRODUCTION

Thomas Friedman (2005), the influential *New York Times* author and columnist, views the just-in-time global supply chain's functioning as one of the essential characteristics of the 21st century's political economy. Friedman goes so far as to devise what he has termed the 'Dell Theory of Conflict Prevention' (using Dell Corporation as a case in point), which posits that with the advent and spread of just-in-time global supply chains in what he terms the 'flat world', there is now an "even greater restraint on geopolitical adventurism than (that flowing from) the more general rising standard of living" which characterized the last 30 years of the 20th century (p. 420). The Friedman postulate stipulates that 'no two countries that are both part of a major global supply chain, like Dell's, will ever fight a war against each other, as long as they are both part of the same global supply chain' (p. 421). He states that such countries grasp the high risk premium they would incur if they let conflict break out and therefore have a stake in protecting the equity they have built up. China, India, Taiwan, among others, are cited as evidence.

While this theory has not been empirically tested, history teaches us that trading partners in the past have been known to fight full-fledged wars, with France and Germany being foremost example in the European theater. The assumption is that the economic interdependence, the improved lifestyle for future generations, provides a shield against hostilities. While it may well be the case among state actors – with the exception of rogue states – non-state actors which engage in terrorism are rather more likely to take advantage of a 'flat' and uniform world and break the chain at any point to disturb the establish global order.

Economic globalization has three primary components: the instantaneous exchange of information, the accelerating movement of currency and investment flows, and the interdependent physical movement of goods, raw materials and intangibles. All of these have had exponential increases due to advances in technology such as the advent and spread of the internet. The global supply chain encompasses all of these components. The use of management information systems has significantly increased the speed and efficiency of the physical movement of goods but the need for security in the face of the threat of terrorism is causing disruptions, delays and alterations of these global flows as impacts are evaluated, responses considered and systems altered to reflect the changing environment. This chapter focuses on the impacts and responses that the post-09/11 terrorist threat has engendered for the global supply chain now operating under conditions of high uncertainty.

> The next terrorist attack is likely to be staged through a supply chain. Given the nature of the terrorist attack on 09/11, the US government has focused its efforts on securing airports and better screening of passengers. As a result, security experts predict that the next terrorist attack will be staged using freight transportation. With 80 percent of global freight moving by sea, terrorists can manipulate weak points in US supply chains to either enter the country or smuggle weapons of mass destruction. (Tohamy, 2004)

Even though American businesses might be targeted more than others, any attack or disruption of the global supply chain will have cascading impacts in all countries that either support or rely on the supply chain. Attacking US components of the supply chain is far more tempting for terrorists, but the effects will clearly not be limited to the US economy. Most terrorist attacks have targeted people in an attempt to disseminate fear, but the potential and trend line for terrorists to become more tactical in their planning and execution will inevitably result in deliberate attacks on the architecture of the global economic system itself. For terrorists that have political or cultural antipathy towards globalization or specific countries, the targeting of the supply chain provides specific cause-effect linkage.

SEEKING BENCHMARKS

We can legitimately ask what is an appropriate comparison for 09/11 or events of alike magnitude in physical damage or loss of human lives, or in the popular imagination. The Enron scandal, happening in roughly a similar time sequence, may in fact have had an equivalent financial impact, though it did not significantly alter the flow of goods. The 10-day dockers' strike at Los Angeles and Long Beach, California in 2002 is perhaps a more useful analogy in seeking some comparative benchmarks. It had a severe, immediate and obvious impact on the supply chain, resulting in estimated losses of $2 billion per day. (Cohen, 2002; Iritany, 2002) It should be noted that the lockout affected companies and economies both upstream and downstream, and resulted in losses and delays lasting many weeks. Overall efficiency suffered even longer.

Some ask, perhaps rhetorically, 'which did more damage to the United States (and the world economy), 09/11 or the collapse of Enron? It is impossible to tell in the short term, but look at how governmental institutions reacted to each of those disasters. . . Both situations have cost billions and billions of dollars. But only one of them scared us' (Ranum, 2004, p. 215).

Compared to terrorism, there is a much longer and broader history of accounting scandals and fraudulent behavior in finance and investment, with arguably much greater overall impact, but certainly less durable concern. The Enron scandal actually did strike fear into the hearts of investors and employees of large corporations and their defined interests. It resulted in the transformation of some accounting practices and levels of transparency (Mulford and Cominskey, 2004). Prosecution and enhanced accountability were pursued somewhat less aggressively by government, the public and industry.

Shutting down a single company has circumscribed repercussions, covered perhaps by insurance or other government-guaranteed schemes. Shutting down a single railway, sea lane or core highway that might be the route for transporting explosives can have extensive repercussions that are not as well contained or predictable. Shutting down the borders, including the ports, impacts not only an entire country, but an entire region and, in the case of the United States, the global economy in its entirety, given the size of the US economy.

An example of how a mass transit transportation system can be shut down occurred in December of 2003:

> [An] incident involving the threat of possible placement of hazardous chemical devices near a Washington, DC metro station resulted in major disruptions to about 40 percent of the system. After several hours of delays, the alleged devices were discovered and deemed innocuous. This situation demonstrates how bomb threats on mass transit systems can have huge negative ramifications to an important commuter route. If a threat is ignored and an attack occurs, the credibility of the mass transit system will have been severely damaged. Yet, frequent hoaxes and baseless threats reduce the seriousness with which industry and government may respond to a provocation. (Alexander, 2004, p. 46)

This incident involved a passenger system, but elements of it are applicable to freight as well. Even a hoax or ruse can cripple a freight line, resulting in destabilizing upstream and downstream delays and economic losses. Not responding to determine the legitimacy of the alarm at all could have catastrophic effects.

Every terroristic threat must be responded to as if it were real under conditions of high uncertainty. If a false alarm of innocuous chemicals can shut down 40 percent of a major metropolitan area for hours, imagine how profound the impact would be of a similar situation at a major port such as Shanghai or Rotterdam or Los Angeles, or an intermodal rail system. For every hour of delay, there could be an amplification going into days, or even weeks of disruption in the supply chain. In the Washington incident, the main impact was to commuters, but undoubtedly businesses were also hurt as employees could neither get to work nor consumers shop. The lasting fear of using the metro persuaded some commuters to find alternative means of transportation or, at the very least, make contingency plans in case of a similar incident. Similar fears, and government regulations, have persuaded businesses to change almost every aspect of their supply chain, from mode of transportation and location of suppliers to choice of logistics management and insurance.

TERRORIST ATTACKS AIMED AT AMERICAN INSTITUTIONS

The inventory of such incidents is numerous both before 09/11 and after, against the American government, companies and interests, but none came close to the severity of 09/11:

> An analysis of American business victimization by domestic and international terrorist attacks abroad illustrates that nearly every type of business sector engaged in by US companies overseas has been targeted . . . These US business targets were singled out because of their symbolism, such as the 'American way of life' visibility as well as for other practical reasons, including vulnerability of target considerations. (Alexander, 2004, p. 23)

Terrorist attacks have targeted both government agencies and American businesses. Indeed, the other primary target of the 09/11 attacks was the Pentagon itself. Other attacks have included the bombing in Beirut, the attack on the USS Cole in Yemen, the bombings of the American embassies in Kenya and Tanzania, and bombings in Dhahran and Riyadh, Saudi Arabia. Even before these, there were attacks against US embassies or government diplomats in Colombia (1948), Washington, DC (1950 and 1954, by Puerto Ricans), Guatemala (1968), Brazil (1969), Frankfurt, Germany (1972) Saudi Arabia

(1973), Iran (1979), Kuwait (1983), Lima, Peru (1990), Karachi, Pakistan (1995), Moscow (1995), Athens, Greece (1996), and Manila, Philippines (2000) (Center for Arms Control and Non-Proliferation, 2005). These do not include attacks against American military bases or personnel, businesses or citizens, of which there are many more, from every corner of the globe. One should also include the anti-globalization protests targeting the WTO in Seattle in 1999, as primary targets of crowd destruction were American business icons.

Among the most likely avenues of attack, the supply chain as whole is the most vulnerable area for any business involved in trade. It is subject to both physical and virtual (that is, computer technology) disruption, and is much more vulnerable than fixed corporate assets. Even fixed locations of suppliers and logistics providers along the supply chain experience high levels of risk because of an increasing loss of control through third party involvement and visibility as the supply chain stretches farther and farther from home base and crosses national boundaries into countries which carry higher geopolitical risk ratings.

Facing the highest levels of risk are the transportation aspects of the supply chain, as they are mobile and cannot be provided with the same level of security as fixed locations.

> The Mineta Transportation Institute reports that between 1997 and 2002 over 195 terrorist attacks occurred worldwide on surface transportation systems, including: buses (41% of all attacks), subways and trains (22%), subway and train stations (10%), bus terminals (8%), tracks (8%), and tourist buses (5%), others (5%), and bridges and tunnels (1%). (Alexander, 2004, p. 45)

Buses have comprised the bulk of these attacks, terrorists previously having civilian casualties as the goal, rather than economic damages. It can be anticipated that such attacks will focus more on the transportation system itself, rather than necessarily the cargo, be it people or goods.

MACROECONOMIC IMPACT OF TERRORIST ATTACKS ON THE UNITED STATES AND LOGISTICS

Overall, the 09/11 attack affected the entire world economy, at a time when it was in an economic recovery phase after the dot.com and internet bubbles. After trading resumed on 17 September 2001, the Dow Jones Industrial Average

> ... declined by 14.3%, the largest weekly fall since 1933. During the nearly two-week period after the September 11 attacks, the Bank for International Settlements reported global equities lost some $3 trillion – about 12% of their value ... The

impact of 09/11 on the world economy was likewise negative. This was particularly true of Japan and Europe. They had already been experiencing recessions prior to the attacks. US neighbors, Mexico and Canada, suffered also in the subsequent economic downturn, particularly in the aviation, tourism and hospitality sectors. (Alexander, 2004, pp. 146–7)

Logistics costs, which already amount to an average of 7 percent of sales at large US companies, are being pushed up by rising fuel prices, transport capacity shortages, and increased security measures on international cargo (*The Financial Times*, 2004). In addition, the US dollar has been weakening, thereby making an import-oriented supply chain more expensive to maintain. Such costs are unfailingly passed on to the ultimate end-users or consumers. Supply chain management is a delicate balance between cost paid and value obtained, at every step of the way. Any inefficiency or disruption translates into direct costs and lowers value tendered.

Terrorism is a unique type of 'glitch' as it requires both industry and governments to respond. Theft of cargo and terrorism are now issues that can only be addressed internationally through collaboration among governments and between the public and private sectors across countries. The US and Europe each sustained more than $15 billion in cargo loss each year since 09/11. 'When a member of the US has experienced a cargo problem in Europe, it has been hard to know who to get a hold of', said NCSC (National Cargo Security Council) Executive Director Joe Baker. The US Department of Transportation first formed NCSC in 1971 to collaborate with industry on fighting cargo theft. The group later evolved into a volunteer non-profit organization (Emigh, 2004).

Homeland security, defined as a border protection and terrorism combating concept, has for most nations become an international problem. While unilateralism is often where policy initiatives begin, their implement of necessity leads to international agreements and collaborative ventures. The weakest link in such a collaborative effort is always the non-complying or non-member state. European Union member states initiated collaborative approaches several years ago on various dimensions of the issue. The EU experience provides a transborder model of collaboration. Mr Koch of the World Shipping Council says:

America cannot solve the container problem alone; it needs more help from the rest of the world than it cares to admit. The issue is not merely about boxes on ships, but about how the mechanisms of world trade operate to maintain efficiency while at the same time enhancing security. Trade flows depend on trust to flourish. But total trust is clearly impossible in a world where death can arrive hidden in a metal box. Only with clever use of technology and international cooperation are the world's big trading countries likely to avoid disruption and expense. Even then, it will be a question of minimizing the threat rather than eliminating it. (*The Economist*, 4 April 2002)

Historically, one is reminded, the foremost threat to the supply chain was piracy on the high seas. It also required a similar collaboration between private industry and governments, as well as governmental international cooperation. Models exist on which to build innovative transborder approaches to the present-day challenges.

THE NEW ENVIRONMENT AND ITS EFFECT ON SUPPLY CHAINS

The overall objective of a supply chain is to have in place a global configuration that results in meeting or exceeding worldwide customer (internal and/or external) expectations at the lowest cost. A global supply chain is much more dynamic and volatile by nature than a strictly domestic one and must be managed with more care. 'In the varying environments encountered internationally, there are a number of challenges and barriers involved in building global supply chains. Many of these are rarely if ever a concern with domestic supply chains. Kauffman and Crimi (2005) list, among others:

- uncertain political stability with a lack of infrastructure, both physical and technological, in some countries;
- high transaction costs due to varying business environments;
- requirements to use in-country agents, partners, or local content requirements;
- lack of potential for repeat purchases;
- limitations requiring bidding for all procurement activities inhibit alliance-building;
- higher logistics and transportation costs;
- different time zones (communication difficulties) which information technology has not overcome;
- long and/or unpredictable supplier lead times;
- protectionism (tariffs, duties, quotas, inspections), though better regulated by the World Trade Organization; and
- limited number of qualified global suppliers and trained personnel.

Rapid change, heightened threats and greater security requirements are a given in the new environment:

> The global business climate has been nothing if not tumultuous in recent years. New regulatory requirements. Businesses now find themselves confronting a host of new government security requirements around the world. Companies remain unclear about what kinds of threats warrant the greatest concern, how they would be

affected if particular kinds of attacks occurred, what marketplace conditions would follow, and when the heightened threat will pass. Complex and interdependent risks. For all the advantages of the extended enterprise and its interdependent supply chains, this organizational model also puts businesses at greater security risk due to the multiple partners and handoffs involved in production and distribution. Globalization and the 24/7 news cycle mean companies now have only minutes not hours or days to respond proactively to a security incident before risking possible damage to brand. (Eggers, 2004)

Globalization itself has created vulnerabilities to both supply chains, border security and brand management. This has resulted in some companies shortening their supply chains to minimize the uncertainty and increase the operations transparency of their chain. Increased transparency or visibility, as it is also termed, allows for greater efficiency, better forecasting of order cycles, and quicker recovery when a disruption occurs. The less predictable the environment, the higher the risk, which generally results in higher costs. The more internationally diversified the supply chain, and the longer, the more variables are at play that raise the uncertainty and risk levels, primarily through reducing the amount of control and visibility and increasing the numbers of partners.

SUPPLY CHAIN MANAGEMENT (SCM)

Supply Chain Re-evaluation and Vulnerability Assessment

The development of global supply chains requires the same information as the development of domestic supply chains but, in addition, it requires excellent information on subjects that include international logistics, laws, customs, culture, ethics, language, politics, governments and currency. In essence, the body of work generally termed 'country risk analysis' provides notional guidelines that must be incorporated in setting up and managing a global supply chain operation since 09/11 (Bouchet, 2004). Team approaches should be used for developing global supply chains, including members of the departments and partner organizations affected by such operations. Kauffman and Crimi (2005) suggest the following process and re-evaluation framework:

1. Form a cross-functional global supply chain development team.
   a. Include all affected parties, internal and external.
   b. The composition may change as development and implementation proceeds.
2. Identify needs and opportunities for supply chain globalization.
   a. Determine the requirements your supply chain must meet.
   b. Determine the current status of your supply chain.

3. Analyse the 'fit' of your current supply chain with your operational requirements.
4. Determine commodity/service priorities for globalization consideration based on needs and opportunities.
5. Identify potential markets and suppliers and compare to current ones.
6. Evaluate markets and suppliers, identify supplier pool.
7. Determine selection process for suppliers.
8. Select suppliers or confirm current suppliers.
9. Formalize agreements with suppliers.
10. Implement agreements.
11. Monitor, evaluate, review, revise as needed.

The re-evaluation of the supply chain as suggested above must parry for future contingencies through preventive security measures. These measures require a reconceptualization and reassessment of performance metrics for the entire chain, just as they can be expected to have differential outcomes and impacts. Figure 9.1, based in Kleindorfer, enumerates how these re-evaluated measures impact on key components of the chain – to wit, reliability, responsiveness, flexibility, expenses and inventory utilization (Kleindorfer, 2004, p. 11).

In addition, a shadow strategy task force (thereby providing an outsider's perspective) should be formed to analyse areas of weakness, both in the company and throughout the supply chain. These task forces should be cross-functional, include partner companies, and look at the supply chain from both an internal and external perspective. A key perspective to build in this effort is the terrorist's view of the supply chain, an exercise far from obvious for more traditionally-minded logisticians. The supply chain must not just be considered in the literal sense but rather in the virtual sense, including any and all vulnerabilities, ranging from shortcomings in technology, required data gaps, geography, culture, political stability, infrastructure, etc. All vulnerabilities should be addressed, especially through communication with other partners in the supply chain that are either responsible for or affected by the vulnerability. For example, if a supplier uses different transportation providers within its own country, it will be difficult to have access to information on background checks on all the transport operators involved in a particular operation. A solution might be to negotiate the usage of a logistics management company to maintain security information on transport providers. This solution, however, adds an additional partner to the supply chain and could therefore create further unanticipated difficulties and costs.

Shortening of Supply Chains

Shortening supply chains theoretically allows for more control, visibility and quicker corrective action:

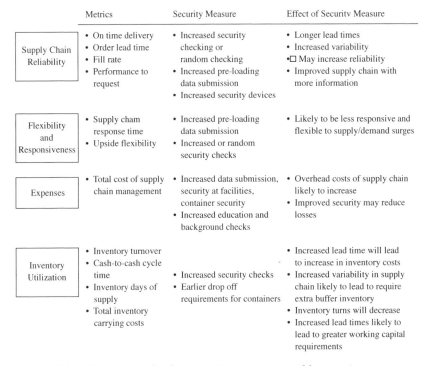

	Metrics	Security Measure	Effect of Security Measure
Supply Chain Reliability	• On time delivery • Order lead time • Fill rate • Performance to request	• Increased security checking or random checking • Increased pre-loading data submission • Increased security devices	• Longer lead times • Increased variability •□ May increase reliability • Improved supply chain with more information
Flexibility and Responsiveness	• Supply cham response time • Upside flexibility	• Increased pre-loading data submission • Increased or random security checks	• Likely to be less responsive and flexible to supply/demand surges
Expenses	• Total cost of supply chain management	• Increased data submission, security at facilities, container security • Increased education and background checks	• Overhead costs of supply chain likely to increase • Improved security may reduce losses
Inventory Utilization	• Inventory turnover • Cash-to-cash cycle time • Inventory days of supply • Total inventory carrying costs	• Increased security checks • Earlier drop off requirements for containers	• Increased lead time will lead to increase in inventory costs • Increased variability in supply chain likely to lead to require extra buffer inventory • Inventory turns will decrease • Increased lead times likely to lead to greater working capital requirements

Figure 9.1 Current supply chain metrics versus possible security measures

> Visibility into the status and movement of goods throughout the supply chain will be a prerequisite, and a new focus on optimizing product lead times will emerge. Visibility is particularly vital in supply chains for highly perishable goods, medicines and market-timed commodities such as apparel. Increased visibility into goods-in-motion will support novel approaches to manufacturing and distribution. (Meyer, 2004)

The longer and the more diverse the supply chain, the more difficult it is to track, coordinate, manage and secure.

Longer, more complex supply chains add uncertainty that must be mitigated as much as possible through management action. This results in a relative loss of efficiency and value:

> From a security standpoint, it is highly advisable to maintain control of all logistics aspects of non-strategic relationships whenever possible. For example, if material is being sourced from Malaysia, from a supplier that the customer does not know well, the contract terms should stipulate 'Free on board (FOB) origin-freight collect.' 'Which allows the customer to control all aspects of logistics activity after the shipment leaves the supplier's dock. Additionally, less familiar shipments can be routed

through specific ports that are better able to accommodate more detailed customs inspections. This could include any ports that have x-ray capability and are members of the US Container Security Initiative' (CSI). (Rhinehart, Myers and Eckert, 2004)

Cost savings from sourcing in diverse locations must be balanced with the increased costs and risks due to higher levels of uncertainty.

One of the most effective means of lowering costs and realizing gains in profit and efficiency is through increased visibility and scrutiny of the supply chain:

> Shippers and carriers alike are gaining more knowledge about the day-to-day nuances of their international supply chains, including the people and vendors working on them. While gathering this knowledge may have a temporarily detrimental effect on supply chain speed, it could ultimately result in some efficiency-enhancing productivity improvements, because the additional scrutiny may reveal some long-hidden performance weaknesses or call attention to the fact that the parties companies have chosen to work with may no longer be the best match for them. (Gulisano, 2003)

Repatriation of Supply Chain to 'Safe-Haven' Countries

It has been considered a solution to reduce uncertainty to 'repatriate' all or parts of the chain to 'safe-haven' countries or regions. Some regions, trade blocs and countries carry a more contained risk of terrorist attacks, either due to geopolitics and to government or industry initiatives. Countries or trade blocs can even turn these into competitive advantages to stimulate trade and investment. By taking certain steps to improve security and modernize trading systems, countries can better position themselves in the global trading system (Nitsch and Schumacher, 2002).

A salient problem is that shorter or regional supply chains are usually more economically vulnerable to the regional forces of recessions, local natural disasters or country-specific acts of terrorism. Attacks can occur at any link in a narrow supply chain and cause more acute initial disruption and impact. For example, attacking Mexico can have a more immediate impact than attacking America directly, especially in terms of logistics. Therefore, regional solutions in a globalized, interdependent, supply-chain-driven world economy might not offer a long-term viable solution.

Repatriation of the global supply chain might paradoxically result in an overall increase in risk to the global economy. Such a strategy excludes transitioning, emerging and developing country markets that are not able to afford initial investments in security initiatives. The resulting trade and investment losses would be born disproportionately by poorer economies, less insulated from terrorism, which would further the cycle of poverty and disparate wealth.

Poverty and economic stratification are two of the key forces fomenting the backlash against globalization. They also create a fertile breeding ground from which terrorist organizations can recruit. Any version of an exclusively safe triadic supply chain (EU, Japan, North America) strategy would be akin to the modern-day version of the proverbial walls of Jericho. A fortress America or fortress Europe policy should be subjected to much critical debate.

Need for an Inventory Buffer

The threat of terrorism requires the establishment of inventory buffers, the size of which will depend upon the length and location of the supply chain. In the case of a disruption of the supply chain there must redundancy to allow for operations to continue during system failure. 'Just in time is okay, but it creates a rigid supply chain and rigid is okay if you're not in uncertain times . . . With new uncertainties, shipping time can vary greatly and you have to balance uncertainty with inventory' (Spiegel, 2003). Increased inventory requirements are another visible cost of securing supply chain systems. Repatriation of the supply chain allows for a smaller inventory buffer. The shorter the supply chain, the shorter the lead time and order cycle. Lead time and order cycle involving transoceanic shipments can be measured in weeks or even months. By sourcing closer to either the retail market or operations, these times can be cut to mere days, but at a higher initial cost. Introducing security as a paramount issue in locational decisions of green – and brownfield plants, as well as distribution centers, is a move away from the economies of scale and scope that have supported firm globalization.

Loss of Customers Due to Supply Chain Disruptions

Lead time is the gap between when an order is placed and when it is received. Estimating lead times in conditions of uncertainty is problematic. Variation in lead times measures the size of the uncertainty relative to demand (Lee and Bilington, 1992). Failures accurately to predict inventory needs either result in excess inventory or stock outs. Excess inventory engenders holding costs; stock outs cause customer loss and destroy business relationships between suppliers and buyers. As with any disruption or inefficiency in the supply chain, ultimate costs are higher.

> Threats of terrorism will of necessity increase lead times geometrically due to uncertainty. Supply chain glitches can lead to both short- and long-term loss in sales and market share, lower sales price due to markdowns of excess inventories, and could prevent the firm from capitalizing on strong market demand due to unavailability of products. Glitches can negatively impact customer service if customers are unable to get the products they want at the time they want them, resulting in

higher customer dissatisfaction and lower customer loyalty. Glitches can hurt the reputation and credibility of the firm, causing customers not to consider the firm as a possible source for meeting their needs. Overall, glitches are likely to decrease net sales. On the cost side, glitches can increase the costs associated with expediting, premium freight, obsolete inventory, additional marketing, and penalties paid to the customer. Furthermore, the loss of reputation and credibility associated with glitches may require firms to increase their public relation expenses to reinstate its credibility and reputation. It can also make it more expensive to raise capital, because investors may ask for a higher premium to lend to firms whose credibility and reputation is questionable. Overall, glitches are likely to increase costs. (Singhal and Hendricks, 2005)

Increased Regional Trade and Reduced Global Trade

Fareed Zakaria wrote some two months after the 09/11 tragedy that the slow-downs at the US borders were imposing large economic costs. In this vein, Goldstein has noted, not without some nostalgia, that 'the 1990s were exclusively focused on openness, speed, and accessibility – with huge economic benefits'. He invoked the reputed Washington-based Institute for International Economics which 'estimates that about half of the productivity boom of the late 1990s was created by ease and openness of transportation, communication and distribution – globalization ... We spent the 1990s taking redundancies out of the system. We are going to spend the next decade putting them back in' (Goldstein, 2004, p. 97).

While the past two decades were a period of increased liberalization of global flows, we have been witnessing the re-emergence of a national security protectionism described by several authors:

> Among Western nations, national security trumps all other concerns. Civil liberties have taken a backseat to security concerns, as governments subject their citizens to constant surveillance ... As a siege mentality sets in, rising nationalist and populist sentiment is the catalyst for heightened levels of economic protectionism. Governments now consider it a high priority to protect jobs and prevent them from going overseas. And barriers to foreign investment and cross-border travel ensure that countries can safeguard their own unique ways of life. (Laudicina, 2005)

It is possible that intra-regional trade in the emerging regional blocs – NAFTA, MERCOSUR, EU, among others – will further increase as a percentage of world trade, if nations rationalize and shorten their global supply chains. Regional blocs are likely to provide enhanced security for supply chain operations because of the proximity of the member states, the common legal frameworks they share, and the greater ease of collaboration. 'Countries no longer believe in the efficacy of multilateral arrangements and prefer alliances with small groups of like-minded countries they feel they can trust' (Laudicina, 2005).

Supply Chain Outsourcing

Since the late 1990s, the trend to outsource logistics to third-party firms has been on the rise. While it has the advantage of division of labor, specialization and discharging the manufacturer and/or distributor of logistical cares, a trust-based relationship is the sine qua non condition for a successful third party relationship (Mariotty, 1999). Gains in supply chain productivity may result from third-party logistics management. Such relationships will benefit from close public–private sector partnerships in matters of security, for example, Operation Safe Commerce (OSC). OSC is a public–private partnership designed to develop best practices for safe and efficient movement of containerized cargo. It must, however, be noted that while 43 percent of companies in a recent survey were considering using third party logistics, 26 percent were unlikely to ever use them. 'This could reflect companies that used 3PL at some stage but found very little value gained, or the complexity of the contract and ownership of the supply chain meant 3PL could not offer enough in terms of savings or expertise to risk another contract' (EyeForTransport, 2005).

As the need to secure supply chains becomes more salient, the enhanced level of security offered by third-party logistics providers becomes a commodity in and of itself. Third-party logistics providers could exploit this comparative advantage in security at the expense of the once all-powerful wholesalers or manufacturers. This is an additional incentive for companies to outsource their logistics (Kumar, 1996).

> TNT manages BMW's North American supply chain from the moment a part is dispatched by a supplier until its installation in one of the Z4 sports cars or X5 sports utility vehicles made in Spartanburg. The arrangement is not unique to BMW: nearly 80% of big European and North American companies outsource parts of their logistics operation to outside contractors, up from 71 three years ago, according to research by the Georgia Institute of Technology. (Ward, 2004, p. 15)

Risk Factors Due to Transportation Mode Must be Considered

All international supply chains have common elements and stages, each with its own inefficiencies, vulnerabilities and risk factors. The infrastructures and market configurations of foreign countries vary greatly, due to customs, culture and legal requirements. Even in a standard international shipment of goods, 'the movement of each container is part of a transaction that can involve up to 25 different parties: buyers, sellers, inland freighters and shipping lines, middlemen (customs and cargo brokers, for example), financiers and governments' (*The Economist*, 4 April 2005). In addition, each mode of transportation has its own inherent levels of risk.

With the ultimate cost of some terrorist attacks being close to incalculable, far more attention needs be paid to logistics, especially intermodal shipping that involves the use of containers where nuclear or biological agents could be hidden. Even the threat of biological warfare from the most absurd source is a possibility, with terrorists merely sneaking in a shipment of mad cows. The drop in the European stock markets (FTSE) immediately following the Madrid train bombings was estimated at US$55 billion. Estimates for the loss from a security breach of one shipping container alone can amount to US$1 trillion. The cost of cyber attacks against companies worldwide reached US$12.5 billion in 2003, and a case of mad cow disease in 2002 caused the Canadian beef industry a US$2.5 billion loss. By infecting herds of cattle with mad cow disease, terrorists could strike a blow to critical components of any economy.

Table 9.1, inspired by Kleindorfer, identifies the range of threats to a global supply chain from source to destination (2004). While at the port, the goods must pass customs clearances, both for the home country and the United States, and comply with the 24-hour manifest rule for ships and related rules for rail and road. The containers must then be loaded onto the selected mode of transportation (usually a ship) and commence movement of goods. The cargo must then clear the US Customs before being transported within the United States to a distribution center. There can be variations with container discharge after it reaches the United States, considering most freight movement is intermodal in nature. Finally, there must be transport to retail locations from the distribution center. Table 9.1 lists the basic stages goods pass through in an international supply chain, with an overview of the vulnerability associated with each. There can be numerous middlemen along the route, both internationally and domestically.

Ships
Ships have been historically vulnerable to hijacking or attack. There is scant security readily available on the high seas, other than what is onboard. The high seas are extremely difficult to police, and response to an attack could literally take hours or days, even after notification to the authorities. Maritime freight makes an attractive target because it is predictable in travel pattern and ships hold a plethora of goods. In addition, terrorists might try simply to run a ship aground or crash it into a port or possibly environmental target if they hijack it. Explosive devices may therefore not be needed. Even a non-oil ship run aground can result in an environmental disaster. If a ship was used for such a purpose, or if it did have conventional or nuclear bombs onboard that were used, it could wreak havoc worldwide. Such scenarios are reminiscent of science fiction or high adventure motion pictures, yet they are not part and parcel of crisis management and scenario response strategies. According to a 2002 Congressional Research Service report, Robert Bonner, US Customs

Table 9.1   Threats to the supply chain links from source to destination

Supply chain link	Threat of disruption or contamination
Source company	Very little control or transparency over suppliers in foreign countries. Often difficult to monitor or police their actions from a remote location, or to know if they have sufficient security measures, especially in terms of hiring. This insecurity adds significant risk if they are allowed access to proprietary information or secured information systems. Could easily be infiltrated by terrorists posing as workers.
Middlemen	A true 'wild card' in the supply chain. Even more difficult to monitor and secure than source companies, especially if they are logistics providers chosen at random by the supplier. Suppliers may routinely change providers, further reducing the effects of security efforts. Note: Middlemen exist at many stages in many supply chains, especially given the market structure that exists in certain foreign countries, where there might be 10–20 or more middlemen involved between production and retail stages.
Source country transport	Easily co-opted in some developing countries, where armed guards might literally 'ride shotgun'. Difficult to track, especially in terms of transportation time and personnel. Could easily be hijacked and the drivers replaced by terrorists after the container has been altered in some manner.
Port of egress	Containers generally sit idle in numerous quantities, which opens up vulnerabilities to terrorists. Security varies between ports, with some receiving favorable treatment from the USA via legislation and customs.
Loading of containers	The ranks of shipyard or distribution center workers could easily be infiltrated by agents, who could then orchestrate alterations to containers or contents.
Customs	Customs agents in foreign countries might lack training or diligence. Again, terrorists could easily either become a customs agent or pose as one.
International transport	One of the most dangerous times in terms of physical attack, primarily referring to ocean transport. The high seas are extremely difficult to police, and before help could arrive, the damage would have been done. There is again a lack of transparency and a very large window of opportunity for terrorists, given the time in transit. Terrorists have effectively used speedboats to attack US warships before in port, in a transoceanic attack, it would probably be a complete success. Another possibility is commandeering a ship, either through piracy, or by having sleeper agents as crew members. A ship could then be docked in a major port in the United States with the intention of destruction of the port, which would have worldwide repercussions in logistics.

Source country links

143

Table 9.1   Threats to the supply chain links from source to destination (continued)

Supply chain link	Threat of disruption or contamination
Customs	Again, agents could be under trained, under staffed, or lax in diligence. It is entirely possible that sleeper agents could infiltrate the Customs and Border Patrol agency or that agents could be bribed. There have been cases of drug smugglers and human traffickers doing both, so why not terrorists?
Unloading of containers	Containers are again left idle for periods of time, with different levels of security, leaving them vulnerable.
Transport to distribution centers	Domestic transport depends on the mode, but there is a general lack of immediate security for any mode. The most common are by road (trucks) and rail; both are vulnerable to direct physical attack. Trucks are more vulnerable to hijacking. Again, a lack of transparency between partners in the supply chain concerning the vehicle operators provides for a lack of security in the case of a hijacking and replacement of the operator by a terrorist.
Distribution center	Generally these are better secured than the cargo during transport, but offer an attractive target. They usually store valuable cargo, as well as have numerous shipments arriving and leaving at any given time, making security clearances difficult. Workers are also focused more on their tasks, especially in terms of efficiency, than security.

Domestic links

Commissioner, stated that after a nuclear attack from a shipping container, 'the shipping of sea containers would stop', with 'devastating' economic effects worldwide.

Piracy still presents a problem for commerce, and is significantly under-reported. Many shipping companies do not report incidents of piracy for fear of loss of business and increased insurance premiums. The location of most current piracy episodes is in the Straits of Malacca and Indonesian waters, not far from Singapore. Indonesia is the world's most populous Muslim country, with active terrorist cells. While the number of pirate attacks dropped world-wide last year, Indonesian waters and stretches of the Malacca Straits continue to be among the most dangerous shipping lanes in the world.

It is estimated that roughly 50,000 vessels, carrying roughly a quarter of the world's maritime trade, pass through the strait every year. About half of all seaborne oil shipments, on which the economies of Japan, China and South Korea depend, also transit there. If terrorists were determined to devastate the world economy, it would be hard to find a better target. Tony Tan, Singapore's deputy prime minister, has pointed out that a ship sunk in the right spot, where the sea lane is only 25-meters deep, would cripple world trade. He also raised the possibility of hijacked ships being turned into 'floating bombs' and crashed into critical infrastructure such as oil refineries or ports.

Malaysia and Indonesia rejected the idea of US patrols in the straits or rapid-response units at the ready. These countries, however, noted they would accept American help in the form of technical advice, equipment, and training (*The Economist*, 10 June 2004).

According to the 2004 piracy report from the London-based International Maritime Bureau (IMB), there were more kidnappings in the Malacca Straits last year than anywhere else in the world. In total, 36 crew members were kidnapped for ransom, with four killed and three injured (*The Straits Times*, 7 February 2005). It would not be beyond imagination for the piracy to be either co-opted or supported by the terrorists.

Rail

Trains are easily disrupted. The previously mentioned incident with the subway system is one example of how a false alarm can have far-reaching deleterious effects. Examples abound. Recently, a suicidal man parking his car on a commuter rail in California killed over 10 train passengers and wounded many others by causing one train to derail and collide with another. It also caused massive delays and extensive damage to the local economy in terms of lost productivity and confidence levels. As with ships, there is little security and a relatively predictable route. Trains are slow moving and easy to access at points along the path. The fact that trains often carry containers with hazardous substances along with consumer freight makes them an attractive target. Accidental toxic spills on trains have caused neighborhood evacuations and could very easily be lethal. A terrorist could attack both the economy and population at once.

Road

According to Chuck Lounsbury, Senior Vice President of Supply Chain for Ryder Systems, 'Trucks almost always cover the last mile in the supply chain. They bring the freight from the rail depot or warehouse to the final customer, so they're more exposed than most' (Kilcar, 2002, p. 30). They are the most vulnerable of all modes of transport. That is because the drivers are generally solitary, leave the immediate vicinity of their vehicles numerous times during transport (when eating, etc), and could easily be replaced with a terrorist agent if abducted. However, truckers are generally the most transparent in terms of monitoring, with constant communication with dispatchers and other truckers, and the shortest window of opportunity for any act to take place. Trucks offer the least 'bang for the buck' for terrorists, as they are relatively small targets and difficult to predict in advance, but they are also the most easily accessible and vulnerable. Information technology is also improving truck movement and transportation monitoring.

Air

Most of the attention placed upon the airline passenger industry has been focused on the movement of passengers, not freight. This is the case because air transportation is not a significant part of the global supply chain for freight (in terms of percentage). The US government has invested large amounts of money in subsidizing the security needs of the industry. Most of this money came from the $10 per passenger surcharge. The EU has been less willing to pick up the tab for increased aviation security costs. Despite industry pleas, European airlines have received less than one-third of the $3 billion in subsidies given to American airlines since 09/11 (Eggers, 2004).

Intermodal

Intermodal transportation is the use of more than one mode of transport to move a shipment to its destination. A variety of combinations are possible. Whenever there is a transfer of ownership or responsibility, the risks are elevated. Intermodal often means that the system is difficult to regulate because it crosses jurisdictional boundaries. On the high seas, the containers come under the aegis of the International Maritime Organisation (IMO), a United Nations body based in London. On land, it passes into the hands of national governments. Michael Wolfe (2004), Principal in North River Consulting Group, indicates that 'intermodal containers, the ubiquitous facilitators of international commerce, are a potential weapon delivery system, a 'poor man's cruise missile.' Weapons delivered by freight systems would put at risk large numbers of lives, significant infrastructure, public and business confidence, and ultimately trade and prosperity.' For global trade, intermodal is often the only option because industrial sites or markets may not be in close proximity to ports or airports. Key issues in the intermodal industry involve exchange of information to facilitate shipment transfers between different modes. Hence, it can be said that intermodal is even more exposed to geopolitical terrorism than single mode transportation.

Risk by Industry

The impact of supply shocks differs depending on the industry. Shocks to the auto industry supply chain will have a major impact on the entire industrial sector, as it accounts for large upstream purchases. Service sector shocks, in contrast, have relatively less impact on the rest of the economy. In the US, several important industries have increasingly come to depend on their global supply chain both for supplying the US market and for export. Retailers and domestically branded apparel, appliance, and footwear manufacturers and distributors have tapped low-cost labor elsewhere, often Asia. Computers, electronics and video, audio and communications equipment depend heavily on offshore supply. More than 40 percent of all US requirements for both consumer and industrial use in footwear, apparel, and computers are made overseas (Fosler, 2003).

> Security of the system (global supply chain) has traditionally focused on reducing shrinkage – the loss of cargo shipments through theft and misrouting. However, heightened awareness of terrorism has redefined supply-chain security – the consequences of an attack on or via a critical global port could be a tremendous loss of life and a crippling of the US economy – and has brought increased attention to the risks containerized shipping presents. (Willis and Ortiz, 2004)

Some industries are more exposed to geopolitical risk. Others are more amenable to security preparedness, prevention and mitigation, but without a doubt industries that rely on containerization are the most at risk.

COST OF SECURITY

General Costs

V.R. Singhal and K.B. Hendricks have shown that supply chain 'glitches' have a direct impact on shareholder value. A disruption in the matching of the supply and demand from logistical failure can have a devastating effect on stock price. It has been shown that the total damage can sometimes be as high as 18 percent of stock value (Singhal and Hendricks, 2002). Relative levels of security also impact trade flows. A 2002 study of 200 countries estimated that a doubling of terrorist incidents resulted in a 6 percent drop in bilateral trade between targeted economies (Nitsch and Schumacher, 2002).

The past two decades saw a shift towards 'just-in-time' manufacturing, where only the bare minimum inventory was kept in order to reduce costs. Higher levels of inventory entail capital costs of both goods in transit and buffer stock. 'Recent estimates indicate that if the United States has to carry 10% more in inventories and pay 20% more for commercial insurance premiums as a result of the increased terrorism threat it would cost 0.1% and 0.3% of GDP respectively or US$7.5 billion and US$30 billion respectively' (Raby, 2003).

Costs of Technology

There are numerous technologies that companies must now invest in. Each partner in the supply chain requires similar investments in terms of technology to access an intranet or extranet that is held in common with other links, but each must also invest in certain technologies depending upon its industry, mostly in order to comply with federal mandates. For example, companies involved in the shipping industry will have to comply with the TWIC initiative. The Transportation Worker Identification Certification (TWIC) aims to establish a uniform biometric ID card for workers involved in the shipping and logistics industries. It will be used to control access to secure areas nationwide, but does not extend to foreign soil.

The quest for efficiency has also resulted in the need to invest in new technology:

> The US based organization for supply chain security specialists, which will become known as the International Cargo Security Council, or ICSC, early next year, is helping its over 1,000 members explore new technologies in areas such as 'smart seals', RFID (radio frequency identification) and logistics management. It will expand its operations to include Europe next, then other regions of the world as well. (Emigh, 2004)

These definitely come with a price tag, which might result in mergers and acquisitions in the logistics industry, as well as the demise of many of the smaller service providers that don't have the capital to invest. As with any industry, when there is less competition the premiums charged increase, which ultimately increase the final cost to the consumer.

Costs of Regulation

Ultimately the cost will fall on the consumer, as it will be passed down the chain from supplier to retail. With each new requirement will come new costs, and most estimates reach in the billions. The question is not only can the technology keep up with terrorist threats, government mandates, and the demand placed on the current infrastructure, but can specific industries, and even some countries, afford it? 'By some estimates, ports face even higher compliance costs, with developing countries confronting particularly large burdens in relation to their GDP. Jamaica, for example, estimates that complying with new port security regulations will cost the country around $100 million' (Eggers, 2004, p. 11). Additional regulations and costs can result in exclusion of certain countries or markets, as mentioned before in this chapter, to the detriment of security for the global environment as a whole.

A brief summary of costs born by the various sectors of the transportation industry in complying with current US federal mandates is included in Table 9.2. Note the relatively small cost of road security, which does not necessarily mean that roads are inherently more secure than other modes, merely that they have not received the level of focus from lawmakers. Since trucks are involved in almost every intermodal shipment in some way, if they are attacked the consequences will impact other modes.

In many ways, the overload and load saturation of the infrastructure are as big as any. 'A single trade can generate 30–40 documents, and each container can carry cargo for several customers, thus multiplying the number of documents still further' (*The Economist*, 4 April 2005).

> C-TPAT has, in my opinion, enhanced the quality and security of the Supply Chain but according to many has not yet shown the speed in which cargo would move into the country, primarily due to the heavy congestion at the ports. This congestion, according to experts, will probably worsen with an expectation to double in the next 10 to 20 years. (Scrobe, 2005)

Customs-Trade Partnership Against Terrorism (C-TPAT) is a government program that represents the commitment of the government and business to

Table 9.2   Cost by transportation sector

Mode of transport	Cost
Ships (maritime industries)	$10 billion over next ten years
Rail	$1.7 billion spent, $6 billion more needed for upgrades
Road	$91 million annually
Air (passenger)	$315 million annually, plus $10 per passenger

Source: Eggers, pp. 11–12.

secure and protect the United States from international terrorism by improving supply chain security and protecting cargo. Certification will reduce
scrutiny and audits by US Customs and can allow eligibility for expedited
clearance of US imports. It is based upon the evaluation of certain logistics
providers and their registration and certification with the government for expedited processing of shipments. 'For those companies that participate in C-
TPAT, the benefits are likely to include: expedited clearances, less scrutiny
during any audit process, and access to self-assessment programs. For most
companies, these benefits outweigh the risks, time, and effort involved in
managing the C-TPAT application process' (Cook, 2003).

The container security initiative (CSI) costs almost entirely fall on the shipping industry, either the ports themselves or the shipping magnates. 'The
Coast Guard estimates the total cost over 10 years for compliance (with CSI)
to be $7.3 billion, most of which will fall on facility and vessel owners for
outlays of hardware, such as perimeter fencing, lighting and closed-circuit
television, and beefing up inspection forces' (Gottlieb, 2004). There are
numerous mandates requiring compliance. The estimated costs for some are
represented in Table 9.3. The hope is that in the long run innovative technol-

Table 9.3   Costs of compliance with key US logistical security mandates

Regulation	Costs for private sector
Container Security Initiative	$7.3 billion (2004 to 2014)
ICAO Aviation Security Plan of Action	$8.5 million (annual)
Maritime Transportation Security Act of 2002 (MTSA)	$7.244 billion (2003 to 2012); $883 million (annual)
24 Hour Rule	$282 million (annual)
International Ship and Port Facility Security Code 2002 (ISPS)	$1.28 billion (up-front); $730 million (annual)
Required Advance Electronic Presentation of Cargo Information	$91 million (total)
Patriot Act Anti-Money Laundering Program 2001	$10.9 billion (through end of 2005) $2.7 billion (annual)
Bioterrorism Act 2002	$367 million (initial cost); $261 million (annual)

Source: Eggers, 2004, p. 13.

ogy will result in greater efficiency and control and help mitigate the costs. For the short term, the costs will continue to escalate at a pace far exceeding gains in efficiency.

TECHNOLOGY AND SUPPLY CHAIN MANAGEMENT

Supply Chain Visibility

The most important thing to consider when designing or restructuring a supply chain is control. The more control a company has, the further its reach up the supply chain, the lower the level of uncertainty, which lowers risk correspondingly. In order to have more control, a company must have good visibility, which can be greatly improved with various forms of technology, such as Radio Frequency Identification Systems (RFID).

> Business and trade networks will invest in greater visibility into the position, movement and status of goods, including the ability to track, demonstrate product pedigrees, prove chain of custody, and optimize stocking and positioning for best possible order fulfillment. This visibility will depend upon integrated data flowing through a seamless, secure infrastructure chain as the leaders move beyond the current 'slap and ship' approach. RFID tag reading accuracy, reliability and repeatability will continue to improve along with unit cost reductions. (Meyer, 2004)

With increased visibility, the team of partners managing the supply chain should be able to discern irregularities as well as inefficiencies, which could result in increased cost savings.

Many powerful forces in commerce are initiating the integration of RFID, including the US Department of Defense and Wal-Mart. These entities will also be responsible for much of the evolution of RFID. It is important that standards are created and harmonized as early as possible, to lower costs and speed adoption of the technology. RFID costs are currently prohibitive for most products, and the technology will not become widely utilized until costs are lowered or the direct benefits from use increase to offer greater value. The greatest benefits to users, other than assisting in compliance with regulations, is better tracking of shipments. RFID can significantly increase visibility, thus allowing for longer extension and greater diversity in the supply chain without loss of control or efficiency.

An important aspect to consider is the need for overall flexibility in the supply chain, including its monitoring. Visibility coming from rigid monitoring systems that are based upon fixed infrastructure are limited in capability. RFID can help to some extent. In the event of an emergency, mobile devices are much more useful than fixed systems. Mobile units can also open up new suppliers, partners and markets more quickly than was ever possible, but generally cost quite a bit:

> Mobile devices will play a key role in enabling new supply chain partners whose technology infrastructure is unreliable or nonexistent. Global suppliers may lack the necessary wired infrastructure, or it may take time to commission the necessary infrastructure for local suppliers, such as a high-speed and reliable data link, application servers and SCM applications. Mobile devices would let a company bypass this infrastructure and shift focus to establishing inter-enterprise workflows to get material flowing to other trading partners. SCM functionality deployed on mobile devices will let new partners (globally and locally) get up and running quickly. Mobile devices will also expand the potential pools of suppliers, distributors and manufacturers that previously were not considered due to lack of IT infrastructure. (Reddy, 2005) Perhaps most important of all, mobile units are relatively easy to replace or update, whereas fixed systems are cumbersome.

SCM Must Focus on Being Resilient

With the assumption that some form of disruption in the global supply chain is inevitable, either from a natural disaster like the tsunami, political discord or terrorist attack, every supply chain should be created and managed with the idea of balancing efficiency with resiliency.

> Disruptions caused by the war on terrorism will continue to be unpredictable and could depend on the medium chosen for subsequent terrorist attacks. Unfortunately, most vendors did not design existing SCM technologies with failures and disaster recovery in mind. The new requirement for SCM technologies is the ability to bring back a company and its supply chains to normal operations after catastrophic disruptions, hence the addition of resiliency to efficiency. Companies will need to trade off between these two drivers. If the supply chain has been disrupted by a terrorist attack, it might be necessary to locate new or additional supply chain partners in order to recover. This will prove problematic. Bringing in new replacement partners is not an easy task. The partner will need to make investments in IT infrastructure and change business processes to fit established norms. This barrier, which makes doing business with established supply chains difficult, is called 'technology lock-in'. Supporting SCM technologies for a particular supply chain can effectively lock out new companies that do not have the same underlying technologies from joining the supply chain. (Reddy, 2005)

General Risk Posed by Technology

To some extent, all logistics managed by computers are at risk at every level of the supply chain. The computers and related hardware are physically vulnerable to direct destruction or violation, whether by a disgruntled employee or a terrorist attack. The networks are vulnerable to hacking from external entities as well, and can be virtually corrupted or destroyed. 'I also think about cyber terrorism; if the data flow is disrupted, all of those JIT (just-in-time) delivery plans and inventory models go out the window,' states Chuck Lounsbury, Senior Vice President, Supply Chain, Ryder System (Kilcar, 2002, p. 30). Software must constantly be updated, opening windows of vulnerability at distinct intervals. The main problem with virtual security is the opposing need to have integrated systems with suppliers and logistics providers to enhance transparency and efficiency. If even one of the partners is less than reliable, all members are at risk due to the integrated systems and external access.

For all the advantages of the extended enterprise and its interdependent supply chain, this organizational model puts businesses at greater security risk than the multiple partners and handoffs involved in production and distribution. A phenomenon known as 'Wolfe's Paradox' suggests that

> ... complex logistics systems incorporating advanced information technology are at once 'more robust and more fragile' than their less sophisticated, less efficient forbears. Well-tuned supply chain management systems excel at handling supply or demand fluctuations within their competence and design capacity. What they cannot do is respond effectively to conditions that far outstrip their normal operating circumstances, such as major spikes in demand – perhaps created by large military deployments – or plunges in supply created by external agents such as significantly tighter, government-imposed security measures. Few if any logistics systems are designed to cope with massive failures of the Internet, telecommunications, GPS, or power supplies. (Wolfe, 2004, p. 16)

Inadequate backup of data is the most salient. If a terrorist action destroys or damages unique stored files, they are unrecoverable.

> In light of the damage inflicted during the 09/11 incidents, previously hesitant companies are investing in expensive backup sites, data storage software and services, and emergency/contingency planning. A number of banks and securities firms adopted a number, or all, of these measures following the bombings of the WTC in 1993. Damage caused by the September 2001 attacks was thereby less pervasive – at some companies – due to the existence of data storage capabilities. (Alexander, 2004, p. 93)

In addition, for the entire time that a computer system is down the supply chain is in disarray, thus, even a remote backup system of hardware is a legitimate and justifiable investment.

The computer information system of a logistics provider is an extremely attractive target for any terrorist or other party that wishes to cause widespread disruption. As each logistics company has numerous clients, by attacking the logistics provider, all of the clients' supply chains are affected. One target provides a very large impact area.

Need for Public–Private Collaboration

The transportation sector in the United States is a harlequin pattern of private organizations.

> A lack of standard security guidelines diminishes supply chain efficiency. Most US ports are owned and operated by the private sector. The port management is responsible for implementing security and contingency plans. A freight carrier like DHL faces different requirements at each port, which diminishes the efficiency of the movement of goods and increases the carrier's administrative costs. (Tohamy, 2004)

Governments the world over have a critical part to play in providing incentives for the private sector to secure the transportation networks. In particular, governments can encourage information sharing, which has historically been a problem among private corporations. They can also provide tax incentives to firms willing to invest in security-related technology. Governments can also reduce the regulatory burdens on cooperating firms. Finally, governments should take the lead in harmonizing global security standards among firms whose operations cross boundaries.

A case in point is the collaboration between the United States government and FedEx, which has in some ways also raised issues of rights to due process of law.

> FedEx has opened the international portion of its databases, including credit-card details, to government officials. It has created a police force recognized by the state of Tennessee that works alongside the Federal Bureau of Investigation. The company has rolled out radiation detectors at overseas facilities to detect dirty bombs and donated an airplane to federal researchers looking for a defense against shoulder-fired missiles. Moreover, the company is encouraging its 250,000 employees to be spotters of would-be terrorists. It is setting up a system designed to send reports of suspicious activities directly to the Department of Homeland Security via a special computer link. (Block, 2005, p. A1, A5). FedEx's rival UPS has publicly stated that they will not disclose customer's private information unless required to do so by law.

Refining Logistics Outsourcing and Reducing Ad Hoc Arrangements

As the relationships become deeper, companies are entrusting logistics partners with more responsibility. At a warehouse in Indianapolis, TNT conducts basic sub-assembly work for Eaton, a truck components maker. 'When we started this contract two years ago, Eaton did not trust us to talk to their suppliers and customers', recalls Ted Wade, TNT's quality manager at the Indianapolis facility. 'But as you develop more trust they are prepared to outsource more functions and allow you further up the value chain' (*The Financial Times*, 7 December 2004).

Given the levels of security mandated by government authorities today, companies can gain real operational and economic value from selecting suppliers that can provide effective and efficient security. They can achieve significant advantages from developing trustworthy arrangements with suppliers that meet tough criteria in such key activities as selecting security-conscious carriers, shipping via secure ports, meeting packaging security requirements, and providing background information on key personnel. (Rhinehart, Myers and Eckert, 2004, p. 52)

Yankee Group, a consultancy, considers there is US$40 billion of inefficiency in today's supply chains. Researchers teamed up to study retailers and uncover some of the root causes. The study looked at 50 retail companies in nine industry segments representing US$500 billion in sales. One percent admitted their current supply chain networks were sub-optimal when it came to achieving transportation cost savings, but when asked if they would change their network design approach, 57 percent said no. As for technology use, 55 percent have a transportation management system, 40 percent have a supply chain execution system, and only six of the 50 used supply chain event management systems (Material Management Handling, 2004).

Most of the burden of recovery for a company in the aftermath of a terrorist event in the United States will fall on the company itself or the logistics management provider if outsourced, as government agencies still have poor coordination with each other and will be primarily focused on civil and social fallout. This further underlines the need for cooperation and transparency with all levels of the supply chain and all its partners.

Port Infrastructure

Older ports need to be updated, but also lack the room to expand to alleviate congestion, which requires building new ports that can be designed with security requirements in mind. A study by the World Bank estimated that simply modernizing port infrastructure and information systems throughout the developing world could boost trade in these countries by 2.8 percent, or $107 billion (Eggers, 2004). Ports must be up to standards in both efficiency and security in order to participate in the global supply chain. As already mentioned, the costs to upgrade US port facilities run in the billions. Shutting down a port after an incident would cost considerably more. The lockout of the docks in California cost $2 billion per day. The immediate impact of closure of the Port of Melbourne, Australia's major shipping port, for one month would be a trade loss of $4 billion. Flow on effects would easily push the full costs to over $10 billion.

Foreign Ports

Compliance with new laws might not be up to par, especially in other countries. This can create problems for supply chain partners further downstream.

A West Coast based clothing importer recently changed contract manufacturers in Karachi, Pakistan. The new manufacturer was unable to provide product details prior to shipping. This lack of product detail curtailed the import supply chain for three months until the Pakistani supplier could meet the new homeland regulatory requirements. Because of this delay, the US importer was forced to find temporary, alternative sources of merchandise, which turned out to be more costly and not up to product specifications. (Cook, 2003, p. 11)

Poorer countries will also have difficulty upgrading their facilities and could thus be excluded from future trade patterns. It must be considered that upgrades can cost $100 million even for a small country like Jamaica, which is a much more substantial percentage of their GDP than for larger countries.

Overburdened Port Systems and Logistics Providers

Almost half of US imports (by value) arrive in containers on ships and are offloaded at US ports. Measured in units, that is nearly 7 million containers a year (Gottlieb, 2004). At the moment, inspectors examine only 2 percent of containers, and often only after the containers have already traveled hundreds of miles from a port to a big city of destination. The potential damage that mandatory routine screening will cause was made clear by the two-day wait at the American-Canadian border after September 11: it nearly caused chaos at Detroit's car factories, which rely on flows of parts from Canada (*The Economist*, 4 April 2002).

During the 2004 shipping season the ports of Long Beach and Los Angeles in California experienced the worst backlog of ships since the ten-day union lockout in 2002. At its peak, 42 ships waited outside the ports, with some experiencing eight-day turnaround from arrival to departure. This disjointed carriers' schedules and delayed hundreds of thousands of containers. The delays actually lasted five months before the backlog was processed. This has lessened the attractiveness of southern California, and increased the need for supply chains to take advantage of other ports on the west coast and even the east coast. These alternative ports of entry are themselves more limited in current capacity, inland routes and infrastructure (Tirschwell, 2005). Alternative facilities can also be constructed to take advantage of new technologies and security initiatives mandated by the US government. When a system is under stress, it is more vulnerable and likely to repair itself more slowly in the wake of a terrorist act or attempt.

CONCLUSIONS

A number of concluding observations, based on our chapter, are worth noting.

First, there should be logistical security standards and systems similar to ISO 9000 norms for the international community. Emergence and harmonization of global logistics security standards implies greater international collaboration. It remains problematic, at best, for corporate actors to comply with conflicting or incompatible national logistical security standards. There is evidence that a global harmonization movement is underway.

Secondly, various organizational models are available in making the global logistical chain more robust. Two such models are possible based upon the American experience: one is publicly led with the full regulatory force of the state, rarer in the United States and more common in the European Union, while the other is privately driven with market incentives and cost recovery (by passing cost on to the consumers). Observers predict that a hybridized model will result, as a new security environment takes hold, with some industries more privately driven while others are more publicly owned and managed. The future remains unclear but the EU model of transportation system harmonization is an inspiring framework.

Thirdly, logistical autarchy of supply chains, with repatriation of chain components in a few secure countries, will likely not yield workable solutions to the threats of global terrorism. By repatriating the chain and isolating developing economies, the gap between developed and underdeveloped countries would be further widened. Moreover, in an era of outsourcing and offshoring, the breaking up of the chain by safety zones would wreak havoc on economies of scale and scope. A recent study of the best locational choices for outsourcing indicates that countries with geopolitical risk, like the Philippines, India, Armenia, Israel, the Ukraine and Brazil, offer great potential as outsourcing platforms. In fact, the global outsourcing index may indicate an inverse relationship between security risks and outsourcing opportunities (Minevich and Richter, 2005).

Fourthly, in the case of the United States, both government and private companies are responsible for security investments. The government relies heavily on privately held ports and states to fund security measures. But the federal government must concede that each US port is a gateway into the rest of the country and to the world; therefore, the public good that results from additional security measures at a port of entry and egress is shared by all. The logic of the market may in fact have to confront what can be termed a pure public good. For example, securing the Ambassador Bridge – which processes around 8,000 trucks per day between Detroit and Windsor, Canada – not only protects the port and the state of Michigan, but also protects the entire US economy from a major disruption.

Fifthly, a logistical security regime is gradually appearing. It is reminiscent of the export control regime designed in the late 1940s and subsequent years. Minimum mandatory security requirements for importers are gradually being defined. For example, the government can require that each importer confirms that the supplier of and the carrier handling each shipment are not on any restricted-party list. If an importer does not provide this guarantee, its freight won't be allowed through a US port.

Lastly, investing in inspection and detection technologies may go a long way in answering the security needs of a new geopolitical environment. With the advancement of detection technologies, it is feasible to inspect each shipment without impacting processing speed. Experts believe that a combination of low-cost, high-speed gamma-ray inspection and high-accuracy x-ray inspection systems at US ports can allow the verification of most incoming shipments. To achieve this level of security, the government must move beyond pilot projects and fund wider deployments of these systems across all ports.

Supply chain management cannot be understood apart from the manifestations of the complex phenomenon of globalization. The global supply chain, in the words of Thomas Friedman, has 'flattened' the notions of geography and distance and compressed transactional time, linking all stakeholders in a value-added chain. This chain is now a central pillar of the global economic edifice. Disrupting it will cause countries and their firms to lose competitive advantage and economic development gains. The global supply chain can therefore be analogized to oil resources. Any country unable to protect its position in the global supply chain will be shut out of this essential resource, much like a global pariah. Osamu Watanabe, Chief Executive Officer of the Japan External Trade Organization, notes "once countries get embedded in these global supply chains, they feel part of something much bigger than their own (national) businesses" (Friedman, 2005, p. 422).

REFERENCES

Alexander, D.C. (2004), *Business Confronts Terrorism: Risks and Responses*, Madison, WI: University of Wisconsin Press.
Andel, T. (2004), 'Warehousing and world peace', *Material Handling Management*, **59**(11) 40.
Block, R. (2005), 'Private eyes in terrorism fight, government finds a surprising ally: FedEx', *The Wall Street Journal*, 26 May, pp. A1, A5.
Bonner, R. (2002), 'Terrorist nuclear attacks on seaports: threat and response', Washington, DC: Congressional Research Service.
Bouchet, M.H. (2004), 'The impact of geopolitical turmoil on country risk and global investment strategy', in Gabriele G.S. Suder (ed.), *Terrorism and the International Business Environment: The Security-Business Nexus*, Cheltenham, UK and Northampton, MA, USA: Edward Elgar, pp. 83–104.
Byers, M. (2004), 'Policing the high seas: the proliferation security initiative', *The American Journal of International Law*, **98**(3), 526–45.

Center for Arms Control and Non-Proliferation (2005), 'Timeline', terrorism project, Washington, DC, www.armscontrolcenter.org/terrorism/101/timeline.html.

Chopra, S. and P. Meindl (2001), *Supply Chain Management: Strategy, Planning, and Operation,* Upper Saddle River, NJ: Prentice Hall.

Cohen, S.S. (2002), *Economic Impact of a West Coast Dock Shutdown,* Berkeley, CA: University of California.

Cook, T.A. (2003), 'A new security mandate', *Supply Chain Management Review,* **7**(5), 11.

The Economist (2002), 'When trade and security clash', 4 April.

The Economist (2004), 'Going for the jugular', 10 June.

Eggers, W.D. (2004), *Prospering in the Secure Economy,* New York: Deloitte Research.

Emigh, J. (2004), 'Supply chain group goes global to combat terrorism', *E-week,* 20 December.

EyeForTransport (2005), 'Outsourcing logistics – the latest trends in using 3PL providers', London, www.eyefortransport.com.

Financial Times (2004), 7 December, www.news.fl.com/home/us.

Fosler, G.D. (2003), 'Straight talk', *The Conference Board,* **14**(2), www.conference-board.org.

Friedman, T.L. (2005), *The World is Flat: A Brief History of the Twenty-First Century,* New York: Farrar, Straus and Giroux.

Goldstein, J.S. (2004), *The Real Price of War: How You Pay for the War on Terror,* New York: New York University Press.

Gottlieb, D. (2004), 'Shippers still adjusting to new trade security rules', *Purchasing,* 9 December.

Gulisano, V. (2003), 'The case for better freight transport security', *Transport Topics,* **3529**(7).

Iritany, E. and M. Dickerson (2002), 'Calculating cost of West Coast dock strike is a tough act', *Los Angeles Times,* 26 November.

Kauffman, R. and T.A. Crimi (2005), 'A best-practice approach for development of global supply chains', presentation to 90th Annual International Supply Management Conference, May.

Kilcar, S. (2002), 'Securing the supply chain', *Fleet Owner,* **97**(8), 30.

Kleindorfer, P.R. (2004), 'Perspectives on risk/security management: with special attention to global supply chain management', presented to RILA–Wharton (RMDPC)–GWU (ICDRM) Roundtable on Global Supply Chain Security, 7 October.

Kleindorfer, P.R. and L. Van Wassenhove (2004), 'Risk management in global supply chains', in H. Gatignon and J. Kimberley (eds), *The Alliance on Globalization,* Cambridge, UK: Cambridge University Press.

Kumar, N. (1996), 'The power of trust in manufacturer-retailer relationships', *Harvard Business Review,* Nov–Dec, 92–106.

Laudicina, P.A. (2005), 'World out of balance: three scenarios for 2015', *The Globalist,* 11 May.

Lee, H.L. and C. Bilington (1992), 'Managing supply chain inventory', *Sloan Management Review,* Spring, 65–73.

Maenza T. (2004), 'Supply chain visibility exposes weak links, hidden costs', UNISYS, www.unisys.com/commercial/insights/articles/articles.htm?insightsID 97843.

Meyer, L. (2004), 'Unisys says quest for profit and security will drive supply chain evolution in 2005', *Business Wire,* 1 December.

Mariotty, J.L. (1999), 'The trust factor in supply chain management', *Supply Chain Management Review*, Spring, 70–7.

Minevich, M.D. and F.-J. Richter (2005), 'The global outsourcing report', *CIO Insight*, **51**, 55–60.

Mulford, C. and E. Comiskey (2004), *The Financial Numbers Game: Detecting Creative Accounting Practices*, Hoboken, NJ: John Wiley & Sons Inc.

Nitsch, V. and D. Schumacher (2002), 'Terrorism and trade', paper for The Economic Consequences of Global Terrorism Workshop, DIW/German Institute for Economic Research, Berlin, Germany.

Organisation for Economic Co-operation and Development (OECD) (2003), 'Security in maritime transport: risk factors and economic impact', Maritime Transport Committee report, www.oecd.org/home.

Raby, G. (2003), 'The costs of terrorism', presented to the APEC Region Conference, Australia, 24 Feb.

Rhinehart, L., M. Myers and J. Eckert (2004), 'Supplier relationships: the impact on security', *Supply Chain Management Review*, September 1, 52.

Ranum, M.J. (2004), *The Myth of Homeland Security*, Indianapolis, IN: Wiley Publishing.

Reddy, R. (2005), 'The evolution of supply chain technologies – part 2', www.tactica-group.com.

Rice, J.B. and F. Caniato (2003), 'Supply chain response to terrorism: creating resilient and secure supply chains', SC Response to Terrorism Project, MIT Center for Transportation and Logistics, 8 August.

Scrobe, P. (2005), 'The Department of Homeland Security to examine the security of the nation's seaports and the cargo entering those ports', oversight hearing, Washington, DC, 15 March.

Singhal, V. and K.B. Hendricks (2005), 'Association between supply chain glitches and operating performance', *Management Science,* May, pp. 1–17.

Singhal, V. and K.B. Hendricks (2002), 'How supply chain glitches torpedo shareholder value', *Supply Chain Management Review*, Jan/Feb, 18–24.

Spiegel, R. 'Two years after 09/11, inventory impacts minimal', *MSI*, **21**(9), 14.

Straits Times (2005), 7 February, Singapore, http://straitstimes.asia1.com.sg.

Tirschwell, P. (2005), 'Lessons of 2002 will apply in 2005', *Journal of Commerce*, 10 January.

Tohamy, N. (2004), 'Are our supply chains less vulnerable now?', accessed 18 October at www.forrester.com/ Research/Document/0,7211,35671,00.html.

United Nations Conference on Trade and Development Secretariat (2003), 'Container security: major initiatives and related international developments'.

Ward, A. (2004), 'Outsiders tighten supply chain', *The Financial Times*, 7 December 7, p. 15.

Willis, H.H. and D.S. Ortiz (2004), 'Evaluating the security of the global containerized supply chain, technical report TR-214', Santa Monica, CA: Rand Corporation.

Wolfe, M. (2004), 'The dynamics of supply chain security', *The Monitor*, Center for International Trade and Security, The University of Georgia, Athens, GA, **10**(2): 16.

10. Brand portfolio: a new marketing competency for diminishing strategic risks

Claude Chailan and Luis Felipe Calderon-Moncloa

The attacks of September 11, 2001 have provoked a huge commotion, and not only from the social or political viewpoint. These events have affected the way of life and the consumption habits of millions of people all around the world, permanently affecting the company–client relationship. Safety in products and services has gained a more central role for the marketing and communication of brands. And this is not only true for airlines; 09/11 has produced a loss of references and consumers' confidence. Consumers' attitudes and choices have manifested a certain distrust, and with this brands have weakened.

Companies realized how vulnerable brands were to major risks, usually risks not related to their good performance. The capacity of brands to link producers and consumers has been rudely challenged, and there have been drastic changes of consumption habits in some markets, such as the accelerated coming onstream of the hard-discounters in Europe, with a new approach to the quality–price relationship and the diminishing power of the brand.

Companies have reacted to this new challenge. Such a weakened and complex environment should increase the role the brand has to play in reassuring the consumers' buying decisions. Brand guarantee and its image are shelter points for consumers: normally, the higher the risk the more helpful the brand. Consequently, brands have learned a different way of communication (for example, emphasizing safety themes, as car-makers do) to change their relationship with the environment or towards the Third World (for example, Nike reconsidering its production policy in order to improve its brand image), but also with globalization (for example, Nestlé's decision to be more respectful of local brands). Brands also start working on ethical matters (The Body Shop cosmetics products), fair trade (Malongo coffee) or social responsibility.

One of the facets of this adaptation of brands and firms to the new situation is the coming onstream of brand portfolios within companies. In this chapter we introduce this new type of management, its importance, its limitations and its major role with respect to the management of the company's marketing and management risks.

INTRODUCTION

From a simple identification means, brand name has now developed into a critical part of the company's strategy. For this reason, companies are willing to consider brands as important assets and invest huge amounts of capital to buy them (Laforêt and Saunders, 1994).

One major historic reason for the brand success is the diminished consumer-perceived risk (Kapferer, 1991; Keller, 1998). The power of brands is founded on consumers' aversion to uncertainty. For a long while, consumers made their food buying decisions based only on the product's visual aspect, ignoring its brand name as they accepted the grocery store owner's opinion as choosing criteria. The grocery store owner was, of course, inclined to recommend products more for his margin than for the product quality (Boyer, 1999). But later on producers introduced clear visible signals that identified their products, and consumers learned to notice the signal before the product's visual characteristics themselves. Brand became more important than the product itself (Riezebos, 2003).

Roselius (1971) identifies two main risk elements perceived by the consumer: probability of making the wrong choice and the importance of the negative consequences of this choice. Roselius shows the important role of brand for diminishing these risks and sets eleven categories of 'risk reducers', based on their efficacy for the consumer. He also shows that three of these risk reducers are the most relevant for consumers to reduce risks (defined as time consumption, personal safety, self-esteem damage, and loss of money) identified at the buying decision moment. These risk reduction variables refer to (1) brand loyalty, (2) choosing a brand leader and (3) point of sale perception.

Even at the present, perceived risk reduction is the first reason consumers have for choosing a brand, and what guides brand management evolution (Kapferer, 2003). When consumers perceive a risk in making a buying decision, they will deploy different strategies for reducing it. Five major risks are considered by consumers:

- Financial risk ('making a bad deal', which increases the importance of the brand compared with the unit price of the product);
- Physical risk (being harmed by the product, especially food);
- Technological risk (being disappointed by the product's performance);
- Psychological risk (feeling guilty or irresponsible for temptation, especially in impulsive decisions);

- Social risk (what peers will say or think about our choices; brand is a sign of community affiliation).

McCarthy (1971) highlights the three primary roles of brands. First, brands make identifying and purchasing simpler. The brand is a signal that gathers, creates loyalty, and unifies known and supposed values (Aaker, 1992). This identity function is basic and fundamental; buyers do not need to invest in an expensive new learning process for every purchase, as their brand memory will allow them to conduct a pre-selection process for a given product category. Brand operates as a signal for a set of characteristics and allows the adoption of a repetitive buying process that reduces the buying time, thus lowering transaction costs. Brand provides, therefore, important information to the buyer and summarizes the product's characteristics that establish the origin of the product. The identification and purchase simplification function is then critical and consubstantial for the brand as it constitutes the first relationship with consumers from a long-lasting perspective (Keller, 1998).

Brand also has a projective, symbolic and imaginary function and provides the consumer with a status. This second function is directly related to the primary role of brands as differentiation means. This is especially true when the quantifiable characteristics of products became very similar and therefore objectively hard to differentiate by the consumer. In this case the differentiation comes more from brand than from the product (Kapferer, 2000). Brand guarantees quality, protection and risk reduction for the consumer by pointing out to its source. By this means the producing company guarantees a minimal standard and performance at any time, in any place. This function allows the producer to tell the buyer the characteristics of its offer; it acts as a deal of trust, which guarantees continuance and a uniform level of relationship between both participants, regardless the reseller.

Brands also allow the use of multiple strategies. Nowadays, the risk reduction function directly related to the brand has been increased by the context, especially after 09/11. This new environment has notably changed the way in which big international companies conceive their brands. In fact, one of the main subjects in the management of risk for certain companies is to decide if they will have one or more brands. Choosing one or more brand strategies is also the focal point for many companies when establishing different sources of competition (Schuiling, 2004). Thus, Strebinger (2002) states that most of the relevant issues when dealing with brands relate to the management of a multi-brand system. This system can be based on a set of isolated brands or on a complex structure of brands from the same family related to each other.

Riezebos (2003) wonders whether it is feasible having a single-brand strategy for the company to focus on and develop from. To ensure continuous success, the operation of a single brand demands permanent innovation, strong research and development (R&D) investment, a unique communicational style and a brand image not based on the product but on associations. This strategy may allow product line extensions within the same category. Riezebos (2003) differentiates between extensions inside the same price layer (horizontal extension, common for mass consumption products) and in different price layers (vertical extension, for durable goods).

The extension strategy based on a single brand may have three objectives:

- an aggressive objective, for market penetration, especially in the development stage of the brand's life cycle or when adapting to a change in demand (that is, Diet Coke);
- a defensive objective to react to a competitors' aggression;
- a market re-launch objective, especially when substituting low price products for added value products at a higher price.

In a monobrand strategy, a brand name may be used for horizontal or vertical extensions. This strategy can be very successful and a well-developed brand can provide a sustainable competitive advantage.

One of the primary weaknesses of this approach is to expose the company to a major risk: a single brand means a single image. If a problem occurs with this brand the whole company's stability will be at stake. The company may anticipate this threat by developing several brands within the same market. This anticipation is essential when the installed brand is highly profitable or when its market shares are well-positioned.

The company may, for instance, look at protecting the installed brand by creating new brands that act in a secondary way, as shelters to the most profitable one. On the other hand, numerous companies realized in the 1990s that operating a single brand within the same product category is not sufficient to be competitive.

> How many brands must we offer to consumers within the same product category? . . . this is the key question for companies willing to internationalise their businesses (therefore) brand portfolio optimisation is a strategic issue because the chosen answer will have a profound and permanent impact on the outcome . . . and because the chosen strategy will allow or impede having a sustainable competitive advantage. (Kapferer, 2000, p. 157)

There are, however, reasons why adopting a multiband strategy is not the best option. First, from a long-term perspective it may be reasonable not to overexpose a brand to preserve its image and/or its specificity within a given product scope. In the luxury goods market, for example, too many line extensions or extension too far from the original brand territory may weaken a brand (as in the case of Pierre Cardin). To refuse a short-term profit for a long-term gain becomes a normal practice in today's corporate world. Avoiding brand image degradation leads companies to limit its use and territory, although it may imply the loss of value or potential of a larger territory than that being operated at that moment.

From a broader social perspective, the overexposition of a brand – as the symbolic definition of an object or a service as well as a model of consumer society (Boyer, 1999 ; Keller, 1998) – may weaken a company. The consumer is also a citizen and the brand may be a social and economic battleground of companies and consumers. Nowadays brands also represent an important political space where virulent battles can be fought (Semprini, 1992). Some movements oppose lifestyles symbolized by brands and oppose, sometimes in a very radical way, a consumer society supposedly represented by companies and their brands (Klein, 2002). This opposition is a fact that must be faced by companies, and must be taken into consideration when developing their brands and their territories in order to avoid vulnerability of a single-brand strategy or extreme exposure.

There are also limitations to a brand expansion because of the intrinsic nature of brands. A brand cannot cover, legitimately and appropriately, the whole existing universe of products. The company's growth implies buying or launching new brands in its attempt to cover markets, segments or targets otherwise inaccessible to a company with a single brand.

A lot of questions can be posed about the selection of the best brand strategy to minimize the risks incurred by a company. Cegarra (1994) was one of the first researchers to investigate the complexity of managing all the company's brands and the definition of an identity system intended to create attributions and organizations between brands and their position. This author identifies four main strategic orientations that explain why a brand portfolio is created: (a) the objective of having global brands, (b) the intention to create economies of scale, (c) the decision to enter many different market segments, and (d) the will to propose a varied offer. But these approaches may seem contradictory because the first two tend to reduce the number of brands and the two last induce the company to increase the number of products. These contradictions suggest the implementation of a system to guide the organization of brand portfolios.

THE BRAND PORTFOLIO CONCEPT

Although it is commonly used by practitioners who ask themselves about the election of the most adequate brand strategies to enter the market, brand portfolio has attracted very little academic attention (Barwise and Robertson, 1992; Kapferer, 2000; Riezebos, 2003). There are very few brand portfolio definitions in literature. Riezebos (2003, p. 184) defines it as "a set of brands owned by one company" and Keller (1998, p. 522) defines brand portfolio as "all the brands, and their extensions, offered by a given company in a given product category". But these definitions make no distinction between the brand aggregate itself and the relationship between brands that is, in our opinion, the essence of the brand portfolio concept. In fact, it is the company's capacity to organize and manage this set of brands, and not the simple fact of brand juxtaposition, which is a long-lasting factor of risk reduction. Only this capacity may provide stability and better risk management based on the separation of brand territories.

Therefore, we propose this definition: 'A brand portfolio is the upper stage for a company's brand aggregation that implies the active management of relationships between these brands'. The main question posed by brand portfolios is that of knowing the relationship between brands within the same company, based on the organization of the corresponding brand territories and the search for a balance to limit the risks the company may incur with a single-brand strategy.

Historically, many firms have ended up with an incoherent set of brands, while others have launched numerous brands to fulfill the need for differentiation, without taking into account the need for positioning those brands in connection to each other (Barwise and Robertson, 1992). The formalization of brands' aggregates, that is, the transformation of an incoherent combination of brands into a proactively generated brand portfolio, has not always been well organized or designed with respect to companies.

At its origins, the transformation of the brand universe surely comes from the big corporations that discovered, in the early 1980s, that they could create value by capitalizing on the transnational concepts carried in supranational brands to attain a critical size (Kapferer, 2000). This new approach reduces the internal brand management costs and also reduces the costs of launching new innovative products. This simple idea has allowed many companies to focus on the strongest brands, or on brands with high growth potential or on highly internationalized brands, and to abandon or minimize all the others.

At the beginning, economic reasons were the main inspiration for this rationalization process: first of all, trying to concentrate all human and economic resources on a few brands and, especially, cutting advertising costs so important in the launching and maintaining process of multiple brands. In the early 1990s, many companies did inform the market of their intentions to reduce their brand numbers, the most extreme case being that of Unilever, which went from 1,600 to 400 brands in the period between 2000 and 2004.

Philippe Véron, CEO responsible for Nestlé's business unit declared:

> Working in the food business, it is impossible to standardize it all. Tastes and culture traits make people more attached to their cooked food brands than to their tooth-

paste. We decided to group our products by their emotional appeal rather than for geographical reasons. Nestlé is, therefore, the brand that groups all the food that a mother will use to nourish her children from birth through adolescence. By this reasoning it becomes legitimate to brand the same name to a baby soup and a breakfast cereal.[1]

Laforêt and Saunders (1999) underline that managing a portfolio is far more important than managing one individual brand. Keller (1998) emphasizes that brand management requires a long-term vision for every brand, where roles and relationships between brands are carefully defined. Keller notes that (1998, p. 532) 'In any brand portfolio management decision the basic criteria are simple but its application could be far more complex' because every brand must have, at the same time, (a) a clearly defined function inside the portfolio and the company's strategy (b) a clearly defined statement of benefits, promises and associations proposed to the consumer.

The brand portfolio concept is a core concern for most world leaders because, as the competitive environment becomes more and more complex, with a high level of risks of every nature, companies do not focus on brand management only but on the definition of links between brands within the company and on the organization of these links.

Alan Lafley, Procter & Gamble's CEO says:

Today our home, baby and feminine hygiene products are convenient for us. Our objective is to extend those lines around our main existing brands eventually by acquisitions. On the contrary, we want to develop our portfolio in our care, beauty and health products . . . An acquisition is only interesting for P & G if it really reinforces our core business and if, at the end of the day, our brands are made stronger by this acquisition. Our responsibility is to develop brands that last all our lives or even longer.[2]

On the other hand, Lindsay Owen-Jones, L'Oréal's CEO states: "We have a complete, balanced brand portfolio. Our eventual acquisitions will only be of companies that complete our niche coverage or our international reach."[3] Gucci, in its turn, takes advantages of its treasury to acquire or launch the Yves Saint-Laurent, Alexander McQueen, Balenciaga, Bottega Veneta, Bédat, Boucheron, Sergio Rossi and Stella MacCartney brands. And Anthony Simon, President of Unilever-BestFoods marketing, underlines that "Unilever's objective is to reduce the number of brands in order to make them stronger. Four strategies support this decision: category, segment, channel and geography."[4] This shows to what extent the brand portfolio is at the heart of the company's strategic analysis.

Strategic choices may become brand choices, choices of brand organization or choices about the kind of relationship between brands that the company wants, and one of the purposes of these choices is to limit the company's risks caused by the exposure of its different brands. But this process includes some contradictory factors, as shown in Figure 10.1. This figure shows the company's willingness and need to have numerous products best able to meet customers' demands, while assuring their expansion and international development – that is, to face first of all the risk of being a single-brand company. Likewise, there is a need to limit the number of brands to avoid facing risks caused by a brand overexposure or over-usage, including the financial risk of dispersing the investment.

The first trend motivates companies wishing to develop to buy or launch more brands in order to enter markets, segments or customers inaccessible with only one brand. This may be an 'inflationist' process in terms of markets as it leads to the creation of many brands. The second trend takes the same companies in the opposite direction, trying to limit the number of brands in order to maximize their need for investments, making their brands stronger and covering more territory.

Brand portfolio management changes the focus of marketing to a superior, strategic decision-making level (Baldinger, 1990; Trinquecoste, 1999), as it implicitly involves focusing on the whole instead of on individual brands (Riezebok, 2003). Figure 10.2 shows some examples of cosmetics companies' brands portfolio.

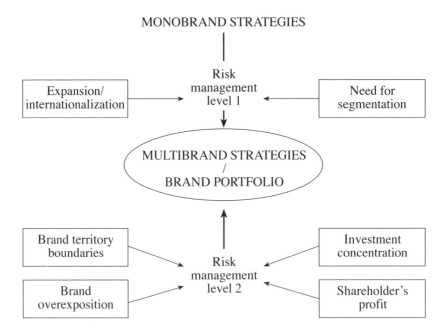

Figure 10.1   Monobrand and multibrand strategies

ESTEE LAUDER	L'OREAL	PROCTER & GAMBLE
Estée Lauder	L'Oréal Paris	Olay
Clinique	Armani Parfums	Covergirl
Aramis	Helena Rubinstein	Max Factor
M.A.C.	Lancôme	Clairol
Aveda	Vichy	Pantene
Tommy Hilfiger	Kérastase	Hugo Boss
Darphin	Redken	Giorgio Beverly Hills
Origins	Matrix	Wella
Prescriptives	Garnier	Sebastian
La Mer	Kiehl's	Gucci
Bobbi Brown	Maybeline	Escada
Donna Karan	Shu Uemura	Ana Sui
Michael Kors	Softsheen-Carson	Trussardi
Stila	Biotherm	Dunhill

Figure 10.2   Cosmetic companies' brand portfolios

According to Barwise and Robertson (1992) brand portfolio is, in principle, an answer to four key management goals: (a) develop global brands; (b) reach multiple market segments; (c) answer to changes in the bargaining power with market channels; and (d) take advantage of economies of scale in advertising, sales, merchandising and logistics. Cegarra (1994) states that the two main purposes of brand portfolio management are, on the one hand, to identify a limited number of the strongest brands to capitalize on and, on the other hand, to assure the survival of all company brands. The increasing recognition of brands as a source of sustainable competitive advantage stresses the importance of conceptual models about organizational brand strategies (João Louro and Vieira Cunha, 2001). Carlotti et al. (2004) assert that the brand portfolio is not only critical because of financial reasons. A brand portfolio allows a company to establish a strategy for every brand, to determine the need for repositioning, to identify the underperforming brands and, finally, to avoid the exposure risks for the company related to a single-brand strategy.

RISK AND BRAND PORTFOLIO STRATEGY

For many companies, the brand combination within a portfolio is a key factor for their development, growth and risk management. It is a crucial phase to understanding companies' competitive advantage (Sharma, 1999; Slater and Olson, 2001) and strategic marketing (Day, 1994; Trinquecoste, 1999). From the intelligent exploitation and management of multiple brands these companies obtain a competitive advantage (Trinquecoste, 1999). A brand portfolio means avoiding the risk of the individual brand by creating a meta-dimension that improves risk management. Juga (1999) and Reynaud (2001) show that by displacing the sources of competitive advantage to an upper level this advantage becomes harder to understand and to imitate.

After the events of 09/11, risk reduction has increased its importance as a main corporate goal, which also increases brand portfolio importance. In fact, multiple considerations have led numerous companies to create a brand portfolio in order to limit certain risks, and this strategical brand management is now practiced by the world's biggest corporations. A more complex environment induces and justifies a strategy of brand juxtaposition to allow companies to continue developing by dominating the exposure of their brands.

This development of brand portfolios raises the question of their balance (Riezebos, 2003) against the single-brand dependency. Darwar (2004) highlights that companies with large portfolios may profit from 'disintegration', that is, the possibility of using IT for reaching individual customers and specific segments. Every brand becomes a tool in the marketer's toolbox whose task is not to manage a brand but the relationship with the client. As Darwar says (2004, p. 34), "brands are not superstars but members of a team".

An organizational model based on the brand portfolio allows the incorporation of the brand-related risk management into the company's strategy. A brand portfolio is in fact the consequence of three phases: (1) brand accumulation/gathering; (2) brand rationalization, that is, definition of criteria used to select them; and (3) theoretical reflection, that is, establishment of an organizational scheme able to manage the brand portfolio, a model to develop the company based on its brand portfolio and the strict definition of criteria to select the brands. Figure 10.3 shows the scheme to build the brand portfolio.

The brand portfolio allows the company to achieve a critical size (especially facing the distribution channels), to face the growth limits of existing brands, and to share, soften and pool some costs (research, industrialization, marketing). The brand portfolio building process is time-sensitive and based on a whole set of experiences. Complementary brands inside a portfolio allow better risk sharing. Also, brand portfolios allow companies to get together different needs and reconcile them in the long term. On the one hand, these are in part the 'external' needs experienced by consumers which lead companies to develop the products proposed but also new brands to emphasize the difference perceived by consumers. On the other, they are 'internal' needs of rationalization related to the search for an economic performance, but also for better risk distribution.

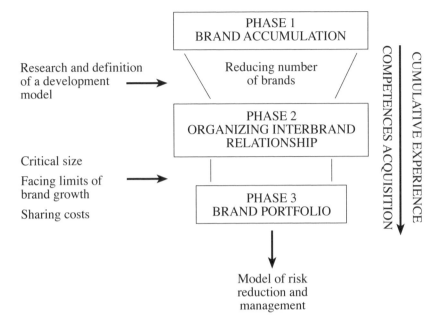

Figure 10.3   Building brand portfolios

Brand portfolios allow arranging and organizing the brand relationships to transform a group of brands with competitive advantages. This allows better control of risks by the company. The contribution of brand portfolio analysis is to bring to light new guiding principles in the way risk is managed inside the companies. It allows going beyond the competition at the brand level to arrive at a meta-level, a dimension capable of creating a competitive advantage that reconciles explicit consumer needs for security and safety with the company's needs for profit.

NOTES

1. *Les Echos*, 21 October 1999.
2. Interview with French financial journal *Les Echos*, 8 January 2003.
3. Interview with French journal *Le Figaro*, 21 February 2003.
4. Interview with French journal *Le Figaro*, 21 February 2003.

REFERENCES

Aaker, D. (1992), 'The value of brand equity', *Journal of Business Strategy*, **13**(4), 27–32.

Baldinger, A.L. (1990), 'Defining and applying the brand equity concept: why the researcher should care', *Journal of Advertising Research*, **30**(3), 1–5.

Barwise, P. and T. Robertson (1992), 'Brand portfolios', *European Management Journal*, **10**(3), 277–85.

Boyer, A. (1999), 'Un marketing sans paradigme', *Revue Française de Gestion*, **125**, 64–80.

Carlotti, S., S. Coe and M.E. Perrey (2004), 'Making brand portfolios work', *McKinsey Quarterly*, **4**, 1–7.

Cegarra, J.J. (1994), 'Gérer un portefeuille de marques', *Décisions Marketing*, **3**, 81–91.

Dawar, N. (2004), 'What are brands good for?', *MIT Sloan Management Review*, **46**(1), 31–37.

Day, G.S. (1994), 'The capabilities of market-driven organizations', *Journal of Marketing*, **58**, 37–52.

Joao Louro, M. and P. Vieira Cunha (2001), 'Brand management paradigms', *Journal of Marketing Management*, **17**, 849–75.

Juga, J. (1999), 'Generic capabilities: combining positional and resource-based views for strategic advantage', *Journal of Strategic Marketing*, **7**, 3–18.

Kapferer, J.N. (1991), *Les Marques Capital de l'Entreprise*, Paris: Les Editions d'Organisation.

Kapferer, J.N. (2000), *Re-marques, les Marques à l'Épreuve de la Pratique*, Paris: Les Editions d'Organisation.

Kapferer, J.N. (2003), 'Réinventer la marque?', *Revue Française de Gestion*, **145**, 119–30.

Keller, K.L. (1998), *Strategic Brand Management: Building, Measuring and Managing Brand Equity*, 2nd edn, Upper Saddle River, NJ: Prentice-Hall.

Klein, N. (2002), *No Logo*, New York: Picador.

Laforêt, S. and J. Saunders (1994), 'Managing brand portfolios: how the leaders do it', *Journal of Advertising Research*, **34**(5), 64–77.

Laforêt, S. and J. Saunders (1999), 'Managing brand portfolios: why leaders do what they do', *Journal of Advertising Research*, 51–66.

McCarthy, E.J. (1971), *Basic Marketing: A Managerial Approach*, 4th edn, Homewood, IL: R.D. Irwin Inc.

Reynaud, E. (2001), 'Compétences centrales: premier pas vers une définition opéra-tionnelle', Xème conférence de l'AIMS, Université Laval, Quebec.

Riezebos, R. (2003), *Brand Management, A Theoretical and Practical Approach*, Harlow: Prentice Hall.

Roselius, T. (1971), 'Consumer rankings of risk reduction methods', *Journal of Marketing*, **35**, 56–61.

Sharma, S. (1999), 'Trespass or symbiosis? Dissolving the boundaries between strate-gic marketing and strategic management', *Journal of Strategic Marketing*, **7**, 73–88.

Schuiling, I. and J.N. Kapferer (2004), 'Real differences between local and interrna-tional brands: strategic implications for international marketers', *Journal of International Marketing*, **12**(4), 97–113.

Semprini, A. (1992), *Le marketing de la marque: Approche sémiotique*, Paris: Editions Liaisons.

Slater, S. and E. Olson (2001), 'Marketing's contribution to the implementation of business strategy: an empirical analysis', *Strategic Management Journal*, **22**, 1055–67.

Strebinger, A. (2002), 'Strategic brand concepts and brand architecture strategy – theoretical considerations', *Actes journée AFM-IRG Les marques*, 1–17.

Trinquecoste, J.F. (1999), 'Pour une clarification théorique du lien marketing-stratégie', *Recherche et Applications en Marketing*, **14**(1), 59–80.

PART IV

Challenges for the Future

11. Corporate global citizenship: successfully partnering with the world

Nancy J. Adler

Remember your humanity, and forget the rest.
Joseph Rotblat, Nobel Peace Prize Laureate[1]

'That victory never leads to peace is not a theoretical affirmation, but an empirical statement.'[2] Fifty years ago, led by Albert Einstein and Bertrand Russell, 11 of the world's most eminent scientists issued the Russell-Einstein Manifesto, warning of the dire consequences that would ensue if the world continued attempting to resolve its most complex and contested issues through war:

> We have to learn to think in a new way. We have to learn to ask ourselves, not what steps can be taken to give military victory to whatever group we prefer, for there no longer are such steps; the question we have to ask ourselves is: what steps can be taken to prevent a military contest . . . [knowing that it would end disastrously for] all parties?[3]

As we enter the 21st century, physicist and Nobel Peace Prize Laureate Joseph Rotblat, at 97 the only living signatory of the Russell-Einstein Manifesto, sagely reminds us what such new thinking entails: 'Throughout the centuries we have tried to ensure that we have peace by preparing for war. And throughout the centuries we had war. . . . It is of the utmost importance to recognize the folly of this policy and adopt a new policy . . . If you want peace, prepare for peace' (Franck et al., 2000, pp. 73–4).

IF YOU WANT PEACE, PREPARE FOR PEACE

In a post-9/11 world focused on creating security in the midst of terrorism, what does it mean to 'think in a new way'? What does it mean to prepare for peace?[3] The Norwegian Nobel Committee, in choosing whom to award the Nobel Peace Prize to each year, has progressively embraced new ways of

thinking about peace. Over the years, the Committee has broadened its definition of peace-makers from limiting it to those engaged primarily in ending
wars after they have broken out, to including those involved in reducing the
probability that violent conflicts ever occur in the first place. The Committee
has expanded its list of Peace Prize recipients, which formerly included only
political leaders and diplomats courageously negotiating resolutions to end
raging conflicts, by adding people and organizations involved in creating and
maintaining the preconditions for peace. These preconditions include establishing democracy in place of totalitarian regimes, broadening human rights,
promoting ecologically sustainable development that supports a flourishing
natural environment, and eliminating poverty and extreme inequities in
income distribution so that every person on the planet can have adequate
access to life's necessities.

PRECONDITIONS FOR PEACE

Democracy and Human Rights

In 2003 the Nobel Committee explicitly recognized human rights and democracy as preconditions for peace when it chose to award the Nobel Peace Prize
to Iranian lawyer Shirin Ebadi for her work supporting 'democracy and human
rights', and especially for her advocacy for women's and children's rights
(Mjøs, 2003).

The Committee emphasized its reasons for giving the Nobel Peace Prize to
Ebadi, the first woman from the Muslim world ever to be so honored, and
explained why it was particularly important to make the award now, at the
beginning of the 21st century:

> All people are entitled to fundamental rights, and at a time when Islam is being
> demonized in many quarters of the western world, it was the Norwegian Nobel
> Committee's wish to underline how important and how valuable it is to foster
> dialogue between peoples and between civilizations. (Mjøs, 2003)

In offering its reasons for selecting Ebadi, the Committee stressed that
whereas there have been several long-running themes in the 102-year history
of the Nobel Peace Prize, 'in the last few decades, the most distinct . . . has
. . . been the increasing emphasis . . . placed on democracy and human rights.'[4]
Ebadi, a conscious Muslim,

> sees no conflict between Islam and fundamental human rights. Islam is a diverse
> religion. How the message of justice is to be realized in practice and how human
> integrity is to be preserved is an essential issue for Muslims of today . . . Here too,

women have an important role to play; no longer is it for elderly men to interpret the message . . . 'Those who kill in the name of Islam . . . violate Islam', says Shirin Ebadi. We know that human rights are being violated not only in Muslim countries. It happens whether regimes are religious or secular, nationalistic or Marxist. (Mjøs, 2003)

Ebadi emphasizes that dialogue among the world's wide range of cultures must be founded on the values that some of the seemingly most divergent cultures hold in common. One of those values is democracy, and, '[o]ne of the most certain findings of modern political science is . . . that democracies do not go to war against each other', Ebadi recognizes that there 'need be no fundamental conflict [for example,] between Islam and Christianity. That is why Ebadi was pleased that the Pope was among the first to congratulate her on the Peace Prize.'[5] Ebadi profoundly understands the importance of democracy and human rights as preconditions for peace.

Sustainable Development and a Flourishing Environment

Again choosing to highlight those who create the preconditions for peace rather than those working to resolve conflicts after they have erupted into war, the 2004 Nobel Committee chose to honor Wangari Maathai, a Kenyan woman who has worked her entire life creating conditions for peace. For the first time in the Prize's more than 100 history, the Committee decided to broaden its thinking and embrace a definition of peace-making that encompasses the health of the natural environment. In announcing Maathai, a lifelong advocate of sustainable development, as the 2004 recipient of the Nobel Peace Prize, the Committee signaled its change in thinking:

> Peace on earth depends on our ability to secure our living environment. Maathai stands at the front of the fight to promote ecologically viable social, economic and cultural development in Kenya and in Africa. She has taken a holistic approach to sustainable development that embraces democracy, human rights and women's rights in particular. She thinks globally and acts locally.[6]

Wangari Maathai, unlike the majority of her Nobel-laureate predecessors, is not an international diplomat; she is the planter of trees. Maathai founded the Green Belt Movement. For nearly 30 years, she has mobilized poor women to plant trees – over 30 million trees.[7] Because of its departure from previous definitions of peace-making, the Nobel Committee explicitly explained the reasons for its expanded appreciation of what leads to peace:

> In recent decades, the Nobel Committee has made human rights a central element of the definition of peace. There were many warnings against such a broadening of the concept of peace. Today there are few things peace researchers and other scholars are

readier to agree on than . . . that democracy and human rights advance peace . . . This year, the Norwegian Nobel Committee has . . . broadened its definition of peace still further. Environmental protection has become yet another path to peace.[8]

What is the relationship between peace and the environment? As the Nobel Committee explained:

> Most people would probably agree that there are connections between peace on the one hand and an environment on the other in which scarce resources such as oil, water, minerals or timber are quarreled over. The Middle East is full of disputes relating to oil and water. Clearly, not everyone outside the region has appreciated the importance to Arab-Israeli relations of the conflicts over the waters of the Jordan, Litani, Orontes and other rivers. Competition for minerals has been an important element of several conflicts in Africa in recent years. Competition for timber has figured prominently in Liberia, Indonesia, and Brazil.[9]

But where does tree-planting come in?

> When we analyse local conflicts, we tend to focus on their ethnic and religious aspects. But it is often the underlying ecological circumstances that bring the more readily visible factors to the flashpoint. Consider the conflict in Darfur in the Sudan. What catches the eye is that this is a conflict between Arabs and Africans, between the government, various armed militia groups, and civilians. Below this surface, however, lies the desertification that has taken place in the last few decades, especially in northern Darfur. The desert has spread southwards, forcing Arab nomads further and further south year by year, bringing them into conflict with African farmers.[6]
>
> In the Philippines, uncontrolled deforestation has helped to provoke an uprising against the authorities. In Mexico, soil erosion and deforestation have been factors in the revolt in Chiapas against the central government. In Haiti, the Amazon, and the Himalayas, deforestation and the resulting soil erosion have contributed to deteriorating living conditions and caused tension between population groups and countries. In many countries deforestation, often together with other problems, leads to migration to the big cities, where the lack of infrastructure is another source of further conflict. (Mjøs, 2004)

The relationship between inadequate and inequitably-distributed resources and conflict are powerful, direct, and devastating in their consequences. With her profound understanding of such relationships, Maathai summarizes:

> We are sharing our [planet's] resources in a very inequitable way. We have parts of the world that are very deprived and parts of the world that are very rich. And that is partly the reason why we have conflicts. Wars and conflicts certainly have many other causes, too. But who would deny that inequitable distribution, locally and internationally, is relevant in this connection? I predict that within a few decades, when researchers have developed more comprehensive analyses of many of the world's conflicts, the relation between the environment, resources, and conflict may seem almost as obvious as the connection we see today between human rights, democracy and peace.

The Nobel Committee concluded its 2004 Peace Prize presentation by emphasizing the need for cooperation; the need for all parties to learn how to cooperate with each other on a global basis:

> Sooner or later, in order to meet environmental problems, there will have to be international cooperation across all national boundaries on a much larger scale than we have seen up to now. We live on the same globe. We must all cooperate to meet the world's environmental challenges.[10]

Considering the global experience and structures needed for such international cooperation, one is struck by the more extensive and integrated global experience of most multinational corporations as compared with the more discrete, geographically-defined experience of most countries and governments.[11] In considering which organizations should be involved in delivering global solutions to global problems, it is incumbent on the world community to more seriously consider the potential contributions of all sectors, including the private sector.

Health, Poverty Reduction and Equitable Income Distribution

Democracy, human rights and environmental sustainability are preconditions for peace, but they are not the only preconditions. Experts are also adding health, poverty reduction and a more equitable income distribution to the list of necessary conditions for global security and sustainability. The Executive Director of the World Health Organization, Gro Harlem Brundtland, a medical doctor and former Prime Minister of Norway, was one of the first to prominently label poverty as the leading cause of illness. At the opening of the 21st century, in her 2000 BBC Reich Lecture, Brundtland first explained the connection between illness and poverty,

> I feel it is necessary to re-establish in people's minds . . . the fact that it is not only . . . that poverty leads to ill health, but . . . ill health also leads to poverty . . . I [therefore] want the fight against poverty to be our global cause as we straddle the millennium. Our goal must be to create a world where we all can live well fed and clothed, and with dignity. We must do this without undermining future generations' ability to do the same.[12]

In the world today,

> about three billion people live on less than two dollars a day . . . That means that 3 billion people live in such poverty that they cannot afford proper housing, proper health care and proper education for their children. Almost half of those people live on less than one dollar per day. That means more than a billion people not having enough to eat every day and at constant risk of malnutrition . . . [Such extreme]

poverty has a woman's face; of the 1.3 billion poorest, only 30 percent are male . . .
Women from poor households are more than a hundred times more likely to die as
a result of childbirth than their wealthier counterparts. (Brundtland, 2001)

According to Brundtland, many of the conflicts in the world 'are not so much
territorial disputes as they are rooted in general misery, the aftermath of
humanitarian crises, shortages of food and water and the spreading of poverty
and ill-health' (Brundtland, 2001). In the wake of governments' attempts to
ameliorate the crises, the situation, instead of improving, often grows worse.
As long as such poverty continues, the world cannot hope for peace, security
or an end to terrorism. As long as we continue to rely on previously tried, and
all too often failed, solutions driven primarily by governmental and intergovernmental agencies, we cannot hope to improve the situation.

Poverty is now not only understood to be a leading cause of illness, it is also
beginning to be understood as a leading cause of conflict and global insecurity. In the 21st century's globally interconnected society, illness in one part of
the world leads to a lack of security worldwide. Health crises originating in the
world's poorest countries no longer remain local, but, as we have seen with
SARS, AIDS, TB and a list of other feared diseases, often rapidly spread
worldwide. As Brundtland (2001) describes,

> Diseases cannot be kept out of even the richest of countries by rearguard defensive
> action. The separation between domestic and international health problems is no
> longer useful, as people and goods travel across continents. Two million people
> cross international borders every single day, about a tenth of humanity each year.
> And of these, more than a million travel from developing to industrialized countries
> each week.

Such globally interconnected patterns are fundamentally changing leaders'
appreciation of what matters in the world, even from the perspective of the
world's wealthiest peoples and nations.

'Health security', as Brundtland (2001) labels it, is now

> as important as national security. Threats to health undermine . . . the world's
> 'human security'. Illness experienced by most of the world's people threatens [not
> only their own] countries' economic and political viability: [it] . . . affects [the]
> economic and political interests of all . . . countries. Several countries – including
> the United States – [along with the United Nations] now recognize that improving
> international levels of health is neither solely a domestic health issue nor an act of
> charity, but rather a matter of national security.

Unfortunately, similar to the management of other preconditions for peace and
security, past approaches that have relied primarily on programs led by
governments, international agencies and non-governmental organizations
(NGOs), have failed so far to successfully address the most crucial issues:

Over the past few years, the human development index has declined in more than 30 countries. Almost one third of all children are undernourished. The average African household consumes 20 percent less today than it did 25 years ago! And development assistance is falling too. Only a few countries have fulfilled past commitments to provide 0.7 per cent of their GDP for development assistance. In actual fact the world average is now closer to 0.2 per cent. (Brundtland, 2001)

Many world leaders are now urgently calling for new approaches, including the unorthodox recommendation that alliances be formed between industry and international agencies to address society's most pressing and important challenges. What is – and more importantly, what could be – the role of the private sector in addressing these challenges and establishing global security? What hope do we have that the private sector will play the constructive role that the world needs it to play?

GLOBAL SECURITY, PEACE-MAKING AND THE PRIVATE SECTOR

Clearly, strides have been made in the world's understanding of what constitutes peace-making. To succeed as a global civilization in the 21st century, however, our ways of thinking about global security and peace-making need to expand once again, this time to more prominently and explicitly include the private sector. This is not because the private sector has better values than the other sectors – it doesn't – but because of the private sector's global prominence as well as its worldwide structures and processes. For the first time in history, answers to questions of societal well-being – including questions of war and peace and of terrorism and security – may well be more in the hands of business people than in those of political, diplomatic, military or humanitarian leaders.

Over the past 50 years, power has shifted dramatically from the public to the private sector. Today, 49 of the 100 largest economies in the world are multinational companies, not countries (Aspen Institute, 2003). Due to this shift in power, traditional perspectives that assumed government and intergovernmental agencies could or would take care of society's welfare are no longer relevant either for society or for the economy; this applies to both the richest and the poorest nations and peoples.

Wal-Mart, for example, is now the nineteenth largest economy in the world, with sales exceeding $250 billion (Mau et al., 2004, p. 128). If it were a country, Wal-Mart would be China's eighth largest trading partner (Friedman, 2005b). Wal-Mart's single-day revenue is larger than the annual gross domestic product of 36 independent countries.[13] With over 1.3 million employees,

Wal-Mart is now the world's largest employer. The company has more people in uniform than the entire United States Army (Mau et al., 2004). What Wal-Mart does in the world matters, not only to its own employees, customers and suppliers, but to the global economy and society within which all companies operate and all people live. Global solutions cannot be conceived of or implemented without taking companies such as Wal-Mart into account.

Business's Contribution: Are CEOs Missing in Action?[14]

United Nations' Secretary General Kofi Annan has challenged businesses to become co-creators of society's success and security: 'Let us choose to unite the power of markets with the strengths of universal ideals . . . let us choose to reconcile the creative forces of private entrepreneurship with the needs of the disadvantaged and the requirements of future generations' (Annan, 1999).

Many, however, rightfully question the role that business has taken. Simultaneously recognizing the importance of business's increasing influence and society's wariness at how CEOs have used that influence, World Economic Forum President Klaus Schwab confronted the world's top business leaders as they convened in Davos, Switzerland:

> In today's trust-starved climate, our market-driven system is under attack. . .large parts of the population feel that business has become detached from society, that business interests are no longer aligned with societal interests . . . The only way to respond to this new wave of anti-business sentiment is for business to take the lead and to reposition itself clearly and convincingly as part of society'. (Schwab, 2003)

Twenty-first century pleas for corporate global citizenship recognize that without the private sector, no attempt to create and maintain a peaceful, prosperous, equitable and sustainable society can succeed. They also acknowledge that much of the private sector will have to rethink its role if it is to contribute in more than narrowly defined, self-interested ways.

Are CEOs rising to the challenge and becoming co-creators of the type of global society that the Nobel Committee, the United Nations and the World Economic Forum aspire to? Many observers bluntly say no. Whether they cite corporate greed and corruption – as brilliantly demonstrated in recent years by Arthur Andersen, Enron, Health South, Tyco, and Worldcom, among many others – or other forms of corporate malfeasance, the private sector is rarely perceived as a primary contributor to global society's security and success.[15]

New York Times editorial writer Thomas Friedman suggests that the private sector's crime is not simply behavior that is ultimately exposed as criminal, but rather CEOs' lack of constructive engagement with the world's most serious problems. As he labels it, many CEOs are simply 'missing in action' (Friedman, 2005a). Equally seriously, many of these missing-in-action CEOs still view commitment to societal well-being not as a strategy for superior performance – both fiscal and societal – but rather as a net drain on their companies' revenues and profits. Locked in an overly narrow definition of free enterprise, they continue to adhere to classical economist Milton Friedman's dictum that the only 'social responsibility of business is to increase its profits' (Friedman, 1970).

PEACE, SECURITY AND ECONOMIC PROSPERITY

Whereas 'missing-in-action' might reflect the behavior of far too many CEOs, it does not accurately describe either all business leaders or all business approaches. Contributions to societal well-being that some companies are making through their core business strategies and processes are so extraordinarily innovative and effective that the Nobel Committee may need to consider expanding its candidate pool for future Nobel Peace Prize recipients to include private-sector initiatives. Perhaps the next Nobel Peace Prize will be offered to a global company, rather than to a diplomat or a tree-planter. Some of the most interesting private sector strategies include business efforts to reduce poverty, wage peace and enhance environmental quality – all while making a profit.

Bottom-of-the-Pyramid Business Strategies: Reducing Poverty and Creating Fortunes

According to management professors C.K. Prahalad and Stuart Hart, 'low-income markets present a prodigious opportunity for the world's wealthiest companies to seek their fortunes and bring prosperity to the aspiring poor' (Prahalad and Hart, 2002, p. 2). Taking a novel approach to bringing private sector expertise to solving some of the world's most crucial problems, Prahalad and Hart guide multinationals on how to reduce extreme poverty – and by extension global instability – while simultaneously earning significant profits. Prahalad and Hart advise global companies to 'see' markets that were previously invisible to them – and remain invisible to most of their competitors.[16] That market is the 4 billion people who earn less than $1,500 annually. These global business strategists dispel the illusion that the world's poorest people do not constitute a market, that they do not possess buying power, and that there are not significant profits to be earned by the companies serving them. By giving the world's poor access to better and more reasonably priced products and services – most of which would not be possible without today's advanced technological design capabilities – bottom-of-the-pyramid strategies have the potential to reduce the risk of disease, terrorism and insurgence caused by poverty. Prahalad and Hart (2002, p. 4) explain that,

> although complete income equality is an ideological pipe dream, the use of commercial development to bring people out of poverty and give them the chance for a better life is critical to the stability and health of the global economy and the continued success of Western MNCs.

Such strategies unambiguously work to the mutual benefit of business and society.

A number of companies are already using bottom-of-the-pyramid strategies to create wealth, reduce poverty, and thus increase global security. Examples include Hindustan Lever (HLL), which created a new detergent, called Wheel, which now has a 38 percent market share in a market that Unilever, the parent company, never realized existed (Prahalad and Hart, 2002, p. 6). Using a new business model that emphasizes volume rather than high profit margins, Wheel

> was formulated to substantially reduce the ratio of oil to water in the product, responding to the fact that the poor often wash their clothes in rivers and other public water systems. HLL decentralized the production, marketing, and distribution of the product to leverage the abundant labor pool in rural India, quickly creating sales channels through the thousands of small outlets where people at the bottom of the pyramid shop. HLL also changed the cost structure of its detergent business so it could introduce Wheel at a low price point. (Prahalad and Hart, 2002)

In its first five years on the market, Hindustan Lever enjoyed a 20 percent growth in revenue and a 25 percent growth in profits per year (Prahalad and Hart, 2002, p. 5). Prahalad and Hart warn that 'the strategic challenge for managers is to visualize an active market where only abject poverty exists today. It takes tremendous imagination and creativity to engineer a market infrastructure out of a completely unorganized sector' (2002, p. 6).

Other bottom-of-the-pyramid strategies are found, for example, in the area of micro-lending. Companies choosing to embrace micro-lending strategy are making a profit by giving the poor access to reasonable borrowing power, and thus access to buying power:

> According to the International Labor Organization's World Employment Report 2001, nearly a billion people – roughly one-third of the world's work force – are either underemployed or have such low-paying jobs that they cannot support themselves or their families. Helping the world's poor elevate themselves above this desperation line is a business opportunity to do well and do good. (Prahalad and Hart, 2002)

The business opportunity comes from the fact that, under the current system, money lenders in the poorest areas charge as much as 20 percent per day interest. Micro-lenders can charge much less and still make a substantial profit. Whereas the Grameen Bank, founded by Bangladeshi economist Muhammad Yunus, is the highly successful pioneer in this field, micro-lending – offering very small loans at reasonable interest rates and within structures that are accessible to the poor – is now a thriving business for the largest banks in a number of countries. 'At the 1999 Microcredit Summit, the United Nations, in conjunction with several major MNCs, such as Citigroup Inc. and Monsanto Company, set a goal of making basic credit available to the 100 million poorest families in the world by the year 2005' (Prahalad and Hart, 2002, p. 14).

Other examples of bottom-of-the pyramid strategies include Honeywell's interest in offering micro-turbines as small-scale distributed energy solutions to extremely poor communities; The Body Shop's policy, led by founder and former CEO Anita Roddick, of trade-not-aid; and Starbucks' (together with Conservation International's), strategy to eliminate intermediaries from its business model and source coffee directly from farmers in Mexico's Chiapas region, thus enabling the company to provide coffee farmers with a reasonable standard of living and the company with a respectable profit.

As Prahalad and Hart (2002, p. 14) help individual companies embrace these new, highly profitable bottom-of-the-pyramid business strategies, they remind the entire private sector that

> It is tragic that . . . Western capitalists . . . have implicitly assumed that the rich will be served by the corporate sector, while governments and NGOs will protect the poor and the environment. This implicit divide is stronger than most realize. Managers in MNCs, public policymakers, and NGO activists all suffer from the historical division of roles. A huge opportunity lies in breaking this code – linking the poor and the rich across the world in a seamless market organized around the concept of sustainable growth and development. Collectively, we have only begun to scratch the surface of what is the biggest potential market opportunity in the history of commerce. Those in the private sector who commit their companies to a more inclusive capitalism have the opportunity to prosper and share their prosperity with those who are less fortunate. In a very real sense, the fortune at the bottom of the pyramid represents the loftiest of our global goals.

Giving Peace a Chance: Industrial Parks as Tools for Peace

Bottom-of-the-pyramid strategies are by no means the only noteworthy approaches that businesses are successfully employing to enhance societal well-being and the possibilities for peace. Industrialist Stef Wertheimer, founder, former CEO, and Chairman of the Board of ISCAR Ltd, a $1 billion-a-year metal-tool-cutting business, offers a very different, yet compelling, approach. Now 74 years old, this Israeli entrepreneur has expanded his vision beyond profits to include peacemaking. Wertheimer has taken on one of the toughest problems in the world, Middle East peace.

In his and many others' opinions, diplomatic efforts to foster peace in the Middle East have failed. Wertheimer now offers an alternative, the Tefen Model, a unique business-based, cross-culturally integrated industrial-park approach that

> stresses creativity through an unusual combination of aims: providing high quality products to a global market, advancing entrepreneurial education and industrial training, fostering new indigenous industries, and showcasing art and culture. To these ends, the [industrial] parks in Israel, Jordan, and Turkey all have incubator spaces, educational and training facilities, museums, and sculpture gardens.[17]

Using the Tefen Model within Israel, Wertheimer has already built a series of industrial parks that bring together Arab, Druze and Jewish Israelis (Fast 50, 2003). Are they successful? By 2002 the four Israeli industrial parks had launched 150 new firms and had created 5,000 new jobs (Wertheimer, 2002). By 2004 the same four industrial parks accounted for more than $2 billion in annual revenue, representing 10 percent of Israel's total industrial exports (Fast 50, 2003).

Will Wertheimer's network of industrial parks ultimately become a major factor in bringing peace to the Middle East? It is too early to tell, but there are already 10 industrial parks either built or planned for throughout the eastern Mediterranean, including sites in Israel, Jordan, Lebanon, Turkey and Gaza. Many people are optimistic about their current and future success. Wertheimer believes that 'industry is the engine of economic stability', and that without economic stability, there can be no peace (Wertheimer, 2002).

As Wertheimer (2002) graphically stated to the United States Congress, 'The Middle East has a way of besmirching the entire world with its conflicts. It is of global interest to quiet this area.' An industrial development plan for this region based on the Tefen Model would produce a variety of benefits, perhaps the most important of which would be

> a reduction of terrorism worldwide. The majority of the world's terrorists hail from [the Middle East] . . . Terrorism thrives in areas of poverty. Narrowing the gap between the financial status of neighboring countries and enhancing a population's standard of living automatically changes attitudes. Job opportunities and a higher standard of living for people in this area will reduce the power that terrorist groups offer to the deprived masses.

American Evan Kaizer's appreciation of Wertheimer's contribution is perhaps the best summary of the benefits this business model could contribute to the world:

Few individuals have achieved the business success of Stef Wertheimer . . . and then have decided to dwarf the importance of their own contributions to the business marketplace, with their commitment to promoting a peaceful coexistence of warring parties based upon respect and economic vitality. We can all learn from his model. (Fast 50, 2003)

Natural Capitalism: Sustainability at a Profit

In addition to innovating poverty-reduction and Middle-East peace-making strategies, businesses are also involved in highly innovative environment-enhancing strategies. According to the *Harvard Business Review*, 'business strategies built around the radically more productive use of natural resources can solve many environmental problems at a profit' (Lovins et al., 1999). Using the label 'natural capitalism', Amory and Hunter Lovins, along with their colleague Paul Hawken, have introduced a process by which business can gain a competitive edge and earn substantial profits by systemically focusing on the health of the natural environment:[18]

> The first stage [of natural capitalism] involves dramatically increasing the productivity of natural resources, stretching them as much as 100 times further than they do today. In the second stage companies adopt closed-loop production systems that yield no waste or toxicity. The third stage requires a fundamental change of business model – from one of selling products to one of delivering services. For example, a manufacturer would sell lighting services rather than light bulbs, thus benefiting the seller and customer for developing extremely efficient, durable light bulbs. The last stage involves reinvesting in natural capital to restore, sustain, and expand the planet's ecosystem. (Lovins et al., 1999, p. 145)

Why haven't most businesses considered such profit-making, environment-enhancing strategies before? Because the benefits often don't show up on the balance sheet. Most businesses treat the natural environment as a free resource. Yet, as Lovins et al. (1999, p. 145) note,

> recent calculations. . .conservatively estimate the value of all the earth's ecosystem services to be at least \$33 trillion a year. That's close to the gross world product, and it implies a capitalized book value on the order of half a quadrillion dollars. What's more, for most of these services, there is no known substitute at any price, and we can't live without them.

If there are such cost savings to be found in natural capitalism, why didn't business embrace it years ago? The answer is not that business values are somehow skewed or abhorrent, but rather that

> scores of common practices in both the private and public sectors systematically reward companies for wasting natural resources and penalize them for boosting

resource productivity. For example, most companies expense their consumption of raw materials through the income statement but pass resource-saving investment through the balance sheet. That distortion makes it more tax efficient to waste fuel than to invest in improving fuel efficiency . . . The compass that companies use to direct . . . [themselves] is broken. (Lovins et al., 1999, p. 145)

Amory and Hunter Lovins and Paul Hawken offer examples of many companies that are already benefiting from natural capitalism. Perhaps only one example, that of the Interface Corporation, a leading maker of materials for commercial interiors, is needed to tell the much larger and highly optimistic story of what business could be contributing to societal well-being. In Interface's

> new Shanghai carpet factory, a liquid had to be circulated through a standard pumping loop similar to those used in nearly all industries. A top European company designed the system to use pumps requiring a total of 95 horsepower. But before construction began, Interface's engineer, Jan Schilham, realized that two embarrassingly simple design changes would cut that power requirement to only 7 horsepower – a 92% reduction. His redesigned system cost less to build, involved no new technology, and worked better in all respects. (Lovins et al., 1999)

How did Interface succeed in such a significant energy-consumption reduction? They used two small, but highly leveraged innovations.

> First, Schilham chose fatter-than-usual pipes, which create much less friction than thin pipes do and therefore need far less pumping energy. The original designer had chosen thin pipes because, according to the textbook method, the extra cost of fatter ones wouldn't be justified by the pumping energy that they would save. This standard design trade-off optimizes the pipes by themselves but 'pessimizes' the larger system. Schilham optimized the whole system by counting not only the higher capital cost of the fatter pipes but also the lower capital cost of the smaller pumping equipment that would be needed. The pumps, motors, motor controls, and electrical components could all be much smaller because there'd be less friction to overcome. Capital cost would fall far more for the smaller equipment than it would rise for the fatter pipe. Choosing big pipes and small pumps – rather than small pipes and big pumps – would therefore make the whole system cost less to build, even before counting its future energy savings. (Lovins et al., 1999)

The second innovation was to make the pipes straight and short rather than crooked and long, which further reduced the friction. Interface accomplished this

> by laying out the pipes first, then positioning the various tanks, boilers, and other equipment that they connected. Designers normally locate the production equipment in arbitrary positions and then have a pipe fitter connect everything. Awkward placement forces the pipes to make numerous bends that greatly increase friction. The pipe fitters don't mind: they're paid by the hour, they profit from the extra pipes

and fittings, and they don't pay for the oversized pumps or inflated electric bill. . . Schilham's short, straight pipes were easier to insulate, saving an extra 70 kilowatts of heat loss and repaying the insulation's cost in three months. (Lovins et al., 1999, p. 145)

The Interface example has implications far beyond both Interface and China for two reasons:

> First, pumping is the largest application of motors, and motors use three-quarters of all industrial electricity. Second, the lessons are very widely relevant. Interface's pumping loop shows how simple changes in design mentality can yield huge resource savings and returns on investment. (Lovins et al., 1999, p. 145)

Inventing small changes, such as those at Interface, 'that are cheap, free or even better than free' (because they generate big savings) rely on whole-systems thinking (Lovins et al., 1999). With whole-systems thinking, 'the right investment in one part of the system can produce multiple benefits throughout the system' (Lovins et al., 1999).

The logic of natural capitalism is compelling. In the 21st century, unlike during the industrial revolution, natural resources, not people, are scarce. Ultimately, the companies that most effectively manage their scarcest resources will win, as will society. Those that don't will cease to exist. Where natural capitalism can eclipse Wangari Maathai's tree-planting efforts is not in its commitment or values, but rather in the private sector's much higher leverage to make substantial and lasting worldwide changes. As more businesses embrace natural capitalism, however, they would be wise to carefully observe the efforts of such leaders as Shirin Ebadi, Wangari Maathai and Gro Harlem Brundtland when searching for approaches that are most likely to succeed.

FROM DESPAIR TO OPTIMISM: AN ECOLOGY OF HOPE

In his 2004 presidential campaign, United States Congressman Dennis Kucinich described his desire to create a Department of Peace as the first step in 'making nonviolence an organizing principle in society' (Kucinich, 2003). According to Kucinich (2003), 'creating a structure of peace ensures that economic structures can be sound, affirmative of human needs, and restorative of human values'. There is no question that the world needs peace to prosper, and prosperity to have peace. The world, however, cannot attain peace without all of society's primary actors actively working to create the conditions for peace. For too long, business has been left out of that equation. Now, as we enter the 21st century, forward-thinking leaders from all sectors are searching for new partnership options that include business as a co-creator of a society we can be proud of.[19] Increasingly, business is taking the lead in some of the most innovative and exciting initiatives that offer hope for the planet.

Arnold Toynbee, in observing societal dynamics, clearly believed society could do better: 'The [21st] . . . century will be chiefly remembered by future generations not as an era of political conflicts or technical inventions, but as an age in which human society dared to think of the welfare of the whole human race as a practical objective' (Mau, 2004, p. 15).

Joseph Rotblat, after all his warnings about the dire consequences of war, also offers reasons to be hopeful: 'I do not believe that there is scientific evidence that biology condemns humanity to war' (Franck et al., 2000 (p. 71 in 1998 edition)).

Former Prime Minister Golda Meir, likewise offers hope for society changing its thinking and behavior, and achieving heretofore unimaginable aspirations:

> War is an immense stupidity. I'm sure that someday all wars will end. I'm sure that someday children in school will study the history of the men who made war as you study an absurdity. They'll be astonished; they'll be shocked, just as today we're shocked by cannibalism. Even cannibalism was accepted for a long time as normal. And yet today, at least physically, it's not practised any more. (Fallaci, 1976)

NOTES

1. Nobel Peace Prize recipient Joseph Rotblat citing the admonition included in the 1955 Russell-Einstein Manifesto as reported in Rotblat (2005).
2. Raimon Panikkar as cited in Franck et al. (2000).
3. 1955 Russell-Einstein Manifesto as cited in Roblat (2005).
4. Mjøs, 2003. Some of the Nobel Peace Prize Laureates who received their awards primarily for their human rights and democracy work include Albert Lutuli of South Africa in 1960, Martin Luther King in 1964, Andrei Sakharov in 1975, Amnesty International in 1977, Lech Walesa in 1983, Desmond Tutu in 1984, Aung San Suu Kyi in 1991, Rigoberta Menchu in 1992, and Nelson Mandela in 1993.
5. Ibid.
6. Norwegian Nobel Committee (2004) in their press release announcing Wangari Maathai as the recipient of the 2004 Nobel Peace Prize (as cited at Nobelprize.org at http://nobelprize. org/peace/laureates/2004/press.html)
7. Ibid.
8. Speech by Wangari Maathai accepting her Nobel Peace Prize in Oslo, Norway on 10 December 2004 (as cited at Nobelprize.org at www.nobel.no/eng_lect_2004b.html).
9. Nobel Peace Prize Presentation Speech by Professor Ole Danbolt Mjøs, Chairman of the Norwegian Nobel Committee, Oslo, December 10, 2004 to Wangari Maathai as reported at: http://nobelprize.org/peace/laureates/2004/presentation-speech.html
10. Norwegian Nobel Committee (2004) in their press release announcing Wangari Maathai as the recipient of the 2004 Nobel Peace Prize, http://nobelprize.org/peace/laureates/2004/ press.html.
11. For a fuller discussion contrasting the geographically local (domestic) structures of most governments and the multi-domestic structures of most international organizations (such as the United Nations) versus the more globally integrated strategies and structures of most

multinational and global companies, see Adler (1994) and Adler and Ghadar (1993 and 1990).

12. Gro Harlem Brundtland speaking on the BBC program 'Talking Points' on Tuesday, 16 January 2001 as found at http://news.bbc.co.uk/1/hi/talking_point/1108388.stm where she broadcast her 2000 Reich Lecture.

13. Wal-Mart's 2002 revenue on the day after US Thanksgiving was almost $1.5 billion, as cited in Mau et al. (2004), p. 128.

14. Friedman (2005a).

15. Among many other articles, see Sorkin (2005) on the Tyco convictions, McLean and Elkind (2003) for a through description of the Enron scandal, Scott (2005) on the initial Enron convictions, Creswell (2005a) for Citigroup's $2 billion payment for its involvement in the Enron scandal, and Creswell (2005b) for JP Morgan Chase's $2.2 billion payment to its investors for its involvement in the Enron scandal.

16. For a fuller and more in-depth discussion of bottom-of-the-pyramid strategies processes and approaches, see the recently released books by Hart (2005) and Prahalad (2005), along with their articles on the topic, including Prahalad and Hart (2002), Hart and Christensen (2002), and Prahalad and Hammond (2002), among others.

17. Wertheimer, 2002. For a further discussion of Wertheimer's Tefen Model and its implications for peace, see 'Trialogue of cultures in the age of globalization' at the Sinclair House Debates, Herbert-Quandt Stiftung Foundation, www.h-quandt-stiftung.de/root/index.php?lang=en&page_id=333, and Ari Goldberg's 'Israeli tycoon urges help for Palestinians', BBC News on-line at http://news.bbc.co.uk/1/hi/business/1944846.stm.

18. In addition to their excellent *Harvard Business Review* article, for an in-depth discussion of natural capitalism, see Hawken et al.'s (1999) *Natural Capitalism: Creating the Next Industrial Revolution*. For further discussion on the role of business in protecting the environment, see the journals *Green@work* and *Reflections* (2000), **1**(4) special issue on sustainability. In addition see Lovins et al.'s (2000) *Harvard Business Review on Business and the Environment;* Nattrass et al.'s (1999) *The Natural Step for Business*; McDonough and Braungart's (2002) *Cradle to Cradle*; and Laszlo's (2003) *The Sustainable Company: How to Create Lasting Value Through Social and Environmental Performance.*

19. For a particularly important and innovative approach, see the Ethical Globalization Initiative (www.eginitiative.org), founded and led by Mary Robinson, the former President of Ireland and former executive director of the United Nation's Human Rights Commission.

REFERENCES

Adler, N. (1994), 'Globalization, government, and competitiveness', *Optimum*, **25**(1), 27–34.

Adler, N.J. and F. Ghadar (1993), 'A strategic phase approach to international human resource management', in D. Wong-Rieger and F. Rieger (eds), *International Management Research: Looking to the Future*, Berlin: deGruyter, pp. 55–77.

Adler, N.J. and F. Ghadar (1990), 'Strategic human resource management: a global perspective', in R. Pieper (ed.), *Human Resource Management in International Comparison*, Berlin: deGruyter, pp. 235–60.

Annan, K. (1999), World Economic Forumspeech initiating the UN Global Compact, Davos, Switzerland, www.aiccafrica.com/PDF%20files/Global%20Compact%20Handout.pdf.

Aspen Institute and World Resource Institute (2003), report ranking business schools and their social impact, 8 October.

Brundtland, G.H. (2001), 2000 Reich Lecture, presented on BBC's 'Talking Points', http://news.bbc.co.uk/1/hi/talking-point/1108388.stm, 16 January.

Caputo, P. (2005), *Acts of Faith*, New York: Alfred A. Knopf.

Creswell, J. (2005a), 'Citigroup agrees to pay $2 billion in Enron scandal', *New York Times*, 11 June.

Creswell, J. (2005b), 'J.P. Morgan Chase to pay investors $2.2 billion', *New York Times*, 15 June.

Fallaci, O. (1976), *Interviews with History*, Boston, MA: Houghton Mifflin.

'Fast 50 – 2003 winners: meet the winners' (2003), complement to the March 2003 *Fast Company* print edition, www.fastcompany.com/fast50_04/2003winners.html.

Franck, F., J. Roze and R. Connolly (eds) (2000), *What Does It Mean to be Human?* New York: St. Martin's Press, originally published (1998), Nyack, NY: Circumstantial Productions Publishing.

Friedman, M. (1970), 'The social responsibility of business is to increase its profits', *New York Times Magazine*, 13 September, pp. 32–3, 122–26.

Friedman, T.L. (2005a), 'C.E.O.s, M.I.A', *New York Times*, op-ed, 25 May.

Friedman, T.L. (2005b), 'It's a flat world, after all', *New York Times*, op-ed, 3 April.

Hart, S.L. (2005), *Capitalism at the Crossroads*, Upper Saddle River, NJ: Wharton School Publishing (Pearson Education).

Hart, S. and C.M. Christensen (2002), 'The great leap: driving innovation from the base of the pyramid', *Sloan Management Review*, **44**(1), 51–6.

Hawken, P., A. Lovins and L.H. Lovins (1999), *Natural Capitalism: Creating the Next Industrial Revolution*, Boston, MA: Little Brown & Company.

Kakutani, M. (2005), 'For Americans in Sudan, good deeds turn sour', *New York Times*, 3 May.

Kucinich, D.J. (2003), 'Iraq and the economy', swearing-in ceremony, Cleveland, OH, www.commandreams.org/views03/0113-05.htm.

Laszlo, C. (2003), *The Sustainable Company: How to Create Lasting Value Through Social and Environmental Performance*, Washington, DC: Island Press.

Lovins, A.B., H. Lovins and P. Hawken (1999), 'A road map for natural capitalism', *Harvard Business Review*, May–June: 145–58.

Lovins, A.B., H. Lovins, P. Hawken, F. Reinhardt, R. Shapiro and J. Magretta (2000), *Harvard Business Review on Business and the Environment*, Boston, MA: Harvard Business School Publishing.

Mau, B. and The Institute without Boundaries (2004), *Massive Change*, London: Phaidon Press.

McDonough, W. and M. Braungart (2002), *Cradle to Cradle*, New York: North Point Press.

McLean, B. and P. Elkind (2003), *The Smartest Guys in the Room: The Amazing Rise and Scandalous Fall of Enron*, New York: Portfolio (Penguin Group).

Mjøs, O.D. (2003), 'The Nobel Peace Prize for 2003', the Norwegian Nobel Committee announcing Shirin Ebadi, the 2003 recipient, 10 December, Oslo, Norway, www.nobel.no/eng_lect_2003a.html.

Mjøs, O.D. (2004), 'The Nobel Peace Prize for 2004', the Norwegian Nobel Committee announcing Wangari Maathai as the 2004 recipient, 10 December, Oslo, Norway, www.nobelprize.org/peace/laureates/2004/presentation-speech.html.

Nattrass, B. and M. Altomare (1999), *The Natural Step for Business*, Gabriola Island, BC, Canada: New Society.

Prahalad, C.K. (2005), *The Fortune at the Bottom of the Pyramid: Eradicating Poverty Through Profits*, Upper Saddle River, NJ: Wharton School Publishing (Pearson Education).

Prahalad, C.K. and A. Hammond (2002), 'Serving the world's poor, profitably', *Harvard Business Review*, **80**(9), 48–57.

Prahalad, C.K. and S.L. Hart (2002), 'The fortune at the bottom of the pyramid', *Strategy + Business*, **26** (1st quarter), 2–14.

Rotblat, J. (2005), 'The 50-year shadow', *New York Times*, 17 May.

Schwab, K. (2003), 'Capitalism must develop more of a conscience', *Newsweek*, 24 February, pp. 41–2.

Scott, A.O. (2005), 'Those you love to hate: a look at the mighty laid low', *New York Times*, 22 April.

Sorkin, R. (2005), 'Ex-chief and aide guilty of looting millions at Tyco', *New York Times*, 18 June.

Wertheimer, S. (2002), 'Statement by Stef Wertheimer', hearing of the United States House Committee on International Relations, Washington, DC, 24 June, www.israelnewsagency.com/stefwertheimer.html.

The Worldwatch Institute (2005), *State of the World 2005: Redefining Global Security*, Washington, DC: Worldwatch Institute.

12. Managing in an era of terrorism

David Gillingham

INTRODUCTION

This chapter views terrorist acts as an extreme form of system failure (Bricklin, 2004). The management of a business in an environment in which terrorist acts may be directed against the firm is therefore seen as a specific application of the management of human errors. The overall analytical framework applied to this situation is the integrated model of error management (Gillingham et al., 1997).

EXTERNAL ENVIRONMENT

From the business perspective, the external environment is the source of terrorism. In most cases the business enterprise will not be the direct cause of terrorist activities. However, the manager needs to understand the external environment in order to be both better prepared for terrorist actions and to be involved as an actor in possible solutions.

While terrorists themselves are rarely from poor or underprivileged backgrounds, nevertheless it is clear that poverty, unemployment, inequality and perceived injustice are the breeding grounds for the causes which terrorists support. There have been terrorist groups active in developed countries but the vast majority of terrorist activities are related to injustices (PLO), nationalist ideals (IRA) and religious fundamentalism linked to other causes (al-Qaeda). Managers cannot change these fundamental problems but they can contribute to the debate, and they can participate in local actions to improve conditions in their markets.

International business leaders can support movements that seem to have a positive effect in reducing terrorism, such as Hernando de Soto's Institute for Liberty and Democracy. Business leaders can also establish charitable foundations to alleviate the major problems that afflict the world; the most obvious example is The Bill and Melinda Gates Foundation. They can also lead initiatives which may be effective in increasing security such as improved airline security and advanced tracking mechanisms for shipping.

CORPORATE ENVIRONMENT

In an environment which has become somewhat riskier, it is important that the organization develops its own system for assessing the risk of terrorist activities on its operations (Schmidt and Quinley, 2002). The challenge is to design systems and manage them in a way that takes account of possible terrorist attacks.

A centralized company will be more at risk than a decentralized company. Not only will a decentralized company have more resilience but it will also be a less attractive target for terrorists. An apparently large company strongly linked to a single national culture is a much more attractive target than a diffused decentralized company with many brands and heavy local involvement.

A company that is seen as caring for its local employees and customers, which is well integrated into the local economy and showing understanding and tolerance of the local culture, is much less likely to be seen as a good target. On the other hand, a company that is seen as part of an invading and imperial power naturally becomes a soft target for terrorists. In this regard companies need to ensure that their advertising and other public activities are not likely to cause offence to local cultures.

MANAGER AND MANAGED

Information Collection

Managers need to ensure that they create an information system that is gathering information, including 'soft' signals that may be the precursors of greater things to come. Companies will need to encourage whistleblowers at all levels to ensure that they are picking up early warning signals. It is important to realize that members of the public may be the first to identify a threat and that the mass media may be the most important source of information once an incident starts evolving (Bricklin, 2004).

In international operations it will be important to have speakers of native languages who are empowered enough to report any signals, no matter how low-level or intermittent they may be. Companies whose dominant culture is centred in a normally safe environment are likely to ignore information from sources outside their home country.

Assessing the Situation

The challenge is to design and manage systems in a way in which risks can be assessed and reduced. Risk assessment needs to be built into the culture of decision-making so that unnecessary exposure to terrorist attacks is avoided. A crucial step will be to carry out a risk assessment. Publicly available information includes data from government agencies such as the British MI5, the Foreign and Commonwealth Office, and the CIA. All of these provide current information and advice on their websites. Commercial agencies also provide custom services such as All Hands Consulting, who provide threat assessment programs and training courses, and STRATFOR, who provide terrorist threat intelligence services. One way of assessing your company's risk is to complete the following checklist:

1. Is your company name associated with a target country (that is, currently those associated with the war in Iraq)?
2. Do you occupy high profile buildings?
3. Do you operate in high risk countries?
4. Do you operate in high risk industries (that is, tourism, energy, transport or banking)?
5. Does your company have a high media profile?

A quick analysis shows that Nestlé would have a low score in all but high risk countries, whereas Microsoft would score more highly. On this basis Microsoft should be prepared to invest more heavily in counter-terrorism than Nestlé.

Assessing the Required Action

There is little doubt that most companies are failing to prepare for terrorist attacks. A British survey found that only 45 percent of companies had business continuity or consequence management plans in place (The Foreign Policy Centre, 2002). A survey in the USA by Guardsmark found that 70 percent of businesses were complacent about the terrorist threat (Continuity Central, 2003). This is probably because the perceived threat is either seen as low or, because of the apparent randomness of attacks, it is seen as unpredictable. In such situations management commonly believes there is little point in preparing action plans. However, thinking through the necessary actions to prevent or respond to a terrorist attack on the company will frequently prepare the company for a range of possible failures, from terrorist violations to simple human error.

The challenge is to manage all employees in a way in which there is a common understanding of the terrorist threat. All staff need to understand that minor security lapses can open the door for a major incident to occur.

The strategy that a company adopts can be guided by the matrix shown in Table 12.1. This compares the risk inherent in the environment with the risk

Table 12.1 Environmental security risk vs company exposure strategy matrix

	Low environmental security risk	High environmental security risk
Low company exposure risk	Do not invest heavily (for example ABB in Germany)	Invest heavily in security risk reduction (for example ABB in Indonesia)
High company exposure risk	Invest heavily in exposure risk reduction (for example McDonalds in Germany)	Invest heavily in both security and exposure risk reduction (for example McDonalds in Indonesia)

resulting from the factors inherent to the company. Certain countries are much more risky than others; where this risk is high it pays companies to invest heavily in reducing the risk to the company from environmental factors. For example, companies can disperse their local operations to reduce risk or move offshore and use local agents. Some companies are more exposed than others to terrorist attacks. If they operate in consumer markets and are associated with certain countries then they are at greater risk. Companies can combat these risks by investing more heavily in security systems and promoting their local connections.

Assessing Probable Consequences

Companies need to work through a range of what-if scenarios in order to predict the likely consequences of a terrorist attack. These scenarios need to be wide-ranging and not constrained by what has happened before. The distinctive feature of terrorist attacks is that they are prepared to do the unthinkable.

UNSAFE ACTS

Quite often terrorist activities are carried out with the assistance of company staff. Hence one defence mechanism is to ensure that the company has appropriate personnel selection and hiring procedures (Czinkota et al., 2004). Employee screening which includes thorough checks on background, including educational qualifications, work history and personal references, becomes an essential part of creating a safer system. However, companies must be equally satisfied that supplier companies have good screening in place.

Many companies are busy places and, like airports, will have large numbers of staff who require access to sensitive areas. They will also have suppliers whose employees will also have access to the companies' facilities and systems. Yet most companies have inadequate security systems. Still others have good systems that are not updated regularly. The end result is that the majority of companies are vulnerable to attack by terrorists because of the everyday occurrence of minor violations, slips and lapses. Where a high risk exists, companies should consider more advanced technological systems which guarantees the swift and accurate identification of all individuals that have access to sensitive areas (tssi, 2005). The challenge is to design systems that detect potential opportunities for terrorists to attack the company.

INCIDENT MANAGEMENT

Defence Systems

Once part of a company's operations comes under attack from terrorists then the system for defending the company should come into operation. Companies therefore need to ensure that their systems can cope with known terrorist actions. The challenge is to design and manage systems that can tolerate terrorist attacks. For example, most companies were able to recover after September 11, but a few – those who had concentrated all their reserves in a single location – were not. Kidnapping is a common tactic used by terrorists, so all companies with personnel in certain countries need to have a plan for how they will deal with a kidnapping, which will need to vary by country and terrorist group. For some the solution will be simply about money; for others it may be much more difficult. Companies need to carefully analyse past terrorist activities to ensure they are well prepared for all eventualities.

Well-informed and well-trained employees are likely to be an effective part of any company defence system (Bricklin, 2004). It was the airline crew and passengers who thwarted the shoe-bomber. The challenge is to create conditions that enable each individual employee to take up activities that result in changed behavior. If all staff are alert to the potential threat then the company is much more likely to prevent, detect in advance, manage and survive a terrorist attack.

Incident Management

Once the incident has started management will need to invoke their emergency plan. In almost all cases there will be heavy media coverage. Indeed, the mass media may well become the most effective means of sharing information.

Individuals close to the incident are likely to be communicating with loved ones by mobile phone and simultaneously tuning into radio, television or the internet (Bricklin, 2004). Managers need to be able to tap into these informal communications if they are to be equally well informed.

It will be important for the CEO to be seen to be in charge and to be seen as caring about those who are personally involved. The company must be seen to be putting public safety and employee welfare first, before the financial interests of the firm. The Tylenol case illustrates this situation very well. Its rapid response in alerting customers not to use Tylenol capsules in 1982, and the total recall of all stock, not only reduced the risks of further deaths but also promoted a positive image of the manufacturer, Johnson & Johnson (Broom, 1994).

Post-Incident Management

Companies must have succession and relocation plans in place (The Foreign Policy Centre, 2002) if they are to recover quickly from a major terrorist incident. They also need to think about how they will manage their public relations. Once again Tylenol provides a good case example. Tylenol re-introduced capsules in new tamper-proof packaging together with an appropriate communications strategy.

Inquiries

When incidents do occur managers need to ensure that appropriate learning takes place. The challenge is to design the organization in such a way that it constantly learns from past terrorist attacks. If a terrorist group is successful against one target then it is likely that the tactic will be repeated against new targets. Hence companies need to develop processes by which they rapidly learn from past incidents inside and outside their company to ensure they are prepared for any eventuality. However it is not uncommon for such incidents to be treated as one-off occurrences, which is seldom the case!

WHAT COULD COMPANIES HAVE DONE ABOUT 09/11?

If companies had been collecting information about terrorist risks then their research would have revealed that the World Trade Center was a likely target, as there had been a previous attack and there was an overt threat of another attack on this target (Weir, 2004). Companies located in the WTC, or nearby, could have relocated to other less vulnerable sites. If they perceived that they needed to stay at this location then they could have reduced their presence, reducing their vulnerability whilst ensuring that they had adequate insurance coverage for their operations and their employees. Most of the companies involved probably did not have emergency plans in place, nor did they have business continuity systems ready to take over operations.

CONCLUSION

Whilst the current risk of terrorist attacks against companies appears to be falling (Kellerhals, 2003) nevertheless businesses must be prepared for all eventualities. Unless the Middle East becomes a more peaceful area it is likely that the Iraq war will have bred a new generation of anti-Western terrorists ready to target Western business interests. Other groups with grievances are likely to take up terrorist tactics at any moment. Furthermore, national governments are limited in what they can achieve. Businesses need to become more involved in counter-terrorism, otherwise they represent a soft target for terrorists (The Foreign Policy Centre, 2002).

The basic premise of this chapter is that whilst we can do little to reduce the overall risk of terrorism we can improve the chances that our company will not be attacked and, if attacked, we can improve its chances of survival. The challenge is to design management systems which are more likely to detect terrorist threats, more likely to thwart any attack, and more likely to survive any attack. The study of the management of human error in other fields provides some guidance to the management of companies in an era of terrorism.

REFERENCES

Bricklin, D. (2004), accessed 7 September at www.bricklin.com/learningfrom accidents.htm.

Broom, G.M., A.H. Center and S.M. Cutlip (1994), *Effective Public Relations*, 7th edn, Upper Saddle River, NJ: Prentice-Hall.

Continuity Central (2003), Portal Publishing.

Czinkota, M.R., G.A. Knight and P.W. Liesch (2004), 'Terrorism and international business: conceptual foundations', in G. Suder (ed.), *Terrorism and the International Business Environment: The Security–Business Nexus*, Cheltenham, UK and Northampton, MA, USA: Edward Elgar, pp. 43–57.

The Foreign Policy Centre (2002), 'The unlikely counter-terrorists', London, UK: The Foreign Policy Centre.

Gillingham, D.W., J. Blanco and J. Lewko (1997), 'An integrated model of error management', *Disaster Prevention and Management*, **6**(3), 186–90.

Kellerhals, M.D. (2003), 'The Washington file', US Department of State, 30 April.

Schmidt, D.L. and K.M. Quinley (2002), *Business at Risk: How to Assess, Mitigate, and Respond to Terrorist Threats*, Cincinatti, OH: The National Underwriter Co.

tssi (2005) www.tssi.co.ukopencms/opencms/tssi/Products_x_Services/identification systems/index.html.

Weir, D.H. (2004), 'Disaster management after September 11: a "normal accident" or a "man-made disaster"? What did we know, what have we learned?' in G. Suder (ed.) *Terrorism and the International Business Environment: The Security-Business Nexus*, Cheltenham, UK and Northampton, MA, USA: Edward Elgar, pp. 201–16.

13. Always consider problems as opportunities

David A.C. Suder

'Our worst enemies are inside us'
Jacques Chirac, French President

INTRODUCTION

There are subjects more difficult to address than others. To speak of terrorism as an opportunity is one of the difficult ones. Still the core management statement 'always consider problems as opportunities' should be explored in this matter like any other.

I recall the time when, as an MBA student, I had been stunned by one of the professors who asked us a surprising question: 'What is the price of a human life?' Everybody in the classroom answered that life doesn't have any price. After a period of silence, this professor asked us, 'So what is a life insurance?'

Our analysis of the question, like the one you might just have had, is correct when thinking on an individual level. However, it doesn't apply when considering the equilibrium of the world. As hard as it sounds, the cost of alternatives will always be compared to define the most relevant solution, even when life has to be the pricing value.

The objective of this chapter is to explain that terrorism as a major problem of humanity is also a unique opportunity for the world. An historical overlook of the driving forces of world stability will help, and is conducted by revisiting the concepts of the enemy to understand the inevitable limits of today's world order. We will then see how political unity will help promote the development of business and why the geopolitical status quo of the pre-09/11 world order was a limitation to the achievement of the global economy.

Terrorism is nothing new in history. What is new is its international dimension and the consequences it will have on our societies and on our economies. In this respect one should consider it as an opportunity, and not as a problem.

CONCEPTS OF THE ENEMY

After the Cold War, three main streams of thoughts have defined the enemy. In 'The clash of civilisations and the remaking of world order', Samuel P. Huntington predicted in 1996 that conflicts would be based on cultural differences and not on ideological or economical factors. His conception of civilization takes objective elements such as language, history and institutions into account but relies mainly on subjective elements such as religion (Huntington, 1993).

For Huntington, the enemy is the civilization to which people do not belong. This concept challenges the will of the western countries to promote values that are considered universal, such as human rights.

Another proposition was made by extension of Marxist doctrines. The theory of dependence argues that western countries maintain their own development through pressure on the Third World. Samir Amin (1992) and Immanuel Wallerstein have extensively developed this theory, which can be summarized as a class struggle on an international level.

The last major stream of thought, the Transnationalists, argue that enemies do not exist anymore and have been replaced by evil networks, consisting of a multitude of threats out of which no one side prevails. Such enemies are driven irrationally and can be associated with the barbarians of the Middle Ages. This approach is, for example, developed by Forget and Polycarpe in their book *Le réseau et l'infini* (1997).

All these propositions have strengths and weakness. Strengths, because they explain historical situations or predicted close future events. Weakness or limits, because none of them is self-sufficient enough to propose a long-term solution.

The civilization model ignores that economic development helps different cultures to converge toward the universal values of democracies. One only needs to observe the recent evolution of Chinese society to reach this conclusion.

The dependence model ignores the work of John Nash. In 1950, he published his 'Nash equilibrium' in the Proceedings of the National Academy of Sciences about turning rivalries to mutual gain. Although enormous efforts still have to be made to erase the consequences of decades of colonialism, recent propositions of the western country leaders show a thorough understanding of the benefit of Nash proposition. It is now widely accepted that the development of Third World countries offers many more advantages than drawbacks. At the same time, world GDP grows twice as fast as that of Europe.

As for the barbarians, one should consider that human evolution has constantly relied on exchange and networking to increase its overall intelligence and efficiency. Individuals might not be much cleverer today than 5,000 years ago, they just profit from the experience of previous generations and the extensive communication opportunities. Networking can't become a threat by itself. As for the ideas, they take us back to some sort of a civilization model (Reeves et al., 1996).

Therefore it is necessary to come back to a more basic definition of the enemy. As Colonel John A. Warden III puts it, an enemy is a system composed of many elements organized around accomplishing a central function. Such a definition fits terrorism in every respect.

THE WORLD HAS AN ENEMY

After the Cold War, conventional enemies disappeared. Alexeï Arbatov, a Russian Ambassador, summarized this situation in one sentence: 'What we've done worst is to deprive you of an enemy.' The world was missing a vital element of its organization since the beginning of civilization. As Archimedes said in the third century BC: 'Give me a support point and I will lift the world'. But the support point of the enemy had faded away.

Instead, the opposition came more and more from minorities, and this trend is likely to continue. Since the Cold War, 129 out of the 187 conflicts took place inside of a national state. Minorities have also used terrorism more and more as the violent way of expressing their opposition. They have, at the same time, understood that no matter what the ideology is, they have an interest to cooperate with each other to increase their striking power. As such, terrorism proposes an alternative to structure world organization. The network of terrorist groups represents a single enemy that needs to be fought as a whole.

However, the main evolution is that this enemy is at the same time inside and outside of the defender. Each state has to face this new paradigm. 'Think global and act local' said Claude Bébéard, ex-president of Axa, a French insurance company. What was proposed to company leaders as a management attitude has been put into practice by organized elements to accomplish a central function, terror.

The United States of America reacted after the 09/11 aggression with a natural and historically conventional attitude toward an enemy. Go and get him by yourself wherever he is. The war in Afghanistan and then Iraq has shown the limits of this ancient approach to the problem and has started to draw the lines of the solution to come.

WHAT WAS LEARNED FROM THE INVASION OF IRAQ?

The war on Iraq made us understand two major changes in the conventional approach toward the elimination of this new enemy. The first is that one state cannot solve the problem of terrorism alone. The second is that one cannot chose between force and diplomacy.

You can't do it alone. Unless one considered (and succeeded) invading all the countries on earth (which presents its own problems) it is not possible to solve the problem of terrorism alone.

The military strength of the United States, which can without contest be considered the strongest in the world, has not been sufficient to stop the enemy in its terrorist form. Forty-three days after the beginning of the war, on 1 May 2003, President Bush announced the end of combat. This would be considered, in a conventional fight against a conventional enemy, the end of the war.

The casualties over that period amounted to 172. The new element is that on 1 June 2005 the casualties were 1,851 (MoD, 2005) – ten times more after the end of the war than during it. This figure shows that a state knows how to fight another state, but it doesn't know how to fight a global and fragmented enemy like a terrorist network.

The clash between France and the US over the invasion of Iraq illustrates that the solution is neither purely diplomatic nor purely military. Both countries knew that the best approach lay in between these two extremes, but still each emphasized one above the other.

These events helped the French, and to some extent the Europeans, understand that force remains the basic element of peace-making. The comfortable solution of relying on the transatlantic friend is not sufficient, and the time had come for the EU to propose a serious alternative. On the other hand, the events helped the US realize that the law of the strongest is not a long-term solution. Military power isn't everything, and perhaps more in the case of terrorism than in any other. Only diplomatic anticipation of the conflict can safeguard the outcome of the war.

THE POLITICAL WORLD FINALLY JOINS THE BUSINESS WORLD

The only way to fight the new world enemy efficiently is to fight it on that very same scale – the world scale. And only a drastic development in world politics can ensure the basis of the structure that will in turn ensure victory. This will lead each state to cooperate with the others. Even the US will not be able to provide national security without the cooperation of other nations.

By considering that the defender needs to adapt its size to the problem, it becomes clear that the United Nations should take over the problem. This will require a political organization more important than the one currently enacted through the integration process of the European Union. This cooperation will require a greater integration of the economical resources to finance the entire process and will be the first step toward the creation of major business opportunities.

As a consequence, political and economical barriers will fall. This has historically increased business. In addition, the regulator is very often at the origin of entirely new markets and it is likely that this will continue to be the case.

This process might sound like an utopia, but it is nothing new. The Paris Peace Conference accepted the proposal to create the League of Nations on 25 January 1919. And US President Woodrow Wilson, one of the main architects of the league, laid down on 8 January 1918 the 14th point of his foundation of world peace: 'A general association of nations must be formed under specific covenants for purpose of affording mutual guarantees of political independence and territorial integrity to great and small States alike' (Wilson, 1918). At that time, the world enemy had a different shape. Now, when the enemy is both inside and outside of each nation state, Wilson's proposition becomes the most relevant alternative.

Globalization is the concentration of time and space. This business phenomenon is becoming a reality for geopolitical considerations. Mathematics tells us that, to control a system, one must be of a greater complexity than that targeted system. As a political phenomenon this is known as integration.

CONCLUSION

The concept of the enemy remains a valid model for international construction, national organization and the integration of states. With terrorism as the new world enemy in its diverse shapes and networks, the political sphere will be forced to increase cooperation and integration. This reaction will finally converge as the League of Nations imagined at the beginning of the 20th century to ensure global security.

This integration phenomenon will procure stability and will in turn increase exchange, growth and welfare. Business opportunities will emerge through the increased action of the regulator and the limitation of economic barriers. Protectionist measures, through security stipulations mounted by regulators, will need to be abandoned because they do not solve the problem.

The truth is that violence is an integral part of human interaction when facing a real or perceived threat. Casualties resulting from this enemy will help create a more stable world order.

How beautiful life would be if violence would not exist, but this is not so. One should weigh this contribution of humanity with the deaths of 55 million people during the Second World War. This was the price of the foundations of the United Nations and the European Union, two institutions that the world should be grateful for. If we consider that the enemy is an inevitable component of humanity, then, in this sense, terrorism is an opportunity.

REFERENCES

Amin, S. (1992), *Les enjeux stratégiques en Méditerranée*, Paris: L'Harmattan.

Forget, P. and G. Polycarpe (1997), *Le réseau et l'infini*, Paris: Economica.

Huntington, S.P. (1993), 'The clash of civilizations?', *Foreign Affairs*, **72**(3), 22–49.

Department of Defense press releases various, accessed from DoD, CENTCOM and CJTF7 and at the British Ministry of Defence website, www.mod.uk.

Nash, J.F. (1950), *Proceedings of the National Academy of Sciences*, **36**, 48–9.

Reeves, H., J. de Rosnay, Y. Coppens and D. Simonnet (1996), 'La plus belle histoire du monde', Seuil.

Wilson, W. (1918), address to the joint session of the US Congress, 8 January.

14. Concluding remarks

Gabriele G.S. Suder

This volume of selected contributions about *Corporate Strategies Under International Terrorism and Adversity* evolves on the basis of Terrorism and the International Business Environment, in which we argue that a 'transitivity' has developed, of (a) globalization, (b) increased systemic vulnerability and complexity, and (c) the development of 09/11-type terrorism that prevails in the international business environment, reflecting that the trade-off between security and business has undergone profound changes.

In the current volume, we have not only studied costs and risks to the international firm, but also modellized adaptation and opportunity scenarios. The volume was organized into four parts. Each of them studied a particular phenomenon that international business has to respond to and deal with. All of them are subject to the complexities and linkages of firms, industries, organizational structures, international relations and markets, but also of terrorism networks.

In Part I, networks were analysed. Mason Carpenter and Alexander Stajkovic looked at 'Social network theory and methods as tools for helping business confront global terrorism: capturing the case and contingencies presented by dark social networks'. The chapter emphasizes the importance of social network theories and social network research methodologies to the study of global terrorism and its relationship with both purely domestic and transnational business organizations. Using the contrasting lenses of bright versus dark social networks, the aim is to show how social network structure and theoretical constructs might be viewed differently from a dark social networks perspective. Building on this conceptual framework, specific methodologies were proposed by which social network may be empirically studied. Our hope is that this framework and analytical tool may foster future research and substantive progress in combating the global terrorist threat.

In the following chapter, 'Speeding up strategic foresight in a dangerous and complex world: a compexity approach', Bill McKelvey and Max Boisot started out with Ashby's Law of Requisite Variety that is updated to 'requisite complexity' and used to analyse the nature of the security challenges that nation states and firms face in the 21st century. Effective counter-terrorism requires more than just 'filling in the dots'. Given the trillions of possible patterns that a few dots can generate, the cognitive challenge of quickly reducing the vast complexity of externally emergent patterns far exceeds the organizational capacities of government agencies, no matter how well equipped these might be. In the real world, the trade-off between generating data and generating meaningful patterns is time-constrained. Under competitive conditions, rapid pattern recognition becomes a weapon in a cognitive arms race between adversaries – whoever generates adaptive responses to external complexity in timely fashion has an advantage. The need for rapid pattern recognition may thus set a limit to the amount of data that can usefully be collected and processed by a human-only hierarchy. This is a new problem that traditional technologies and ways of organizing were never designed to cope with.

In chapter 4, both authors study 'National security as a socio/computational process'. Under competitive conditions, rapid pattern recognition becomes a weapon in a cognitive arms race between adversaries. The need to generate adaptive responses in a timely fashion sets a limit to the amount of data that can usefully be collected and processed by a human-only hierarchy. This is a new problem that traditional technologies and ways of organizing cannot cope with. Two new methods are suggested: (1) to reduce Ashby's external complexity (as seen in Chapter 3), contextual tensions, different vantage perspectives and corroboration over time are used to simplify external pattern proliferation in timely fashion – moving from possible to probable and actionable patterns; and (2) to create, activate, and speed up the formation of internal complexity as a means of rapidly reducing external complexity, a socio/computational semi-autonomic human connectionist network consisting of two elements is developed: (a) distributed intelligence is created via the use of a large number of heterogeneous human agents using state-of the-art detectors and mobile phones, and (b) neural network and structural equation models located in a central intelligence organization are advocated.

With Part II, we study the strategic behavior of international firms. 'Terror incognito: international business in an era of heightened geopolitical risk' is the chapter in which David Wernick explains the broad agreement that the terrorist attacks of 09/11 altered the international business environment in a fundamental way. Indeed, surveys of senior US and European corporate executives post-09/11 have shown that terrorism has risen from a peripheral concern to a major preoccupation and that expenditure on security-related equipment and services has increased sharply since the attacks. Beyond the threat of direct attacks against personnel and physical assets, international firms now face a number of new macro-level concerns, among them disruption risk caused by attacks against key suppliers and the critical commercial infrastructure (for example airlines, sea freighters and information networks) that underpins the global economy. There is also a growing worry that hastily enacted governmental antiterrorist regulations could disrupt well-oiled supply chains and add layers of bureaucracy and uncertainty that impede business performance. Traditionally, terrorism has been viewed by academics and corporate risk officers as a country-specific threat akin to expropriation, labor unrest and other forms of political risk. This chapter argues that such a formulation is anachronistic in a world where economies are increasingly integrated, technology is cheap and ubiquitous, borders are porous, and terrorist groups are increasingly lethal, decentralized and global in reach. As such, new approaches are needed to assess and manage a wide range of geopolitical risks confronting international firms, of which transnational terrorism is the most serious.

Chapter 6 provides insights into 'Country risk spillovers in the Middle East: a prelude to the road map for peace and the war on terror'. Ilan Alon and D.L. McKee study the fact that political upheavals in the Middle East are not uncommon. They include domestic conflicts, such as the Islamic revolution of Iran, and external hostilities, such as the Arab–Israeli wars. These events affect the perceptions of foreign investors who shy away from these countries since they seek stable environments for their moneys. While the effects of political risk events on foreign direct investment have been investigated by numerous researchers, the influence of one country's political occurrences on investors' perceptions of a neighboring country has been largely ignored. The purpose of this study is to investigate such an influence by examining the political risk spillovers between selected nations of the Middle East. Nations selected include Egypt, Iran, Iraq, Israel, Jordan, Kuwait and Saudi Arabia. The chapter finds that strong correlations exist in bankers' perceptions of country risk in these countries.

With the sequence of these chapters, we moved from political risk to country risk. Next, we read about 'Terrorism and financial management' and risk issues. Raj Aggarwal's chapter explored how terrorism is changing the nature of the finance function in companies. Cutting financial flows to the bad guys has been a key goal of US and other governments especially since 09/11. With the passage of the USA Patriot Act, US companies and financial institutions must now comply with tough new regulations regarding financial transfers. Firms may also have to operate with higher levels of working capital, reduce financial leverage, fortify defenses against takeovers and place much greater emphasis on risk management and information system security. These new requirements to fight terrorism also mean changes in supply chains, finance operations and corporate strategy. These are significant changes and have important implications for all senior finance executives and members of boards of directors.

Part III of the book examines corporate management and performance issues that encompass internationalization and location decisions, global supply chain management, and brand portfolio challenges.

Chapter 8 analyses the important challenges of choosing or changing a business location that may influence the degree of direct and indirect consequences of terrorism on business operations. 'Location decisions, or: modelling operational risk management under international terrorism' is hence a chapter that is based on the main theories of internationalization, resource management and of operational risk studies. It studies risk avoidance and risk aversion behaviors of manufacturing firms and categorizes modes of entry by cost and opportunity, and risk and return, and positions those into relation with the international value chain and the return of investments into particular typologies of locations. Operational risk management can limit potential loss through the mapping of entry and exit strategies or modes of adaptation to market situations, given the intra-firm risk assessment of locations on the basis of tacit and explicit knowledge criteria. From the relations established in the model of this chapter result the probability (in terms of operational risk management) with which each location receives a certain type of investment. The approaches developed best lead to a cartography exercise that allows for a strategy away from highly concentrated operations and towards a certain flexibility and diversification of risk: for certain operations, for example, a semi-globalization made in multidimensional intermediate stages of localization and integration may allow a respect of the 'ecology of places'. The model developed here ideally allows an easy classification of location categories along return aspects, in order, on the business level, to "take decisive action to eliminate the threat they [the terrorists] pose" (Bush, 2002 on Homeland Security issues) and to anticipate these also in terms of the flexibility necessary when applying entry, adaptation or exit strategies, for example when turning to risk aversion if the risk-return evaluation is not conclusive.

John McIntyre and Eric Ford Travis, in the following chapter, explained that the global supply chain, in the words of Thomas Friedman, has 'flattened' the notions of geography and distance and compressed transactional time, linking all stakeholders in a value-added chain. This chain is a central pillar of the global economic edifice. Disrupting it will cause countries and their firms to lose competitive advantage and economic development gains. The global supply chain can therefore be analogized to oil resources. Any country unable to protect its position in the global supply chain will be shut out of this essential resource, much like a global pariah. The authors found in their chapter 'Global supply chain under conditions of uncertainty: economic impacts, corporate responses, strategic lessons', that first there should be logistical security standards and systems similar to ISO 9000 norms for the international community. Secondly, various organizational models are shown to be available in making the global logistical chain more robust. Also, logistical autarchy of supply chains, with repatriation of chain components in a few secure countries, will likely not yield workable solutions to the threats of global terrorism and taking the case of the United States, both government and private companies are shown to be responsible for security investments. They also discovered that a logistical security regime is gradually appearing and investing in inspection and detection technologies may go a long way in answering the security needs of a new geopolitical environment.

Chapter 10 examined 'Brand portfolio: a new marketing competency for diminishing risks'. The 09/11 attacks have affected the way of life and the consumption habits of millions of people all around the world, permanently affecting the company–client relationship. Claude Chailan and L.F. Calderon-Moncloa look at the manner in which companies have reacted to this new challenge. Nowadays, the risk reduction function directly related to the brand has been increased by the context. This new environment has notably changed the way in which big international companies conceive their brands and the role the brand has to play in reassuring the consumers' buying decisions. One of the facets of this adaptation of brands and firms to the new situation is the coming onstream of brand portfolios within companies. In this chapter was introduced this new way of management, its importance, its limitations and its major role with respect to the management of the company's marketing and management risks.

Part IV examined the challenges that we may expect for the future, and treats issues that remain open and will be shaped by potential further developments in international terrorism and the manner in which corporations react to its consequences. Three authors gave us insights from different standpoints. David Gillingham shared his observations on 'Managing in the era of terrorism'. This chapter views terrorist acts as an extreme form of system failure. The management of a business in an environment in which terrorist acts may be directed against the firm is therefore seen as a specific application of the management of human errors. The overall analytical framework applied to this situation is the integrated model of error management.

'Corporate global citizenship: successfully partnering with the world', is an appeal by Nancy Adler, who looks at the role of business in the reduction of risk by means of peace, reduced poverty and economic prosperity. The chapter 'Always consider problems as opportunities' by David A.C. Suder concludes this volume. The aim of this chapter is to explain that terrorism as a major problem of humanity is also a unique opportunity for the world. An historical overlook of the driving forces of world stability sheds light on this hypothesis, and is conducted by revisiting the concepts of the economy so as to better understand the inevitable limits of today's world order. We consequently see how political unity will help promote the development of business and why the geopolitical status quo of the pre-09/11 world order was a limitation to the achievement of the global economy.

Terrorism is nothing new in history. New is rather its international dimension and the consequences that it has and that it will have on our society and on our economies. Corporate strategies under international terrorism and adversity will help the business and civil community to adapt.

Index